Manipulation on trial

The unprecedented movement in the price of silver during 1979 and 1980, from $8 per troy ounce to $50 and back to $10, resulted in charges of monopolization and market manipulation being brought against the Hunt brothers of Dallas. These charges led to a lengthy trial in 1988 and a judgment against them of some US$200 million.

This book seeks to elicit broadly applicable lessons from this complex and fascinating case. Drawing upon interviews with the judge, jury, attorneys, and expert witnesses (the author having so served), *Manipulation on trial* focuses on the economic analysis of the Hunts' large positions in futures contracts and the Hunts' alleged influence on the price moves. The author investigates the elusive definition of manipulation in sophisticated markets, the difficulties of interpreting statistical evidence, the imprecision in calculating damages, and the hidden assumptions behind inferences concerning intent. He concludes that these problems induce courtroom procedures to oversimplify the economic analysis and cause the law on market manipulation to be created retroactively. Yet the failure lies not with the legal institutions, but with the futures exchanges, which have not developed in advance the rules to minimize large-scale trading during periods of unusual price moves.

This book will be of interest to all academic economists working on commodity and financial markets. It will also be of interest to the staff of futures exchanges and regulatory agencies, and to lawyers who practice or teach in commodities, securities and antitrust law.

Manipulation on trial

Economic analysis
and the Hunt silver case

Jeffrey Williams
Stanford University

CAMBRIDGE
UNIVERSITY PRESS

CAMBRIDGE UNIVERSITY PRESS
Cambridge, New York, Melbourne, Madrid, Cape Town, Singapore, São Paulo

Cambridge University Press
The Edinburgh Building, Cambridge CB2 8RU, UK

Published in the United States of America by Cambridge University Press, New York

www.cambridge.org
Information on this title: www.cambridge.org/9780521440288

© Cambridge University Press 1995

First published 1995
This digitally printed version 2008

A catalogue record for this publication is available from the British Library

Library of Congress Cataloguing in Publication data
Williams, Jeffrey C.
    Manipulation on trial: economic analysis and the Hunt silver
    case / Jeffrey Williams
        p.   cm.
    Includes bibliographical references and index.
    ISBN 0 521 44028 9
    1. Silver – Prices – United States.   2. Commodity exchanges – United
States.   3. Commodity futures.   4. Commodity futures – United
States – Case studies.   5. Speculation – United States – Case studies.
6. Hunt, Bunker, 1926– .   7. Hunt, Herbert, 1929– .   8. Hunt,
Lamar, 1932– .   I. Title.
    HG307.U5W55   1995   332.64′42421′0973 – dc20   94–44565   CIP

ISBN 978-0-521-44028-8 hardback
ISBN 978-0-521-06347-0 paperback

Contents

Figures

Tables

ix

Preface

The Hunt silver case refers to the trial in 1988 in which the jury found Bunker Hunt, Herbert Hunt, Lamar Hunt, and several of their associates liable for manipulating the silver market during 1979 and 1980 and awarded the plaintiff Minpeco, a Peruvian government-owned metals marketing firm, $192 million in damages. The Hunt silver case unites the extraordinary price moves of a major commodity, the esoteric trading strategies within futures markets, the remarkable Hunt family, and the legal fencing culminating in a six-month trial. *Minpeco v. Hunt* and the companion proceedings brought by the Commodity Futures Trading Commission's Division of Enforcement will always attract people wanting to understand commodity markets or complex litigation.

Because my main academic interest is commodity markets, and because I, who served as an expert for the defense, have continued to be intrigued by the litigation initiated against the Hunts, I have written this book. I may be suspected of bias, but the experts for the winning side, not surprisingly, are less inclined to reflect on the strength, consistency, and hidden assumptions of the various types of economic analysis I describe here. To be sure, I continue to believe that much of the economic evidence did not indicate a "corner" of the silver market and I continue to be troubled that some little-understood but perfectly normal aspects of commodity markets were portrayed as perversions. To me, now, the issue worthy of reassessment is the nature of economic argument in a courtroom setting, namely the selection of economic evidence, its style of presentation, and its influence on the verdict.

My service as an expert witness has given me access to many documents, from the Hunts' daily trading records to the trial transcripts, necessary for any account of the case. More important, I have had the cooperation and interest of many individuals involved with the litigation. The attorneys with whom I worked, besides sharing the lessons they learned about the role of economic analysis, have provided me with their pre-trial and post-trial motions concerning economic analysis. The principals on the other side, lawyers as well as economists, have discussed candidly with me what they considered to be the strengths and weaknesses of the various arguments used and have given me any documents I have requested. Similarly, the CFTC Division of Enforcement's two experts have discussed their approach to the economic analysis. The presiding judge, Judge Morris E. Lasker, has offered some insights into the case. Most of the jurors were interviewed a few months after the trial by Minpeco's attorneys, who have shared with me what they learned about the jury's reception of particular expert witnesses. Minpeco's attorney chiefly involved with expert testimony, Thomas Gorman, has kindly written the Foreword that follows this Preface.

Because this book is not an attempt to fight the case again, I have not mirrored the trial's adversarial nature by devoting entire chapters to the plaintiff's case and others solely to the defense. Instead, after an introductory chapter putting the Hunt silver litigation into the legal context of manipulation cases and a second chapter chronicling the events during 1979 and 1980, the book offers five essays on central issues in the case, organized and divided in ways not in parallel with the trial. The five essays discuss the identification of manipulation, the testing for causes of the price rise, the determining of what the price of silver would have been without the Hunts' trading, the inferring of manipulative intent from the Hunts' actions, and the predicament of economic analysis in the courtroom. In each of these essays, my intention is to clarify the main arguments employed by either side through a discussion of the broader issues those arguments raise. In each of these essays, my hope is to offer an insight about the case not obvious during the course of the trial.

All the legal professionals involved with the Hunt silver litigation have remarked on its exceptional complexity in regard to both laws and facts. In addition to manipulation law, the Hunt case involved antitrust law, racketeering law, and fraud-on-the-market doctrine. All lawyers interested in these specific legal areas should find this book relevant, as should any lawyer involved in a case in which expert witnesses are important. Likewise, all economists specializing in futures markets, securities markets, monopolization, and antitrust should find this book useful, as should any economists who might serve as an expert witness in another field. Although the specific legal setting and the specific commodity markets have a U.S. focus, those readers from outside the U.S. should find that the substantive issues are universal. Any lawyer or economist concerned with how technical ideas can be communicated to non-specialists should find lessons in this book.

Economists played an unusually prominent role in *Minpeco v. Hunt* and the case brought by the CFTC Division of Enforcement. Economists were needed as expert witnesses because the main victim of the alleged offense, namely the silver market, could not speak for itself. Not only did the economists' points of view figure strongly in both the testimony and closing arguments, but the economists themselves served as the link through several changes of attorneys for the defense and provided a key legal strategy for the plaintiff. Mr. Gorman has credited his economist expert, Professor Hendrik Houthakker, with recognizing the arguments regarding fiduciary responsibility that forced a number of brokerage houses to settle on generous terms, spurring Minpeco's case against the Hunts. Economists, he has concluded, if hired as experts, should play a more integral role in determining legal strategy.

The prominence of the economists does not, of course, imply that they were the most important witnesses. Holding that distinction are the Hunts themselves. Even so, the economists' various arguments are both sufficiently separate from the other testimony and sufficiently relevant to other litigation to justify the emphasis in this book.

This book is not, however, an exposé of expert witnesses as mouthpieces for lawyers. All the economists in the Hunt case approached the subject objectively and determined their own testimony. I sometimes name individuals, because specific individuals originated particular ideas and because specific individuals impressed the jury. Yet my emphasis is on the nature of the arguments and the style of presentation.

Nor is this book a complaint about the power of juries with no background in commodity markets, econometrics, or finance. The jurors made considerable effort to follow complex testimony and to reach a reasonable verdict. The pertinent issue is why scrupulous academics differed so much in their conclusions and why the jurors interpreted those conclusions as they did.

Rather, this book is a response to those who refer to the Hunt case in a few sentences of sweeping judgments and broad generalizations. The evidence was voluminous and often ambiguous, and the economic arguments often nuanced if not inconsistent. Those attempting to learn from the Hunt silver litigation should be helped by a concise record of the economic analysis presented.

In studying the Hunt case, it must always be remembered that the trial itself was unusual, since most civil cases settle, as *Minpeco v. Hunt* itself nearly did just before the trial started and again as the jury deliberated. That the case did not settle magnifies certain issues, such as the presentation of statistical analysis to the jury. Fortunately, for at least two reasons, this danger of magnifying particular issues is less acute when analyzing the nature of economic evidence and the role of economist expert witnesses in the Hunt silver litigation, in which, from an early stage, the economists' testimony looked to be significant. First, even if trials are rare, the likely course of expert testimony influences the lawyers' objective analysis of the strength of a case when they discuss any settlement with their clients. Second, had *Minpeco v. Hunt* settled, the CFTC Division of Enforcement's case against the Hunts would likely have proceeded to a public verdict. With the filing of experts' official written reports, the substance of the Division of Enforcement's case can be examined, the very style of its analysis being of interest for future manipulation cases.

A complication for the recapitulation of evidence here arises from the separate allegations made by the CFTC Division of Enforcement and Minpeco. Because the CFTC hearing was delayed in deference to *Minpeco v. Hunt* and then halted after Bunker and Herbert Hunt declared bankruptcy, the text emphasizes Minpeco's strategy and the testimony of its expert witnesses. The text likewise follows Minpeco's definition of the supposed conspirators.[1] (The CFTC Division of Enforcement did not, for example, include Lamar Hunt.)[2] Because the largest holdings by far were those of Bunker Hunt, Herbert Hunt, and their investment arm IMIC, who were included whatever the list of the supposed conspirators, none of the graphs or tables here would be materially different whatever the list of conspirators followed. (To avoid awkward locutions such as "the Hunt brothers and the alleged co-conspirators, who might not be defendants," the text here uses the shorthand "Hunts.")

Given that the expert witnesses differed slightly in the starting and ending dates for their analysis, for convenience and clarity, I have standardized everything to the year May 1, 1979, through April 30, 1980, in the graphs and tables here. All evidence after 1979–1980 ends with 1987, to reconstruct the information available at the time of the trial. These choices affect none of the controversies, which concern the methods of analysis rather

---

[1] Minpeco's list of the supposed conspirators can be divided into two groups. In the so-called Hunt group were the brothers Bunker, Herbert, and Lamar Hunt; certain family members, Elizabeth (Hunt) Curnes, Houston Hunt, Ellen (Hunt) Flowers, Barbara (Hunt) Crow, Douglas Hunt, Lyda Hunt, Albert and Mary (Hunt) Huddleston, and Dale Huddleston (father of Albert); and Hunt-controlled entities, particularly International Metals Investment Company (IMIC), Hunt Holding, and Hunt Minerals. In the so-called Conti group were Naji Nahas and accounts controlled by him, particularly Litardex Traders; Mahmoud Fustok; Banque Populaire Suisse (BPS), which acted as agent for Fustok and others; various corporations and individuals domiciled in Switzerland, particularly Gillion Financial; and Norton Waltuch and his personal accounts at Conti Commodity Services, Inc. In all, Minpeco identified 48 separate accounts.

[2] Also, as noted by Judge Lasker in his decision on defendants' motion for judgment notwithstanding the verdict, there was insufficient evidence of the defendants' control over all 48 accounts. Any of those to be excluded (such as Dale Huddleston's) are, however, too small to have altered the economists' analysis or the jury's verdict.

than the specific period, and permit the methodologies to be compared more easily.[3]

Although some technical terminology is inevitable, I have provided a glossary of commodity market terms and have kept the discussion of futures markets and econometrics as accessible as possible. One of my conclusions, presented in Chapter 6, is that the intercession by experts to explain futures markets hid from the jury the experts' own assumptions about those markets. Another of my conclusions, presented in Chapter 4, is that the defense underutilized a major idea about tests for causes of the price rise because the economists expressed the idea only in the idiom of econometrics. I hope not to make that mistake here.

Because some of the interpretations presented here derive from interviews, another concern is the *ex post* rationalization of the trial. Just as the witnesses' statements, especially the Hunts', had been hardened by depositions and the passage of time, the lawyers and economists interviewed later may have become rigid in their understanding of the course of the trial and the persuasiveness of particular types of evidence. (All remember, even after six years, some of the tiniest details of the evidence.) Even the members of the jury when interviewed some months afterwards must have simplified their description of their deliberations, if only to make some order out of a chaotic process. Such selective memory is especially likely in a case with so much evidence and such myriad connections.

I distributed the entire manuscript (differing from the published version by minor copyediting) to the economist expert witnesses and legal professionals, asking them whether they were comfortable with my characterization of their arguments. Those whom I had interviewed I directed to specific passages, for I had offered as a condition of the interview their right to approve any such material. Several of them suggested changes in wording or emphasis, which I have made. This circulation in advance does not, however, mean they necessarily agree with my interpretation of the effects of their various arguments, let alone the broader lessons I propose in the essays.

As I hope I have made clear, I have received much specific information and many general insights while interviewing those involved in the silver litigation. For such help, I wish to thank Hendrik Houthakker, Robert Kolb, and Pablo Spiller, Minpeco's economist experts; James Burrows and Pete

---

[3] To avoid encumbering the text, I do not provide page references to trial testimony or reports to the CFTC unless the subject is specific. Nor do I reference those data from public sources such as exchanges' yearbooks. Nor do I document the Hunts' trading records. Although incredibly time-consuming to reconstruct (a task that was done separately by the CFTC Division of Enforcement, Minpeco, and the defense), these were not in dispute at the time of the trial. The phrase "has said recently" indicates the source as an interview.

Kyle, the CFTC Division of Enforcement's experts; Robert Pindyck, the brokers' expert; David Copeland, Joel Katcoff, Aaron Rubinstein, and Robert Wolin among the Hunts' attorneys; Thomas Gorman, one of Minpeco's attorneys; and Judge Morris E. Lasker. My particular appreciation goes to Joel Katcoff and Thomas Gorman, for without their cooperation and encouragement, this book would not have been possible.

The individuals who participated in the silver litigation at least had a reason to be interested in my manuscript. To those friends and colleagues on whom I inflicted every detail of the Hunt case, I give my special thanks: Heidi Albers, Thomas Cauley, Stephen DeCanio, Roger Gray, Robert Lurie, Anne Peck, Diana Strazdes, Kris Waumans, and Brian Wright. Diana Strazdes worked so long and with such determination editing the text (any felicity of style is due to her) that she deserves to be called this book's co-author.

Nalini Kuruppu and Daisy Sanchez on the staff at the Food Research Institute typed the initial text. Nalini Kuruppu and Liz Robinson, enduring endless revisions, made the graphs all I could desire. Anne Dunbar-Nobes did an excellent job with the copy-editing. I thank them all.

Foreword

At the conclusion of *Minpeco v. Hunt*, Judge Morris E. Lasker said that books could be written about the novel procedural and evidentiary issues involved in the case. Expert witnesses on both sides of the case agreed that the economic issues developed in the case were also novel. Yet little of the extraordinary scholarship from the trial has been preserved.

Fortunately, Jeffrey Williams, in this remarkable volume, records important segments of the knowledge developed in the Hunt silver litigation and raises significant questions for future discussion. The book is based not only on his own work as an expert witness in the silver litigation, but also the trial transcript and post-trial interviews with the lawyers and economist expert witnesses who served on both sides. We all owe Professor Williams a debt of gratitude for his efforts and achievements.

The discussion of the economic issues developed in the silver litigation is clearly of great significance. In scope and complexity, those economic issues and their intersection with the legal concepts of manipulation under the commodity laws and price fixing and monopolization under the antitrust laws may be unprecedented.

Perhaps more important than the preservation of the economic issues, however, are the questions raised by *Minpeco v. Hunt* and by Professor Williams in this volume: (1) What is "manipulation"? (2) What is the role of the expert in litigation and at trial? (3) What is the role of the jury in complex trials? Each of these questions has been the focus of considerable debate. Each is raised and discussed at length here.

Initially, in discussing the definition of manipulation, Professor Williams highlights many of the key concerns. The book correctly points out the divergent views adopted by the lawyers for each side and the approach taken by the Court to this question. The defendants repeatedly focused on a "classic corner" in the commodity markets where the shorts come "hat in hand" to the longs to cover their positions. The defendants largely ignored the price-fixing and monopolization issues in the case. In contrast, the plaintiffs generally ignored the defendants' "classic corner" argument. The plaintiffs chose to focus on a broad conspiracy/manipulation/price-fixing scheme that created an artificial price. The Court employed a different approach, using in its instructions to the jury the traditional legal intent-based definition.

As Professor Williams notes, these positions do not precisely define "manipulation." Rather, the divergent positions of the parties and the court appear to be like Justice White's famous statement about pornography. As Professor Williams notes, that position can leave market participants, and later judges and juries, to speculate about what is prohibited by the law.

Yet there is merit in the present legal position of using a flexible, rather than a precise and rigid definition of manipulation. Rigid definitions are easily circumvented and effectively disregarded by the market place – frequently by the time they are drafted. For this reason laws dealing with manipulation frequently do not precisely define the concept. For example, not long ago the Congress and the Securities and Exchange Commission expended a great deal of effort trying to craft a statutory definition of insider trading, which is currently prohibited by a broad anti-fraud rule. No acceptable definition was ever crafted. Similarly, an American Bar Association task force has spent a great deal of time trying to define the concept of manipulation under the securities laws. But a precise definition has not been drafted.

The reason the Congress, the ABA, and the courts have not crafted an all-encompassing definition of "manipulation" (or even insider trading) is suggested by *Minpeco v. Hunt*: The concept is a constantly evolving one. Prior to the debacle in the silver markets, it was thought that the silver market was too large to manipulate. Clearly, that idea was correct if manipulation was thought of in terms of a classic corner. Yet, the price in the silver market skyrocketed and the Hunt jury had little trouble determining that the Hunts and their allies fueled the skyrocket.

If the jurors in *Minpeco v. Hunt* were correct – and I believe they were – their decision suggests that the Hunt manipulation accomplished what market professionals had previously believed to be impossible. Achieving what was thought to be impossible clearly points to a new form of manipulation. Viewed in this context, *Minpeco v. Hunt* teaches more than the simple fact that the wisdom of market professionals was wrong or even that the Hunts and their allies should be credited with crafting a new type of manipulation. The silver litigation suggests that the flexible, open-ended concept of manipulation should continue to prevail over any fixed formula rigidly defining manipulation. Otherwise, the creation of the next new form of manipulation will be encouraged rather than deterred.

This is not to suggest, however, that the concept of manipulation should be vague and undefined. Market participants, and later judges and juries if necessary, are entitled to know what is prohibited. There must be guideposts that define prohibited conduct. Professor Williams points out many of the guideposts and cogently explores the pluses and minuses of each. These factors, tested in the crucible of a major trial, provide invaluable guidance for the future and merit further thought and research.

Two additional questions concern the role of the expert witness and the use of lay juries in complex trials. It is popular lore among many lawyers that "experts cancel each other out." Frequently each side in litigation tries to hire the most experts with the best credentials, invoking an alternative to the "cancel out" theory: "the more the better" theory. Both theories suggest that expert witnesses are not of real significance.

The jury's decision in *Minpeco v. Hunt* suggests that both theories should be discarded. The plaintiffs only presented one expert on the merits while the defendants offered the testimony of three. All the expert witnesses had impeccable credentials. Clearly the jury did not follow either the "cancel out" or the "more the better" theory.

Post-trial interviews with the jury suggest that the testimony of the expert witnesses was carefully considered and dissected by the jurors. The jurors diligently evaluated both the material that was presented and the credibility of the witness presenting that material. Those interviews suggest that, if properly presented, expert testimony can be of substantial assistance.

The jury's reaction is confirmed by my own experience in the case. The economic experts made a very significant contribution, not only on the precise economic issues but in shaping the factual and legal questions. Underlying the complex facts and the commodity and antitrust law questions was the futures markets and the business of using those markets. The economics of those markets from the viewpoint of economists and market participants permeated every facet of the litigation and trial.

The participation of the experts, not only at trial but at each stage of the case, was critical. For example, in opposing motions for summary judgment made by the defendant brokerage houses, one of the key issues was the knowledge of the brokers about manipulation. A key element in Minpeco's successful opposition to those motions (and the later favorable settlements with the brokers) was information from David Lloyd Jacobs, former Chairman of Consolidated Goldfields. As an expert witness, Mr. Jacobs provided a businessman's view of what a market participant must have known based on information about the markets that would have been available to market professionals at the time. Mr. Jacob's insights, coupled with those of one of Minpeco's economic experts, helped build the factual record establishing the brokers' knowledge.

The silver litigation thus suggests that expert witnesses are far more important than many believe. The assistance by experts from both academia and business is not only important but may be critical in resolving complex commercial cases. Those experts should, in my view, be involved at an early stage in the litigation to help focus the discovery. Focusing the discovery at an early stage should have the added benefit of facilitating the litigation and perhaps cutting down on some of the needless discovery currently conducted in many large cases. The cost of employing the experts may be offset by the savings in discovery expenses and the enhanced results.

Likewise, during the trial the experts can provide substantial assistance in shaping the fact arguments, presenting testimony, and assisting in preparing cross-examination. For example, although Minpeco only offered the testimony of Professor Houthakker on the merits, Professors Kolb and Spiller provided invaluable assistance throughout the trial in formulating the issues, preparing the economic testimony offered, and developing the cross-examination of the defense experts.

Finally, as Professor Williams suggests, there is a question of whether a lay jury can understand and decide complex issues such as those involved in the silver litigation. Interviews with the jury suggest that they can.

Yet, as Professor Williams notes, frequently the economic issues in the silver litigation were not completely developed for the jury or were presented in a truncated or conclusory fashion. The explanation for this may be based more on the fear of the lawyers than the limitations of the jury. Over and over, as Professor Williams documents in this book, there was a grave concern that "the jury will not understand" because an issue is too complex, too difficult. Those fears are contradicted by the interviews with the jury.

The fears persist, however, based largely on anecdotal evidence. In my view, "the jury will not understand" myth should be discarded. One of the vital tasks of a good trial lawyer is to present the case in a clear, concise, cogent fashion so that the trier of fact (whether it is a lay jury or a judge) can understand it and be persuaded to return a favorable verdict.

Too often the claim that "the jury will not understand" is either a cover-up for the fact that the lawyers do not fully understand their case (and who can effectively present what is not understood) or a substitute for the time and effort it takes to present the case properly, or both. Effective presentation by the trial lawyers coupled with innovations by the judges, such as "mini–summations" at defined points in a long trial and note-taking by the jurors (techniques used by Judge Lasker in *Minpeco v. Hunt*), will facilitate jury comprehension and an effective presentation of the case – the trial lawyer's job.

As a final note, I should acknowledge that it is unusual for a lawyer from one side to make a contribution (no matter how small) to a book by an expert who was on the other side in a trial. The issues raised by the silver litigation and the scholarship that was involved in the case, however, should go beyond being on opposite sides in a legal dispute. Questions concerning the definition of manipulation and the proper role of an expert or the use of a jury in complex litigation are important issues. Although the silver litigation did not resolve any of those questions, it did suggest some answers and provides ideas for future discussion, as Professor Williams demonstrates in this book.

Thomas O. Gorman

Cole Corette & Abrutyn
Washington, DC
December 1994

1   Why the Hunt silver case?

In the summer of 1979, silver traded in the range of $8 to $9 per troy ounce, the highest price in dollar terms seen up to then. That range soon seemed unremarkable, for in early September the price of silver rose sharply to $16 per troy ounce; in early December it increased to above $20; on the morning of January 21, 1980, it reached a previously unimaginable $50 per troy ounce, the peak seen in Figure 1.1. The fall from that extraordinary peak occurred even more rapidly. Trading just above $30 until the beginning of March 1980, silver collapsed to $10 per troy ounce on March 27. Although the price passed $20 again in September 1980, the general pattern since has been downward. For a period in 1992, silver traded below $4, and at the time of writing (1994), in the range of $5 to $6.

Commodity prices are notoriously variable. In the past twenty-five years, prices of wheat, corn, and soybeans have risen as much as 75 percent upon news of a severe drought. Crude oil has at times risen 100 percent in a few months. In the same 1979–1980 period that witnessed silver's price rise, the prices of gold, platinum, and palladium rose up to 200 percent. Nevertheless, silver's 500 percent increase from the summer of 1979 to January 1980 remains the most pronounced for any commodity traded on an organized exchange.

Considering the estimated 12 billion troy ounces of silver then above ground in all forms excluding rare coins, antiques, and fine jewelry, some $400 billion of wealth worldwide was first created and then destroyed between late August 1979 and late March 1980. Two explanations have been offered for this price spike: first, that worldwide political and economic troubles prompted a flight to precious metals, and second, that the Hunt brothers of Dallas, in conspiracy with several others, manipulated the market. According to the latter explanation, the Hunts attempted the largest, longest, and most audacious manipulation in history.

Beyond question, the period of silver's price spike marked an exceptional confluence of political and economic events. For instance, the unrest in Iran

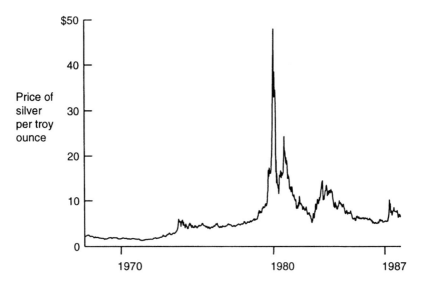

Figure 1.1. Silver prices, 1968 through 1987

following the fall of the Shah and the return of the Ayatollah Khomeini during early 1979 brought queues at gas stations throughout the U.S. in the summer and saw the capture of the American Embassy and the hostage-taking in the fall. The Soviet invasion of Afghanistan in late December 1979 led the U.S. to embargo grain shipments and boycott the 1980 Moscow Olympic Games, and nearly ruptured diplomatic relations between the two superpowers in mid-January 1980. Throughout 1979, inflation in the U.S. accelerated, the dollar sagged against the major currencies, and in early 1980, the American economy fell into recession.

Equally beyond question, the Hunt brothers and their alleged allies (those who traded through the ContiCommodity brokerage house by way of a Swiss bank) controlled a large amount of silver during the seven-month price spike – over 250 million troy ounces, an amount comparable to one year's production from the world's silver mines. The principals were N. Bunker and W. Herbert Hunt (a third brother, Lamar, bought in smaller amounts and less frequently). Bunker and Herbert Hunt had had an interest in silver since 1973, often trading silver futures contracts on either the Chicago Board of Trade (CBOT) or Comex in New York, and sometimes taking delivery, by which means they had accumulated 42 million troy ounces of bullion by June 1979. From June through August 1979, they added considerably to their already large positions. As of August 31, Bunker Hunt alone had 12,188 contracts calling for delivery just in March 1980, representing 60.9 million troy ounces worth $673 million at prevailing prices and making him the largest private investor in silver.

Even though the Hunt brothers were billionaires with vast interests in oil-related companies and real estate, the course of silver prices over 1979–1980 dwarfed all other influences on their finances. At the peak on January 21, 1980, their personal profits (since May 1, 1979) exceeded $5 billion. Because they spent much of these profits in taking delivery of coins and bullion in London and Zurich as well as Chicago and New York, they found themselves increasingly short of cash as the price of silver fell after January 21 when the exchanges, worried by the increasingly erratic movements in the price of silver, restricted trading to the liquidation of existing positions. By the end of March, the Hunts' ability to raise cash was exhausted, and their brokerage houses, also on the verge of insolvency, forcibly liquidated the Hunts' remaining futures positions. Ultimately, the Hunts lost hundreds of millions, perhaps billions of dollars on their silver investments.

After the price collapse of late March 1980, the Hunts found themselves in financial, public-relations, and legal trouble. In April they required a $1.1 billion loan to consolidate their silver debts, with family holdings in oil properties pledged as collateral. In April and May 1980, they were called to testify before House and Senate hearings to account for their actions in the silver market. In May 1981, L. J. Davis's "Silver Thursday," published in *Harper's*, presented the Hunts' previous trading in commodities markets as a practice run for a corner of silver. In 1982, Stephen Fay's *Beyond Greed* portrayed them as masterminds of a conspiracy to monopolize the silver market. By then, other parties' losses on silver led to the filing of many lawsuits against them. Their own losses on silver, spread across the accounts of many relatives and trusts, attracted the attention of the Internal Revenue Service, which disputed the accounting and claimed hundreds of millions of dollars in back taxes.

Among the lawsuits claiming that the Hunts had manipulated the silver market, two were particularly serious. In 1985, the Commodity Futures Trading Commission's Division of Enforcement began formal proceedings against the Hunts, seeking a multimillion dollar fine and a lifetime trading ban. The CFTC Division of Enforcement's hearings, begun in late 1987 before an administrative law judge, were superseded by a civil case in the Federal District Court in New York City. The plaintiff in that civil case was Minpeco SA, a parastatal Peruvian metals marketing company, which had lost heavily on its first venture into silver futures contracts in August through December 1979, and which had brought suit against its brokers and against the Hunts in 1981.

In 1987, when their motion to be dismissed from Minpeco's suit was denied and a trial appeared imminent, the brokers settled with Minpeco. The Hunts did not, and a trial commenced in February 1988. That August, six months later, the jury found the Hunts liable for conspiracy, manipulation, monopolization, racketeering, and fraud on the market. Although less than the $450 million that Minpeco requested, the $132 million in damages assessed against the Hunts, along with disappointments in their oil properties and their tax disputes with the Internal Revenue Service, forced Bunker Hunt and Herbert Hunt into bankruptcy.

Minpeco v. Hunt was not only the last act in the drama of the rise and fall of the Hunts' vast fortune, but also the most important manipulation case ever tried. Previous cases had concerned manipulations alleged to have taken place in the last hours or days of trading in a particular delivery month on a single exchange, whereas the Hunts' distortion of prices supposedly ran for many months throughout the world silver market. The Hunt trial lasted six months and involved dozens of witnesses, experts, and lawyers – all after six years of exceptionally complicated judicial consideration of foreign jurisdiction, the applicability of antitrust law, and the fiduciary responsibility of brokers.

Unfortunately, *Minpeco v. Hunt* by no means resolved the issues that prompted it. After waiting eight years, Minpeco received incomplete restitution for the damages it claimed. The trial did not lead to any new techniques for detecting incipient manipulations; indeed, the trial added a new and nebulous type to the list of possible manipulations. Most frustrating to those concerned with commodity markets, the Hunt trial did not resolve the extent to which the Hunts caused the price spike. The trial itself was filled with the ambiguity, contradictions, and inconclusiveness found in the turmoil in the silver market during 1979 and 1980.

Minpeco v. Hunt and the related proceedings before the CFTC involved considerable economic analysis, an analysis of a complicated historical period and a complicated market. This book considers how that economic analysis served the legal proceedings and explores whether the unstated differences between economic analysis and legal analysis contributed to some of the ambiguities and contradictions within the trial. Before the economic analysis is examined, however, it is necessary to understand why there could have been an allegation of manipulation, why circumstantial evidence about the workings of the silver market were so central to the testimony, and why economist expert witnesses were needed. To put forth that broader context is the purpose of this introductory chapter.

1.1   What is "manipulation"?

The legal offense of "manipulation" seems obvious enough in the simple dictionary meaning of "adapting or changing (accounts, figures, etc.) to suit one's purpose or advantage." Yet the translation of that definition to commodity markets is far from straightforward. All participants in commodity markets trade with a purpose, namely to make money for themselves. All seek advantage, by spotting trends or trading techniques before others do. All endure incessantly changing circumstances. In such a setting as commodity markets, there is no generally accepted definition of manipulation, the result for the applicable law being, as a leading treatise puts it, "a murky miasma of questionable analysis and unclear effect" (Russo, 1983–93, Chapter 12, §5). To make the same point, McDermott (1979, p. 205) uses different diction: "The law governing manipulations has become an embarrassment – confusing, contradictory, complex, and unsophisticated."

The Commodity Exchange Act, which makes it a felony for any person "to manipulate or attempt to manipulate the price of any commodity in interstate commerce" neither defines nor provides examples of manipulation, except that done "to corner or attempt to corner any such commodity."[1] As Perdue (1987) documents, legislators sponsoring the Grain Futures Act of 1922 and the Commodity Exchange Act of 1936 intentionally kept the definition elastic. Those legislators antipathetic to speculation in any form viewed the trading of anyone not a regular handler of the physical commodity as a "manipulation" of those markets. Others viewed a speculation that prices would fall as a "manipulation" of producers' rights to a high price. As Stassen (1982) argues, the legislative finding that "sudden or unreasonable fluctuations in the prices [on organized commodity exchanges] frequently occur as a result of … speculation, manipulation, or control"[2] – a legislative finding necessary in the constitutional climate of the early 1920s to justify Federal regulation[3] – was not based on systematic study of speculators' activities on actual commodity exchanges.[4] (As it happens, the great majority of regulatory actions brought under the law have involved commercial dealers who were hoping for a rise in price.)

The legal definition of manipulation has instead been derived through specific cases, involving very different commodities and circumstances. Not surprisingly, the cumulative definition is imprecise and only shifts the problem of definition to other terms. One Appeals Court has defined manipulation as "the creation of an artificial price by planned action."[5] The

---

[1]   U.S. Code, Title 7, Chapter 1, §13(b).
[2]   U.S. Code, Title 7, Chapter 1, §5, before changes in 1982.
[3]   *Chicago Board of Trade v. Olsen*, 262 U.S. 1 (1923).
[4]   Authorized because of such views about commodity markets, the Federal Trade Commission's exemplary study (1920–6) of the grain trade examined prices but did not have the data to connect price movements to individual traders.
[5]   *General Foods Corp. v. Brannan*, 170 F.2d 220 (7th Cir., 1948), p. 231, which involved the May '44 CBOT rye contract. Because this case was the first in which "manipulation" was to be judicially construed, the Commodity Exchange Authority, part of the Department of Agriculture (of which Brannan was Secretary), urged a definition that the U.S. Supreme Court had used in an antitrust case, but the Appeals Court rejected that specific case as inapplicable (Greene and Rogers, 1951).

vacuous expression "artificial price" has come to mean a price that does not "reflect basic forces of supply and demand,"[6] yet no uncontroversial list of those basic forces exists.[7]

Three manipulative schemes have been identified by those trying to generalize the case law (Edwards and Edwards, 1984; Johnson, 1981; and Johnson and Hazen, 1989–94). These may occur alone or in some combination:

1. A "corner" or "squeeze," in which someone, taking advantage of the anonymity of futures trading, establishes a large futures position calling for delivery in a particular delivery month. Waiting until those who have the contractual obligation for delivery have little time remaining, the cornerer surprises them by appearing eager to stand for delivery. Meanwhile, having obtained much of the deliverable grade locally available, the manipulator leaves those committed to make delivery the unenviable choice of paying express charges for transportation or buying back the futures contracts at a premium.

2. A "rumor" manipulation, in which someone with a previously established position in the physical commodity or in futures convinces other traders through false reports that a shortage in that commodity will occur, for example, through a rumor of a freeze. The rumor must be believed by others only long enough for the manipulator to close out his position at top prices.

3. An "investor-interest" manipulation, in which a series of trades and statements made by the manipulator convinces others of a broadly based desire to hold the commodity, thereby increasing its price. Until others realize that the underlying interest is merely temporary, the manipulator can sell her holdings at a high price.

The Hunts took large numbers of deliveries on futures contracts, as in a classic corner. Nevertheless, those making the deliveries did not seem particularly squeezed; price relationships did not indicate a tight restriction on bullion for delivery in those specific months. The Hunts advised many others to invest in silver, as in a classic investor-interest manipulation. Nevertheless, they were open about their own interest in silver, they did not entice many others to invest (many small investors left the silver market), and they

---

6   *Cargill, Inc. v. Hardin,* 452 F.2d 1154 (8th Cir., 1971), p. 1163, involving the May '63 CBOT wheat contract. See Smith et al. (1973) for commentary.

7   Easterbrook (1986, p. S117) argues that "an effort to isolate which 'forces of supply and demand' are 'basic' and which are not is doomed to failure. If people want to purchase wheat to admire its beauty rather than to mill it into flour, they may be weird, but their demand is real. People may want warehouse receipts for wheat in order to bake bread but they may also want them (as they want Treasury bills) for their close equivalence to money."

did not sell out at a high price. Faced with these less-than-perfect fits but without abandoning these other types of manipulation, the plaintiff in *Minpeco v. Hunt* suggested that the Hunts conducted a fourth type not previously identified in commodities law:

4.   A "price-effect" manipulation, in which a trader holding an opinion about the commodity's long-run value buys (or sells) it in sufficient quantity to influence the current price, knowing that such an effect on price will occur.

The first three types of manipulation are harmful because the price (or price relationships) signal a socially wasteful shipment, investment, delay in consumption, and so forth. The prospect of any of these first three manipulations might also keep traders away from the market, which would reduce its usefulness for others. The harmful effects of the fourth type of manipulation are less obvious, however. If the actions of many small traders collectively equaled that of a large trader, they would have an equivalent price effect, but not one deemed socially harmful.

Among these four types of manipulations, the one particularly associated with futures markets is the corner. Because of the liquidity and standardization of contracts that futures markets achieve, many traders "sell short," that is, commit to make delivery during a specified month of something they are in no position to deliver. (The "shorts" hope later to buy back their contract at a lower price, just as those who first buy, namely the "longs," often hope to sell at a higher price before taking physical delivery.) Because of this system of continuously updated good-faith deposits, those who cannot deliver the commodity have a compulsion to buy back the contracts whatever the price. A cornerer exploits the fact that as some short sellers procure the commodity or buy out their contracts from the cornerer, the price rises, making it more expensive for those who remain. McDermott (1979) suggests that a cornerer's actions correspond to what is called "hindrance" in general contract law – one party to a contract making it impossible for the counterparty to fulfill the contract.

An investor-interest manipulation is the type to which the term manipulation is most commonly applied in securities law (e.g., Loss and Ruebhausen, 1937; Berle, 1938; and Mermin and Pickard, 1947).[8] Often associated with this type of manipulation are so-called penny stocks, those characterized by high-pressure sales practices and a thinly traded market, in which the one or two market makers often have connections to the issuer of the security (De Toro, 1989). Also, the notorious "pools" of the 1920s attempted, through "wash sales" and "cross trades" among members of the

---

[8]   For the parallels between regulation of commodities and securities, see Wolff (1969) and Bromberg and Lowenfels (1980–93).

pool, to persuade others of an inherent interest and liquidity in some security, which the pool would hope to unload at top prices.

Recently, securities law has grappled with whether the fourth type – a price-effect manipulation – is truly a manipulation, especially in the context of corporate takeover battles (Silberberg and Pollack, 1983 and 1984). As part of a hostile tender offer, the raider publicly offers a premium over the prevailing price, fully intending that such an effect on price will allow it to purchase a controlling interest. The defending management devises so-called poison pills, with the full intent that their price effect will dissuade the raider from its bid. The courts seem to be reaching a consensus that a price effect by contestants in a takeover battle is not a manipulation (Poser, 1986). In the instance of speculators who perceive a company to be a likely takeover target and who buy a large number of shares, one judge in the district with jurisdiction over the Hunt case has observed that if such actions "constituted manipulation within the meaning [of the securities laws], most large-scale transactions in a single security would be prohibited."[9]

In sum, "manipulation" is made to cover a wide range of actions and circumstances, whether in securities or commodities markets. Regarding the controversial actions, there is often considerable ambiguity as to whether they were detrimental to the market or whether any harm was intended. Regarding the circumstances, many of the suspicious price responses emerge under unquestionably legitimate trading. "Manipulation" is a particularly vague offense.[10]

As it happens, the other charges against the Hunts – racketeering, monopolization, and fraud on the market – are also notably vague. The RICO statute, which outlaws "a pattern of racketeering," does not define "pattern."[11] (The Hunt case illustrates the ambiguity. Does each trade constitute an act of racketeering, or each delivery month, or the entire manipulative scheme?) To many observers (e.g., Freeman and McSlarrow, 1990), the RICO statute is so vague as to violate due process. Regarding the lack of clarity in the charge of "monopolization," suffice it to say that a huge antitrust literature observes that the term has the same definitional problems as "manipulation."[12] The final charge of "fraud on the market" by its very name is even hazy about the identity of those harmed and the causal con-

---

[9]   *Trane Co. v. O'Connor Securities*, 561 F.Supp. 301 (S.D.N.Y., 1983), p. 305.
[10] In general, the void-for-vagueness doctrine would make such a statute unconstitutional (Amsterdam, 1960; Jeffries, 1985). Yet in *Bartlett Frazier Co. v. Hyde*, 65 F.2d 350 (7th Cir., 1933), cert. denied, 290 U.S. 654 (1933), the original Grain Futures Act was not rendered void for its indefinite definition of manipulation.
[11] The Racketeer Influenced and Corrupt Organization Act (RICO) is codified in 18 U.S. Code §§1961–68.
[12] The monopolization charge was under Section 2 of the Sherman Act. The conspiracy charge was under Section 1: "Every ... conspiracy in constraint of trade or commerce ... is declared to be illegal" U.S. Code, Title 15, Chapter 1, §1.

nection between the accused's trading and those harmed.[13]

Because of the imprecise definitions of "manipulation," "pattern," "monopolization," and "fraud," the charges against the Hunts, despite referring to specific statutes, amounted to allegations under the common law. Under the common law, the judge defines the offense with the particular case at hand in mind and the jury applies the definition to the facts of that case. In essence, *Minpeco v. Hunt* illustrates what happens when the common-law notion of the conscience of the community confronts highly esoteric and technical subjects with which the jurors have no experience.

1.2   Why the emphasis on circumstantial evidence?

All manipulation cases concentrate upon circumstantial evidence. As Mark Cymrot, one of Minpeco's attorneys, observed during the trial, "No one would ever confess to having conspired to manipulate a commodity market so you have to show compelling proof through circumstances. You have to piece together the circumstances so that there's no other reasonable explanation than a conspiracy."[14]

The circumstantial evidence typically involves the historical context of the allegedly manipulated market. For example, Great Western Food Distributors was judged to have manipulated the December '47 refrigerator egg futures contract,[15] because the price for that contract at the end of its trading life was abnormally high relative to the price for January '48 delivery and to the price for fresh eggs, based on the historical experience of those relationships.[16] Similarly, the Cargill case involving May '63 wheat concerned the behavior of that contract during the last two days of its trading life – its price rose sharply relative to the July '63 contract.[17] For manipulation to be found, the price rise had to be judged as "abnormal" in comparison to the previous nine years of wheat trading. Moreover, other explanations of the unusual prices had to be considered. Cargill placed orders to liquidate its position in the last fifteen minutes of trading at a sequence of ever higher prices. Because such limit orders were not proscribed, Cargill's action had to be placed in the context of trading practices in futures markets. In the Indiana Farm Bureau Cooperative case involving the last days of the July

---

13   New York General Business Law §§352.

14   *Wall Street Journal*, 13 June 1988.

15   The use of "December '47" instead of "December 1947" is meant here and elsewhere to emphasize that a futures contract with its own identity is involved.

16   *Great Western Food Distrib., Inc. v. Brannan*, 201 F.2d 476 (7th Cir., 1953), commented upon Rosenak et al. (1953). A very similar allegation of a corner in eggs arose over the December '52 contract, *G.H. Miller & Co. v. United States* 260 F.2d 286 (7th Cir., 1958). Eggs on the Chicago Mercantile Exchange never had many market participants, so a single trader could stand out, intentionally or not.

17   *Cargill, Inc. v. Hardin*, 452 F.2d 1154 (8th Cir., 1971).

'73 CBOT corn contract,[18] the behavior of corn prices during other periods was investigated and the day-by-day trading of all the large traders, including eleven corn merchants, eight exporters, and five speculators, was reconstructed (Hieronymus, 1981).

The interpretation of the historical context is always less than certain, as, echoing Gray (1981), Davidson (1985, p. 1294) has noted: "The future behavior of a normal market is not bounded by the market's historical experiences. Every year some product reaches its record high price while some other product falls to a record low." When a commodity's price is close to its historical average, it might be because a manipulation kept it from being unusually low.

Further complicating the consideration of the circumstantial evidence, a manipulation is an effect, not simply an act. Case law has not evolved to take a specific action or lack of action as incontestable evidence of manipulation, such as buying more than fifty futures contracts on the last day of trading in a delivery month or not selling the physical commodity when prices record at least a 10 percent premium for immediate delivery over delivery one month later.[19] As the court decisions have emphasized, acts deemed manipulative in some contexts are unquestionably legitimate in others. Acts become manipulative by combining with other acts and by contributing to an artificial price.

Thus, some judgment is required to detect a manipulation from circumstantial evidence. A sudden increase in price (or price relationships) does not by itself reveal whether a manipulation took place. The judgment becomes in large part an exercise in reasoning about what a manipulation would do to prices, namely "the predictable effects of the offense" in Pirrong's phrase (1994, p. 1014). But, as neither Pirrong nor many other commentators have recognized, a similar exercise in reasoning is needed about the alternative explanations, such as an export boom, a technical refining bottleneck, or an unusual spatial configuration to crop failure. To detect manipulation it does not suffice to find the circumstantial evidence that would be expected during a manipulation, rather the circumstantial evidence should be relatively more likely to appear during a manipulation than during, say, an export boom. However, such a comparison requires even more care in inference and judgment.

The existing literature, moreover, considers the likely effects of manipulation through static models, whereas commodity markets are dynamic and ever changing. The importance of this feature can be illus-

---

[18]   *In re. Indiana Farm Bureau Coop Assn.*, CCH Commodity Futures Law Reporter ¶20,964 [1977–80 Transfer Binder] (CFTC 1979), affd., ¶21,796 [1982–84 Transfer Binder] (CFTC, 1982).
[19]   According to Harrington (1981, p. 274), "commodities manipulation is too complex an area of the law for facile rules."

trated with the problems caused for two otherwise reasonable definitions of manipulation. Perdue (1987, p. 348) recommends defining manipulation "as conduct that would be uneconomical or irrational, absent an effect on [the] market price." She has in mind such conduct as a trader who stands for delivery on some futures contracts, the commodity having been shipped to the location, graded, and placed in the exchange-certified warehouse at considerable expense, only to remove it from the warehouse to ship it elsewhere for a lower price. Friedman (1990) offers a refinement of Perdue's focus on the alleged manipulator's conduct to inquire whether a trader could have pursued a course of action that would have left him in the same position but would have been less restrictive for others. Friedman would condemn the trader who took delivery and reshipped at a loss, not because of the loss but because the trader could have arranged with those making deliveries to avoid the expense of placing the commodity in and removing the commodity from the warehouse.

In the incessantly changing environment of commodity markets, a shipment from an exchange-certified warehouse might arrive at another location only to fetch less than previously available at the other location, despite an alleged manipulator having no manipulative purpose when making the shipment. Conversely, a manipulator might have the additional good fortune of prices rising everywhere while the shipment is in transit. (Cargill, defending itself over the May '63 CBOT wheat contract, pointed to its profits as proof of "economic" trading, not the "uneconomic" trading of a manipulator.) A trader might have delayed negotiating with others despite the imposition placed on the others because of an expectation of further advantageous price changes – changes that the trader did not intend to cause. Conversely, a manipulator might accommodate some other traders early on, hoping others will be lulled into a more profitable squeeze. Clearly, it is difficult to deduce a trader's intention regarding particular acts from the outcome of those acts.

1.3   Why the need for economic analysis?

Although the main circumstantial evidence comes from the supposed victim, a particular market such as the silver market cannot speak for itself. Experts in commodity markets must testify instead. In the Hunt case, a tax advisor, several accountants, two representatives of the exchanges, and nine economists (seven of whom testified) prepared reports on the silver market.

First on record were the CFTC Division of Enforcement's two experts, Professor Albert Kyle from the University of California, Berkeley, and Dr. James Burrows of Charles River Associates, Boston. (It was unusual for the CFTC Division of Enforcement to employ outside experts at all.) Each wrote a lengthy report, the equivalent of direct examination, for the hearing before an administrative law judge. Professor Kyle presented price relationships, such as the coin/bullion differential and the price of bullion for immediate delivery relative to the price for much later delivery, as consistent with manipulation. Dr. Burrows, relying on Charles River Associates' expertise in mining costs and industrial uses of metals, discussed the changes in silver supply and demand as being inconsistent with the price changes during 1979. Their reports, written independently, provided a two-pronged argument for the Hunts' having manipulated the silver market.

Three experts responded for the Hunts with formal reports submitted to the CFTC in September 1987: Professor Stephen Ross from Yale University, Professor Franklin Edwards from Columbia University, and I, Jeffrey Williams, initially from Brandeis University and later from Stanford University. We three shared data sets and met several times but did not work jointly. As the defense experts for the civil trial, we divided up subjects rather more consciously. Professor Ross advanced the political and economic interpretation of the price rise. Professor Edwards testified about the prices in silver futures for distant delivery dates as evidence that the price would have been high without the Hunts. I concentrated on price relationships, comparing silver to other metals and bullion to coins; I also explained regression analysis to the jury while arguing that the Hunts' day-by-day trading was unrelated to changes in the price.

As Minpeco's sole expert, Professor Hendrik Houthakker from Harvard University testified about all aspects of the economic evidence. His testimony ranged from statistical studies of silver prices to comparisons of the Hunts' futures position with bullion in exchange-approved vaults. He also drew attention to specific acts, such as the deliveries taken, as evidence of manipulative intent.

At the start of the trial, the plaintiff employed Professor Robert Kolb from the University of Miami to introduce the jury to commodity markets. He and Professor Pablo Spiller of the University of Illinois performed much of the statistical analysis used by Professor Houthakker and suggested lines of cross-examination. Both expected to testify as rebuttal witnesses, but the plaintiff's lawyers, sensing their case was going well, opted to forgo such testimony. Professor Robert Pindyck of MIT also was not called upon to testify, because the brokerage houses for whom he had conducted his analysis settled with Minpeco in the fall of 1987.

The two weeks that the economists spent before the jury represented the lengthiest testimony except for that of the Hunts themselves. The economist expert witnesses addressed all the key aspects of any civil case, namely the nature of the offense, the defendants' intent to commit the offense, the causal connection between the defendants' actions and the damage to the plaintiff, and the monetary valuation of that damage. The economists spoke to the "ultimate issue": Did the Hunts manipulate the silver market?

This book, apart from the next chapter, which recounts in more detail the events in the silver market during 1979 and 1980, is organized around the economists' testimony on these key aspects of defining the offense, determining the causal connection, calculating the damages, and inferring intent. A theme developed in all the essays is that the economists, whether witnesses for the plaintiff, the CFTC Division of Enforcement, or the defendants, based their analysis on unarticulated assumptions, assumptions about the nature of manipulation, the purposes of futures markets, and the formation of commodity prices. Assumptions are a necessary beginning to any analysis by an expert. Often they encapsulate the cumulative knowledge of the expert's field. The problem comes when they are hidden. An expert's hidden assumption cannot be compared to other assumptions the same expert makes in other parts of the analysis nor with assumptions other experts make. With the assumptions unarticulated let alone examined, the expert's analysis can suffer from internal inconsistencies or be conducted at cross purposes to other experts' analyses. Hidden assumptions introduce another layer of ambiguity.

The first of the essays (Chapter 3) centers on the studies made of price relationships for indications of manipulation. The plaintiff's experts listed the following as indications of manipulation: the silver/gold ratio, the coin/bullion differential, the price spread with more distant delivery dates, and the within-day variability of prices. Besides arguing that these price relationships were not separate indicators, the defense experts presented correlations among bullion prices to show the geographic extent of the market and introduced evidence about price relationships from several other metals. Unfortunately, no expert put forward a clear definition of manipulation or explained the range of normal price relationships. Hence the discussion was often internally contradictory and misdirected. The defense experts concentrated on evidence relevant to a classic corner without realizing that the plaintiff was claiming the Hunts had conducted a price-effect manipulation. The plaintiff's expert presented evidence regarding the antitrust charge that was consistent with the idea of a corner. One of the CFTC Division of Enforcement's experts conceived of the case in terms of a short-term corner and its other expert in terms of a long-term price effect.

The second essay (Chapter 4) concerns the statistical analysis used to relate the Hunts' trading or general political events to the price of silver. The economists' various approaches to this issue contained within them strong assumptions about the nature of causality and the speed with which something would affect prices. By relating the Hunts' trading to the level of prices and by ascribing much of the concurrent movement in gold to the Hunts, the plaintiff's experts presented regression analysis purporting to show that the Hunts had caused the price rise. By relating the Hunts' trading to the day-by-day changes in the silver price and by ascribing all the movements in gold to political news, the defense experts presented regressions purporting to show no connection between the Hunts' trading and the price rise. Even though the lawyers emphasized these results in closing arguments, their actual statements consisted of brief appeals to the various experts' expertise in econometrics and these appeals affected the jury more than the details of the testimony. But the ineffectiveness of the testimony was not necessarily a result of the jury's lack of experience with statistical analysis. The experts, especially the defense experts, failed to translate several important non-technical points into an idiom more instructive than econometrics.

The third essay (Chapter 5) focuses on the apparently conflicting testimony about what the price of silver would have reached had the Hunts not been present in the silver market. As Hieronymus (1977b, p. 56) has emphasized, in the incessantly changing circumstances that are characteristic of commodity markets, "a distorted price can never be identified with precision and certainty." Even so, the economists' estimates of the price of silver but for the Hunts ranged from $8 to $45 per troy ounce with several in between, a range in price that would suggest seemingly irreconcilable differences. Actually, the experts did not contradict one another as much as emphasize different aspects of the determination of the price of silver, in large part because a comprehensive picture eluded any analyst. The members of the jury, left with the task of choosing among the experts, could do so properly only by seeing the elusive comprehensive picture; their task, however necessary, was next to impossible.

The fourth essay (Chapter 6) concerns the inference of intent from the Hunts' actions, testimony about which was prominent among the expert witnesses. Inferences were made about their trades on days during which price-move limits applied, their placement of many of their futures positions in so-called straddles, and their negotiating of so-called exchanges for physicals with commercial dealers. The experts' testimony on these arcane subjects frequently depended on a hidden assumption, such as whether some action was common in commodity markets, which prevented the jury making an independent judgment about intent. More insidiously, from the experts' explanations of complex transactions, the jury may have gained the impression that anything to do with futures markets is suspicious.

The concluding essay (Chapter 7), which reports on the jury's reaction to the various experts and comments on the jury's verdict, explores the influence of economic analysis in this and, by extension, other manipulation cases. In the Hunt case, the contributions of the economists were largely misinterpreted or ignored, in part because the manner in which economists tend to analyze a problem (especially an allegation like manipulation) is fundamentally different from, and at times incompatible with the way the legal system assesses evidence and determines cause. Those differences between economic reasoning and legal reasoning, between economic analysis and trial procedure, which went virtually unrecognized by the participants, crucially affected the outcome of the Hunt trial.

Of course, the expert witnesses in the Hunt case were merely part of the attorneys' presentations on behalf of their clients. Under the advocacy system, attorneys put forward the best possible case. The lawyers emphasize their expert's credentials, coach their expert to project a forceful yet thoughtful demeanor, emphasize in their closing argument their expert's strongest points for their case, and emphasize the opposing expert's weakest responses. The attorneys seek throughout to adapt expert testimony to suit their purpose or advantage, that is, to "manipulate."

1.4   Why the legal ambiguities?

In the degree of unprecedented price relationships and in the magnitude of positions, the closest parallels with the Hunt silver case would be the controversies surrounding Cargill's positions in the Chicago Board of Trade's corn market in September 1937 and the International Tin Council's default on the London Metal Exchange in October 1985.[20] In September 1937, Cargill (a grain merchandising firm then of regional scope and now of worldwide significance) held futures contracts for delivery in September (the last old-crop delivery month) of more corn than that available in Chicago or surrounding areas. The price of corn for delivery in September reached an unprecedented premium of 75 percent over new-crop corn available in December, and Cargill never explained convincingly why it needed corn at that premium. The CBOT stipulated a price for an imposed liquidation of the contracts; both the CBOT and the CFTC's predecessor agency brought charges of manipulation against Cargill and conducted a series of administrative hearings (Broehl, 1992).

The International Tin Council (ITC), as part of a treaty among many producing and consuming countries, operated a buffer-stock scheme. Supporting the tin price through purchases of physical metal and through many forward contracts on the London Metal Exchange (LME), together amounting to two-thirds of annual new production, the ITC influenced the market from 1982 until October 1985, when it suddenly announced itself unable to meet its financial and contractual commitments. The price collapsed 40 percent, the ITC's banks and brokers staggered under £300 million in losses from their extension of credit, the venerable LME suspended trading in tin and barely survived (Anderson and Gilbert, 1988).

Such flamboyant episodes seem to be the few occasions that commodity exchanges and their members attract outside scrutiny. By their nature, these

---

[20]   See Markham (1991) for a comprehensive list of manipulation cases.

episodes present difficulties for economic analysis (whether or not as part of a legal proceeding), for they occur only with a confluence of events. Because the 1936–1937 corn crop had been devastated by drought whereas the maturing crop looked abundant, a price premium for old-crop corn would have been expected in September 1937. To what extent did Cargill exaggerate the price relationships? Tin consumption had been increasing less than new production for a number of years, not to mention that the U.S. government looked more inclined to sell from its own enormous stockpile. To what extent did the ITC's activities consolidate trends that would have occurred regardless? It is clear that over 1979–1980 the price of silver behaved strangely and the Hunts held large positions. Nevertheless, are those two facts causally connected? Had late 1979 and early 1980 been marked by major oil finds outside the Middle East and by a thaw in the Cold War, would anyone have noticed the Hunts' large positions in silver?

The flamboyant episodes of commodity prices also present difficulties for legal analysis. Cargill long felt it was unjustly punished for anticipating the course of corn prices following a short crop, and felt all the more aggrieved when the two large parties opposite it in the futures market were not symmetrically found to be manipulators. Although clearly intending to "stabilize" tin prices, the ITC was not confronted with the obvious charge of manipulation, but was sued for misleading its creditors about the extent of its positions and for simple breach of contract.[21] Even if in 1979–1980 the Hunts did to some degree cause the strange price relationships, it is not obvious that they intended to take excessive advantage of the style of trading in futures markets or to harm other participants in the market. Had Minpeco sold its silver not in October but at the peak in January, it would not have filed suit.

Commodity markets inevitably create big winners and big losers, often by small differences in the timing of entering and exiting the market. When can it be said that the winners' own trading contributed to those winnings? That is, when do the losers have a reasonable legal right to compensation?

A corner transpires when the manipulator insists that those on the other side of the futures contracts deliver according to the contracts' strict terms. In other areas of the law, insistence on contractual rights would rarely be considered an offense, and if so, one in which the counterparty would be relieved of obligations but not able to seek damages (Yorio, 1989). "To hold that the long has unlawfully squeezed is to permit the shorts to escape responsibility for their contractual obligations" (Davidson, 1985, p. 1288).

---

[21]   Even though the ITC had presented itself as having the financial backing of the many governments, the English courts ultimately ruled that sovereign immunity allowed the signatory countries to abrogate commercial contracts and debts. So much for the popular idea that an international agency would have an advantage in stockpiling commodities because of an impeccable credit rating.

When the developing system of settling futures contracts by the payment of monetary differences came under attack as gambling, the exchanges defended themselves by emphasizing that either party could insist on the contract culminating in delivery.[22] Actually, a great advantage of futures contracts is that they can be offset before delivery. A corner might be said to be the violation of some traders' expectations of being able to offset and not deliver (Burt et al., 1963). (Van Smith [1981, p. 1607] takes the view that those "who insist on delivery should be presumed to intend to manipulate.")[23] Yet early law involving futures markets was troubled that during an offset a principal to a contract could be substituted without the other party's knowledge.[24]

The plaintiff Minpeco never traded directly with the Hunts. Even had the Hunts' and Minpeco's orders arrived on an exchange floor at the same moment, the anonymity achieved by futures markets would have left them unaware that they were dealing with each other. In most other broad business crimes, only parties with a direct and visible connection have the legal standing to sue.[25] For example, in antitrust disputes, normally only the alleged monopolist's own customers may sue, even though others may have been harmed more (Kellman, 1985, pp. 402–14). Who has standing to sue over an alleged manipulation?

Another difficulty for legal analysis is that the prices under scrutiny move incessantly. In standard antitrust situations, the price for a company's specific product is clearly under its control and, once posted, the price might not change for months. In manipulation cases, many others besides the alleged manipulator are frequently trading in the marketplace for the identical item. What is one party's causal relationship with prices? Even if the alleged manipulator were the only trader on his side of the market, every futures contract has a counterparty. How can the effect of one party's trading be distinguished from other parties' trading?

Allegations of manipulation arise in markets where traders constantly search for a tiny price discrepancy or an opportunity to move more quickly

---

22 See Federal Trade Commission (1920, Vol. 5, pp. 272–321) and Irwin (1937) for a history of this legal emphasis on delivery, and Architzel and Connolly (1981) for the unintended implications for the new futures contracts with "cash settlement."

23 In a theoretical model, Kumar and Seppi (1992) suggest manipulators may trade in the physicals market to influence the index at which those futures markets with cash settlement rather than physical delivery conclude the contract. So far, no allegation of such a type of manipulation has reached the courts.

24 *Corbett v. Underwood*, 83 Ill. 344 (1876); *Irwin v. Williar*, 110 U.S. 499; *Higgins & Gilbert v. McCrea*, 116 U.S. 671 (1886).

25 One exception is securities law in instances of false disclosure, such as incorrect accounting statements, when those trade relying on the price as a proper measure of value can sue. (Those who bought other securities, believing a whole industry was performing well, cannot sue, however.) This application of fraud-on-the-market doctrine is controversial, as Black (1984), Wemple (1985), and Carney (1989) discuss.

than others. The situation differs from typical antitrust cases involving price fixing, in which some agreement obstructs the jockeying for small advantages. In settings where clever trading is the norm, the line separating acceptable from unacceptable practice cannot be easily drawn, yet it can be easily crossed.[26] For instance, in January 1980, the Hunts gained some advantage in the large exchanges for physicals they conducted with the major silver dealers, but, considering the dealers' precarious cash reserves, they could probably have extracted even more. The advantage came to less than one percent of the value of the silver. Was that excessive? As Gray (1980) puts the question, when does aggressive trading become market tampering?

These questions require both legal and economic analysis, two styles of analysis that do not comfortably interact. Trial procedure revolves around a distinction between the "facts" and the "law." Juries determine the facts, judges instruct on the law. Yet *Minpeco v. Hunt* demonstrates how much the interpretation of any fact, even the selection of that fact from among all the circumstantial evidence, depends on the interpretation of many other facts. For example, the interpretation of the Hunts' decision to stand for delivery of silver bullion depended on interpretation of the normal use of futures markets, the tax consequences of a substantial gain through a price rise, the reasons for that price rise, the estimated availability of bullion refined from coins, and the estimated flexibility in refining services; those factors in turn depended on one another. Nor did *Minpeco v. Hunt* separate the circumstantial evidence from the offense and from the perpetrator.[27] If the price of silver had risen sharply but no one individual had large positions, as happened in the gold market, the price spike would not have been called a manipulation and no case would have gone before a jury. Because the most convincing evidence of an offense was the sheer magnitude of the defendants' positions when combined, it is hard to imagine the Hunt jury finding some of the defendants not liable.

Trial procedure also emphasizes a distinction between "facts" and "opinions."[28] Expert witnesses alone can offer opinions, which is to say, inferences drawn from a set of facts. Following a ritual, each economist in *Minpeco v. Hunt* catalogued all the commodity prices, trading records, exchange board minutes, warehouse statistics, and so on, that he had

[26]   Similar demarcation problems arise in antitrust cases involving predatory pricing.
[27]   Intent is also not an issue separate from the offense, as Fischel and Ross (1991) emphasize. A criminal case might consider whether the defendant killed out of self-defense or premeditated murder. The investigation would focus on the killer's state of mind but would begin with the facts that the defendant fired a gun and someone died, an indisputably bad outcome. In a manipulation case, the trader's state of mind determines whether there was a harmful act, as if no one would have died had murder not been the shooter's intent.
[28]   All witnesses must draw inferences to some extent. As Jones (1994) argues, the distinction between fact and opinion is itself a distinctive creation of the legal profession.

examined, and then pronounced a yes/no opinion about whether these factors were consistent with a manipulation of the silver market. No economist was required to detail the steps of his inference from those facts. It was as if greater importance attached to the number of related markets the expert examined than to the sequence through which the expert reasoned from a definition of manipulation, to the manipulation's likely effects in any related market, to the measurement of the effect in the related market, and finally to the probability of that type of manipulation in the silver market.

The vagueness in the definition of the offense, the emphasis on circumstantial evidence, the reliance on experts, and the style of the legal proceeding combine to make a manipulation case highly specific to the traders and market involved. Of course, every case is specific to the extent that it involves a unique set of facts. Yet individual cases provide precedents for other cases. Jeffries (1985) argues that the value of an individual case as a precedent can be measured by whether it reduces the uncertainty about proper behavior for those who intend to abide by the law.

Jeffries's test can be applied to the Hunt silver case in the following way. Imagine running the trading desk of a commercial firm with a position in a futures market large enough to rank by some common measure as the largest. You do not want to be noticeable nor suffer any losses, but you have some legal doubts about whether or how you should reduce your position. Some actions (or lack of actions) may not be legal. Does the Hunt silver case as reported in the following chapters reduce your uncertainty about the division between legal and illegal behavior? If it does not, *Minpeco v. Hunt* will have added to the murky miasma of the law on commodity markets.

Bunker and Herbert Hunt bought their first silver futures contracts in 1973. Within a year they began to acquire bullion by occasionally taking deliveries on their contracts. By January 1, 1979, they had accumulated some 37 million troy ounces of bullion as well as 25 million troy ounces in futures positions, controlling silver worth $375 million at prevailing prices.

The Hunts were attracted to silver out of an abiding doubt that governments act in the interests of private investors. Bunker Hunt had suffered the 1973 nationalization of his share in the mammoth Sarir oil field in Libya. At home, the brothers saw their financial assets threatened by increasing inflation and a declining dollar, trends they interpreted as the U.S. government abrogating the responsibility it took on when it issued bonds. Although not among those cranks wanting a collapse of the world financial system and a return to silver currency, they nonetheless concluded that physical assets were less likely to depreciate than financial assets. In silver they found a close equivalent to a financial asset, yet one beyond the influence of governments. (Gold bullion, another candidate for this role, could not be owned by U.S. citizens in 1973.) The Hunts therefore formulated the strategy: buy silver, not U.S. Treasury bonds.

Actually, as a hedge against a decline in the value of financial assets, physical assets of any sort, whether gold, silver, copper, oil, soybeans, sugar, or coffee, performed handsomely in the early 1970s, as the Hunts well knew. Their own sizable (and controversial) positions in soybeans and sugar had proved reasonably profitable. Their main asset, oil, had appreciated significantly.

The Hunt family's wealth resided predominantly in two firms: Placid Oil, which owned mostly reserves and leases, and Penrod Drilling, which owned thousands of oil platforms and drilling rigs. These firms and the family's other holdings were controlled by elaborate individual and group trusts extending through different generations, some 200 distinct companies and trust funds in all (Rowan, 1980a). The Hunt silver interests had an aspect of

20

family participation and, in typical fashion, these investments were placed through many accounts and names. However, unlike Placid Oil and Penrod Drilling, silver trading did not have the family's full participation. Although Bunker Hunt's four children had silver positions during 1979, the Hunt sisters had none and Lamar was much less active than his two brothers, who at times traded together and other times traded separately.[1]

The Hunt brothers were attracted specifically to the silver futures markets because of the convenience that such organized exchanges traditionally provide to traders. The trading floors of futures exchanges offer anonymity and exceptionally low transactions costs. The exchanges' system of daily "marking to market" allows investments to be highly leveraged.[2] The exchanges' standardized contracts give traders considerable flexibility to close out the position, take delivery of warehouse receipts representing the physical commodity, or transfer the contract to another delivery month. These attributes of silver futures markets were extolled in a number of investment guides of the period, notably Smith (1972) and Browne (1974), who went even further, recommending silver in any form.

In the summer of 1979, Bunker and Herbert Hunt doubled their already large positions in silver futures contracts. With two Saudi partners, they also incorporated a vehicle named IMIC, which had the sole purpose of purchasing silver and which by the end of the summer had accumulated futures positions controlling nearly 50 million troy ounces. They advocated silver to others, several of whom initiated large positions through the brokerage house ContiCommodity Services.

These were the controversial acts that led to *Minpeco v. Hunt*, for shortly after the Hunts and their associates took these positions, the silver market began the wild ride shown in Figure 2.1. Did the Hunts cause this sharp price increase and sharp fall? Or were they merely swept along, becoming victims themselves of the turmoil in the silver market?

To determine whether the Hunts caused the turmoil in the silver market is not a straightforward task because many others were involved with the market at the same time, including the commercial dealers, the exchange officials, and the regulators at the Commodity Futures Trading Commission. Similarly, many other markets recorded a sharp increase and sharp fall in price at the same time, including the other precious metals gold, platinum, and palladium. The same question could be asked of the participants in these other markets as of the Hunts: Were these others causing or reacting to the events in the silver market?

This chapter chronicles the turmoil in the silver market as systematically

[1]   There are three sets of children of the eccentric patriarch H. L. Hunt; those referred to here and throughout this book are all members of his "first family" (Hurt, 1981).

[2]   Many of the terms special to futures markets are defined in the Glossary.

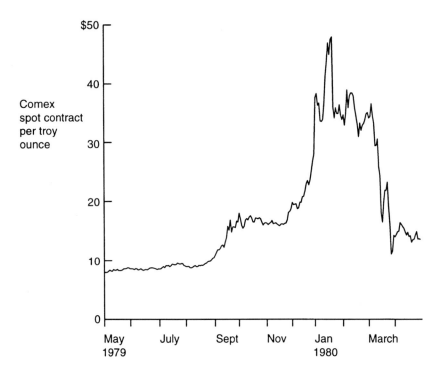

Figure 2.1. Silver prices daily from May 1979 through April 1980

and dispassionately as possible. Each segment into which the chapter is divided covers a different cluster of events and characters. Section 2.1 describes the silver market up to May 1979 while introducing the workings of futures markets. As Figure 2.1 indicates, the twelve months from May 1979 through April 1980 can be split into four distinct phases in silver prices: summer to late August, late August to mid-December, mid-December to January 21, and January 22 through April 1980. Sections 2.2 through 2.5 describe each phase in turn. The risk to brokerage firms and clearing-houses on "Silver Thursday," March 27, 1980, provoked a number of official inquiries, which are discussed in Section 2.6. Section 2.7 recounts the suits and countersuits, delays and settlements, from 1981 to the eve of the trial in 1988. Section 2.8 anticipates how some of the issues apparent in the chronicle were introduced at the trial, the testimony itself being examined in subsequent chapters.

Proper analysis of the events from May 1979 through April 1980 requires an understanding of the order in which they occurred. Unfortunately, none of the lengthy testimony at the trial provided the jury with the sequence of the Hunts' actions in relation to political and economic events, the day-by-day movements in the price of silver, and the decisions of the exchanges and other major traders. The sense that participants in the silver market reacted to continually changing conditions was lost and the Hunts' actions were generally presented as unaffected by such conditions.

2.1 The nature of the silver market in early 1979

As of early 1979, the most visible markets for silver were to be found in London, Chicago, and New York. London housed two markets, the London Metal Exchange (LME) and an informal body of bullion dealers (Gibson-Jarvie, 1983). Although transactions in London occurred throughout the day, prices were reported at the morning and afternoon "rings" conducted at the LME and at the afternoon "fix" among the bullion dealers. The volume of silver traded in London was far exceeded by that traded at the two organized markets in the U.S., the Chicago Board of Trade (CBOT) and the Commodity Exchange in New York (Comex). These two futures exchanges reported price changes continuously during trading from 9.40 a.m. to 2.15 p.m. in New York and 9.40 a.m. to 2.25 p.m. (New York time) in Chicago.

Although the CBOT was (and remains) the larger exchange, Comex in 1979 had a silver futures market nearly twice as large. Comex offered markets in gold, silver, and copper; although gold had recently passed silver as its volume leader, the silver market was essential to Comex's health as an exchange. Trading in silver futures on Comex dated from 1963, and active trading from 1967. In 1969, the CBOT, which had long dominated the grains, initiated trading in silver, its only viable metals market. Even so, the fact that two exchanges in effectively the same time zone could each have a viable futures market in the same commodity, namely silver, was most unusual (Silber, 1981).

The birth of these two silver futures markets related to the activities of the U.S. government, which from 1934 until 1968 dominated the world silver market, first by supporting a price floor through huge purchases placed in stockpiles or minted as coins, then by defending a price ceiling by redeeming so-called silver certificates, both of which discouraged private trading. The U.S. government's cessation of day-to-day control in 1968 had two consequences relevant to events in 1979–1980. First, the U.S. government retained a silver stockpile of nearly 180 million troy ounces, mostly in bullion.[3] Second, huge numbers of the U.S. silver coins in circulation were saved for the value of their silver, in small lots in the back of dresser draw-

---

[3] As of early 1979, 39 million troy ounces was held by the U.S. Mint and 139.5 million troy ounces in the National Defense Stockpile. For several years, the managers of the stockpile had recommended disposal of the silver.

ers, from where they could reappear in commercial channels.

As with other commodities, the two silver futures markets intertwined with what is known as the physicals market. Those transacting there included the mines and refineries of scrap that provide silver bullion; the photography, electronics, and jewelry firms that use it; and the large-scale dealers in precious metals, who both buy and sell bullion and other forms of silver. The large-scale dealers all belonged to one of the organized exchanges – indeed, they were among Comex's most influential members.

To those unfamiliar with futures markets, the very name causes confusion. "Futures" abbreviates "contract for future delivery." The clearer abbreviation would have been "contracts market," for a futures market operates much as if the contracts were traded in their own right. These contracts are not passed physically, but are simply entered on or removed from the books of the exchange's clearinghouse. If a trader buys one and later sells another for the same delivery month, the convenient recourse is to clear them from the account and settle only the difference in price. Thus, many futures contracts do not culminate in delivery. Of course, some do, and in that way the futures and physicals markets are linked.

A conventional forward contract calls for delivery of a commodity of a particular grade, at a precise date and location, with a precise counterparty of known credit risk. A futures exchange transforms a forward contract into a futures contract by standardizing its terms and ensuring its performance. The Comex and CBOT silver futures contracts called for delivery of 5,000 troy ounces of bullion, in ingots of .999 purity.[4] The ingots themselves would not be delivered, but rather a warehouse receipt representing specific ingots at an exchange-approved vault, which were managed by major banks in New York and Chicago and which, by 1979, contained most of the commercial stocks of bullion.

A futures exchange ensures performance through a system of original and variation margin. "Original margin" is a good-faith deposit required of both parties to initiate the position. Original margin can be kept small because of daily "variation margin" paid by one party to the other by way of the clearinghouse. If the price has fallen, the party committed to take delivery pays variation margin equal to the price fall; if the price has risen, the party committed to make delivery pays variation margin equal to the price rise. Such "marking to market," in effect, re-negotiates the contract's price each day, so that neither party has a reason not to fulfill the contract.

By standardizing contracts and reducing counterparty risk, a futures exchange achieves transactions costs as low as 0.1 percent of the value of

---

[4]   In 1971, the New York Mercantile Exchange (NYMEX) designed a futures contract calling for the delivery of a bag of U.S. silver coins in the face amount of $10,000, but by the late 1970s trading in it was moribund.

the commodity in the contract. Active futures markets achieve the happy state in which the low costs of transacting attracts more outside business, the volume encourages more short-term trading on the exchange floor in the style of market making, and the liquidity increases for everyone.

Within the standardization of contracts, futures markets offer a multiplicity of delivery dates. On Comex in 1979, typically twelve different delivery dates were traded simultaneously, roughly one for every other month-long interval up to two years into the future.[5] On the CBOT, the delivery months generally alternated with Comex's, as can be seen in Table 2.1. Thus, at any moment, no single futures price but rather a constellation of them prevailed. For example, at the close of trading on Comex on May 1, 1979, the expiring May '79 contract traded at $7.906 per troy ounce, the July '79 contract at $8.040, the September '79 contract at $8.163, and so on to a delivery month of March '81, at $9.096.

These simultaneous prices for bullion for delivery at different future dates should be seen as part of a much larger web, which, at any one time, encompasses the price of bullion for immediate delivery, the prices for bullion at other delivery dates and at locations other than exchange-approved vaults, the prices of coins and scrap, and the prices for services such as storage, transportation, and refining. The expression "the price of silver" is therefore merely a handy abbreviation, which inevitably glosses over the changing relationships within the web of prices. Perhaps no single concept is as important for comprehending the Hunt trial and the experts' testimony as this idea of a web of prices.

Any one price within this web reflects the influence of its neighbors, because traders will monitor the price relationships for arbitrage opportunities. For example, in early 1979, a handful of traders specialized in monitoring the differences between futures prices on Comex and on the CBOT. Whenever they saw that the prices for the same delivery date had moved to a greater differential than the price of transporting bullion between vaults in Chicago and New York, they bought in the under-priced location and sold in the over-priced location, thus minimizing the price difference between Chicago and New York. Similarly, arbitrage keeps the price relationship among coins, bullion, and the refining fee in line.

A particularly important arbitrage connects the simultaneous prices at the same location for different delivery dates. Because bullion does not spoil, lose moisture, or attract insects, the transformation of bullion on hand today into bullion available in the future is accomplished merely at the cost of interest expenses and small vault fees (including insurance). If the price for

---

[5] From early in the development of futures trading in the mid-nineteenth century, the delivery window has been a calendar month, with those committed to deliver having the choice of the particular day within the month.

Table 2.1. *Trading in silver futures on May 1, 1979*

Delivery month	Comex			CBOT		
	Closing price ($)	Day's volume	Open interest	Closing price ($)	Day's volume	Open interest
May '79	7.906	793	2389	7.960	9	15
June	7.970	3	20	8.040	13697	18312
July	8.040	19358	30128	8.120	22	13
Aug.	—	—	—	8.170	4287	14994
Sept.	8.163	2407	22514	—	—	—
Oct.	—	—	—	8.290	1254	9305
Nov.	—	—	—	—	—	—
Dec.	8.324	4576	27348	8.375	1433	11088
Jan. '80	8.375	806	25581	—	—	—
Feb.	—	—	—	8.490	1655	13634
March	8.478	2587	26429	—	—	—
April	—	—	—	8.590	2025	18289
May	8.581	2020	19766	—	—	—
June	—	—	—	8.690	2013	16671
July	8.684	230	17690	—	—	—
Aug.	—	—	—	8.790	1077	11739
Sept.	8.787	315	10915	—	—	—
Oct.	—	—	—	8.990	479	9056
Nov.	—	—	—	—	—	—
Dec.	8.943	106	1984	8.995	239	7654
Jan. '81	8.994	9	434	—	—	—
Feb.	—	—	—	9.100	171	10572
March	9.096	18	560	—	—	—
April				9.205	67	13777
May				—	—	—
June				9.310	39	10474
July				—	—	—
Aug.				9.415	56	3424
Sept.				—	—	—
Oct.				9.520	41	176
Nov.				—	—	—
Dec.				9.630	18	44
Total		33228	203546		28582	169237

Prices are per troy ounce. Volume and open interest (the number of contracts outstanding at the close of the day's trading) are in lots of 5,000 troy ounces.

a distant delivery month is higher than that for a nearer delivery month plus interest expenses and vault fees, any trader can take delivery at the earlier date, contract to make delivery later, borrow money using the warehouse receipt as security, pay the vault fee, and enjoy a profit at the end. Not surprisingly, it is extremely rare for "spreads" between pairs of delivery months to be above interest expenses and vault fees, that is, "full carrying charges." (The price spreads prevailing at the close on May 1, 1979, shown in Table 2.1, accord within $0.001 per troy ounce of the prevailing interest rates for those intervals plus the average vault fee.) The reverse arbitrage is not physically possible, because silver cannot be transferred from the future to the present.[6] Thus, the web of prices can display a premium for immediate delivery but virtually never a premium for later delivery of bullion.

Because futures markets allow trading at such low transaction costs, they are often employed as part of arbitrage operations, especially by firms dealing in physical commodities. A dealer might spot an opportunity to purchase coins at a further discount to bullion than prevailing refining rates. Acting quickly, it buys the coins and sells a corresponding amount of futures contracts. Hoping that later someone else will be in a hurry for coins or for bullion refined from the coins, it employs the standardized futures contract "as a temporary substitute for a merchandising contract that is to be made later " (Working, 1962, p. 442). Dealers in silver and most commodities tend to be "short" in the futures market, that is, to have committed to make delivery.[7] Speculators (namely those who do not handle the physical commodity) tend to be "long," that is, to have committed to take delivery. (Futures jargon makes these adjectives into nouns, referring to the traders as "shorts" or "longs.")

The many possible arbitrage operations place futures prices at the center of the web of prices. Futures prices, especially in the most actively traded delivery months, often are the first to change. For this reason, futures markets are often credited with "price discovery." Often dealers quote prices for the informal physical market with a close eye on the futures prices. For example, the widely disseminated price for bullion given daily by Handy & Harman is essentially the price of the nearest futures month on Comex as of 11.55 a.m.

For several years before 1979, even as silver prices moved up and down relative to other commodities, the relationships within the web of silver prices remained stable. For instance, the scrap refining fee moved little and

---

6   Mines, secondary refineries, and transport firms all have an incentive to deliver earlier at any such premium; such adjustments are an indirect reverse arbitrage.
7   Dealers who use the futures markets are said to be "hedgers." This terminology suggests a desire to avoid risk. That may be some dealers' motive, but the motive is less important than the fact that dealers use futures contracts in conjunction with positions in other markets (in the example here, in the coin market).

hence the coin/bullion differential remained much the same. The differential between prices for different delivery dates rarely deviated from full carrying charges. This stability of price relationships encouraged two uses of the silver futures markets that had little connection to silver for its own sake: to take positions on interest rates and to minimize taxes.

In 1979 the silver futures markets were used as a futures market in interest rates. At full carrying charges, the spread between any pair of delivery dates is the product of the price of silver and the applicable interest rate. Provided the price of silver does not move appreciably, a position in interest rates can be closely approximated by a "straddle" of delivery months in silver (Jones, 1981), say a long "leg" in the July '79 contract (that is, a commitment to take delivery in July) and a short "leg" in the September '79 contract (that is, a commitment to make delivery in September). Of course, such trades concerning interest rates could be accomplished directly through financial futures markets. In 1979, however, these had just begun and were much less liquid than those in silver.

In 1979 the silver futures markets were also used (as they had been since the early 1970s) for minimizing taxes (Levy, 1981). Widely advertised by major brokerage houses to non-professional traders with incomes subject to a high marginal tax rate, the scheme, in its most advanced form, employed so-called butterfly straddles. A typical butterfly straddle in place in late November 1978 would have comprised: long 200 July '79 contracts, short 400 December '79, and long 200 May '80 contracts. Despite appearances, such butterfly straddles entailed little risk. If the price of silver rose, the long positions would make money but the short position would lose virtually the same amount; if the price of silver fell, the profit on the short position would be offset by a loss on the long positions. The advantage was that any loss could be realized in the 1978 tax year while any gain could be postponed into the next tax year; were the position held more than six months, the gain would qualify for the much lower rate applied to long-term capital gains. This use of the silver futures markets was costing the Internal Revenue Service hundreds of millions of dollars per year.[8]

Tax-motivated butterfly straddles had three important consequences for the silver futures market in early 1979. First, the popularity of straddles increased the liquidity in the silver markets yet that liquidity was apt to dry

---

[8]   By early 1979, the IRS had announced that it would contest all reported losses that had been part of a butterfly straddle. Some tax advisors recommended that their clients avoid the controversy but others maintained that the technique could continue with outright spreads (one leg long, another short) or with spreads between commodities. The tax-postponement game continued in one form or another through 1981, when the law was changed to require all futures positions to be marked to the prices on December 31 of each year, forcing all gains to be realized for tax purposes. Rudnick and Carlisle (1983) explain the changes.

up at short notice, especially if spreads failed to remain at full carrying charges. Second, because later delivery dates postpone a taxable event, silver futures markets sustained much more active trading in the distant "back months." Third, butterfly straddles to shelter an income of even a few hundred thousand dollars required upward of 1,000 contracts, nominally representing millions of troy ounces. To allow such trading, neither the CBOT nor Comex imposed limits on the size of positions in silver, unlike the grain markets where no one trader (except dealers) could have a position of more than 600 contracts.

As will be seen, six characteristics of the silver market in early 1979 became relevant to the Hunt silver litigation:

1. The ease of trading in futures contracts made it possible to establish large positions relatively anonymously and with a minimal commitment of cash.
2. Silver futures markets had no official limits on the size of positions.
3. As in other futures markets, commercial dealers and individual traders had made contracts to deliver bullion they did not possess.
4. Huge amounts of silver existed as stocks, although much of it in coins rather than bullion.
5. Because of the stable relationships in the web of silver prices, silver futures markets were employed for trades motivated by interest rates and tax-minimization. These positions added to the liquidity of the silver market, but were likely to be transferred to other commodities at the least provocation.
6. Because organized exchanges were active for silver in more than one location, the exchanges' officials were aware that trading could divert to a competitor.

2.2   Growth of the Hunts' positions in the summer of 1979

In contrast to those who transacted in silver futures merely to take positions on interest rates or to reduce taxes, Bunker and Herbert Hunt apparently began by treating silver futures as an actively managed long-term investment. During the first part of 1979, they carried on their trading style of previous years. First among their patterns, they held large positions in futures, always above 5,000 contracts and always net long, so that they made or lost substantial sums as the price went rose or fell. Second, they tended to trade several times per week, most often adding contracts but sometimes offsetting and closing them out. Third, they concentrated their positions in the nearby delivery months. Fourth, they tended to wait until just before a contract entered its delivery period to roll their positions into a later month, usually the next offered on that exchange. Fifth, they often stood for delivery, in the general pattern of 500 contracts once every five months. Sixth, they paid little attention to the tax ramifications of rollovers, a "taxable event."[9]

This trading style, which prevailed through the first part of 1979, offered a bonanza to brokerage houses. Instead of a position originally placed in a distant contract that would be rolled over less than once a year, the rollovers into the nearest contract offered six commissions, totaling easily over $1 million annually. The brokerage houses, notably Bache, also provided funds for carrying bullion at profitable interest rates. Not surprisingly, individual brokers often solicited the Hunts, which may be one reason why the brothers opened so many accounts at so many brokerage houses. The lure of commissions may also have blinded the brokerage houses to the risks to their own solvency created by the Hunts' large positions.[10]

In June 1979, the Hunts changed their style of trading. They began to roll over soon-to-mature contracts into much later delivery months in the next tax year, and they began to add straddles. This change in trading style was represented at the trial by the plaintiff as the start of the manipulation. An alternative explanation is that a new tax advisor, hired in May 1979, sought to limit the expenditures on commissions, to limit short-term taxable gains,[11] and to employ straddles for minimizing taxes.

During a few weeks beginning in mid-June 1979, the two Hunts placed large straddles – 7,290 for Bunker Hunt and 5,964 for Herbert Hunt. All had the long leg the closer, that is, the two Hunts could have demanded delivery of 66.270 million troy ounces of bullion before they in turn were required to deliver that amount. Straddles with the long leg in the March '80 contract dominated, numbering an incredible 10,314 contracts.[12]

In July 1979, the two Hunts formed International Metals Investment

---

9   The Hunts' trading pattern at this time can be seen in the trades that Bunker Hunt executed on the CBOT between March and May, 1979. On March 15, 1979, his several personal accounts had among them 1,680 April '79 contracts, and 900 June '79 contracts, what with 3,907 May '79 (Comex) contracts, a huge total of 6,487 contracts. On March 16, he began rolling the April '79 contracts into June '79 (that is, selling April '79 while buying June '79). Most of these rollovers he executed on March 29, the last day before delivery could have begun on the April '79 contract. He repeated the style with the June '79 contract, executing a series of rollovers between May 11 and May 24, again mainly into the nearest CBOT contract. Meanwhile, during those ten weeks he had increased his overall position on both exchanges by 1,411 contracts, although on some days selling 100 or 200 contracts.

10   The Hunts also held 5 percent of the shares in Bache.

11   In a conversation with CFTC officials on October 23, 1979, Bunker Hunt mentioned tax reasons for wanting to delay rolling over or liquidating his March '80 position until January (House Committee on Government Operations, 1980, p. 116).

12   Lamar Hunt placed straddles on September 21, 1979, just after closing out what had been profitable positions in September '79, then December '79 contracts. In late December, he closed out part of the losing legs of these straddles, completing a sequence in accord with the use of the straddles for tax minimization.

Corporation (IMIC), registered as a corporation in Bermuda in partnership with two Saudi investors, Ali Bin Mussalam and Mohammed Aboud Al-Amoudi. After the four principals put up $10 million in cash and $20 million in other securities, with another $70 million that could be called upon, Bunker and Herbert Hunt approached the Dallas office of Merrill Lynch, through whom they and relatives had long traded commodities and securities. In a meeting in late July, Herbert Hunt represented that IMIC intended to become a precious metals dealer and to stand for delivery on silver futures contracts, for which IMIC might seek financing through Merrill Lynch. Ultimately, Merrill Lynch's executive committee approved a trading limit that permitted IMIC to commit all its paid-in capital to original margin (at the amounts prevailing) in silver, with no other reserves or diversification.[13] IMIC bought on the order of 500 contracts nearly every day from late July through early September, spacing those purchases more or less evenly across the delivery months from September '79 through August '80. The Hunts' share of IMIC increased their net long positions in silver by approximately 5,000 contracts, an amount comparable to the expansion of their positions from May to July.

Also affecting the silver market during the summer of 1979 was the build-up of other investors' positions through ContiCommodity Services. Conti's Norton Waltuch had acquired several new clients, notably Naji Nahas, based in Brazil but with many connections in the Middle East, and Banque Populaire Suisse (BPS), based in Berne and Geneva. Actually, BPS was trading through several specially constructed subsidiaries and on behalf of its own clients, many of them Arab investors such as Mahmoud Fustok, who appreciated the anonymity of the Swiss bank and the convenience of what, in many cases, were accounts managed by BPS's traders.[14] Mr. Waltuch, by handling his clients' orders personally, became from mid-July through mid-September a major buyer on Comex, where, reportedly, rallies began even as he approached the exchange's floor.

Both the CFTC Division of Enforcement and Minpeco alleged that the so-called Conti group conspired with the Hunts to manipulate the price of silver. Supposedly, the Conti group targeted the December '79 contract, while the Hunts concentrated on the February '80 and March '80 contracts. Stephen Fay, in *Beyond Greed*, presented the Conti group as the culmination of Bunker Hunt's efforts to recruit Arabs for his manipulation scheme. True, Bunker Hunt had previous contact with Norton Waltuch, Naji Nahas, and Mahmoud Fustok, for all shared an interest in racehorses and several times conversed at racetracks or auctions. Bunker Hunt had also made sev-

---

[13] Merrill Lynch accepted IMIC's account provided IMIC traded only through it.
[14] Some of this trading was through ACLI Commodities (which also handled some accounts for the Hunts), but the name "Conti group" has been applied to all.

eral trips abroad to spread the word about silver, including one in the spring of 1979 to the Arabian Peninsula. In August, he attended a dinner in Deauville, France, hosted by Mr. Fustok. Whatever the subjects discussed during these meetings, neither the CFTC Division of Enforcement nor Minpeco nor Fay found any evidence of a formal plan to manipulate the silver market or to divide the spoils. What can be said is that Mr. Waltuch and his clients acted with the Hunts in the sense that they, too, placed a large bet on an increase in the price of silver.

By the end of August, the combined accounts of the Conti group and Bunker and Herbert Hunt (along with those of Hunt relatives) were net long 33,691 futures contracts. (Table 2.2 provides the holdings by group and relative to the whole futures market.) Because of the straddles in the two Hunts' accounts, the gross long positions were even larger. Of these, 39,836 called for delivery between December 1979 through May 1980. The 39,836 contracts, 27 percent of the open interest in those six delivery months, represented a claim for 199 million troy ounces, whereas certificated stocks of silver not already in the Hunts' and the Conti group's hands amounted to merely 14,162 contracts.

The increase in the Hunts' and the Conti group's futures holdings from June through August 1979 relative to the whole market occurred in part because smaller longs exited the market. At the same time, the principal commercial dealers increased their short positions, which, presumably, were backed by silver in some form. The Hunts and the Conti group had not enticed into the market many small, speculative shorts without experience in locating physical silver. Rather, the conditions were set for a struggle between several large longs and several large commercial shorts.

Manipulative schemers or not, Bunker and Herbert Hunt, in the summer of 1979, had doubled their already colossal bet on the price of silver. In just their personal accounts, including their half of IMIC and their existing holdings of bullion, they had positions approaching 140 million troy ounces (a level they kept more or less until the following March). At prevailing prices, the value of the silver they controlled exceeded $1.3 billion, a large fraction of their net worth. With every $1 movement in the price of silver, they gained or lost $140 million, an amount substantial even to them. Far from seeking prudent diversification, the Hunts had become heavily committed to a single commodity.

2.3   Exchanges' worries during the fall of 1979

On August 22, 1979, the price of silver for September '79 delivery closed at $9.537 per troy ounce. On each of the next eighteen days, with one exception, the closing price reached a new high, rising to $15.90 per troy ounce on September 18. Until December 1979, the spot price remained in the

Table 2.2. *Futures and forward positions of alleged conspirators on August 31, 1979 (contracts for 5,000 troy ounces, those short in parentheses)*

Delivery month	Three Hunt brothers and IMIC	Other Hunt relatives	Conti group	Total	Their % of open interest
Sept '79	589	0	962	1551	73.55
Oct.	530	180	0	710	7.59
Nov.	0	0	20	20	0.00
Dec.	2462	583	7771	10816	25.34
Jan. '80	275	0	0	275	3.30
Feb.	6221	254	0	6475	32.20
March	13553	139	200	13892	46.55
April	80	109	0	189	0.84
May	9334	112	24	9470	38.40
June	990	0	0	990	4.85
July	(5419)	0	(200)	(5619)	26.96
August	226	0	0	226	1.58
Sept	550	0	(24)	526	4.34
Oct.	0	0	0	0	0.00
Nov.	0	0	0	0	0.00
Dec.	(3205)	0	0	(3205)	15.89
Jan. '81	0	0	0	0	0.00
Feb.	0	0	0	0	0.00
March	(1275)	0	0	(1275)	15.23
April	(250)	0	0	(250)	1.52
Total long	36815	1377	8977	47169	13.68
Total short	(13254)	0	(224)	(13478)	3.93
Net long	23561	1377	8753	33691	8.84

The open interest (the number of contracts outstanding at the close of the day's trading) includes Comex and the CBOT but not the LME for which statistics are not available. The principal longs' positions as a percent of open interest are accordingly reduced (by 264 contracts). The entry in the last row in the last column is the sum of the gross long and the gross short divided by twice the open interest across all delivery months.

vicinity of $16 to $17 per troy ounce. During this period, the relationships within the web of silver prices for different qualities, locations, and delivery dates altered from those prevailing earlier in the year. Bullion, for instance, strengthened relative to coins. The prices of contracts for delivery through May '80, the last month in which the principal longs had major holdings, strengthened relative to those for later delivery. These new price relationships, which also remained stable to December, were signaling a premium of perhaps $0.10 to $0.15 per troy ounce for the proximate delivery of bullion, perhaps prompted by the longs' evident intentions to take delivery. Indeed, deliveries on the September '79 contract were heavy.

The surge of late August to mid-September brought many worries to exchange officials, for a sudden price change contradicts the appearance of an "orderly" market and can cause some parties to abrogate their futures contracts. As prices passed $11 per troy ounce on September 4, 1979, the Comex Board of Governors held an emergency meeting, at which it decided to raise original margin on silver futures. It considered altering the margin rules again on September 6, 17, 18, and 19, and ultimately required much larger original margin on new positions. At its regular meeting on October 3, the Comex Board set up an independent committee to monitor their market and suggest rule changes. This Special Silver Committee held a meeting on October 25, at which it decided to increase original margin on all positions, and met again on October 29, November 6, and December 18, at which it interviewed the principal longs. Tension existed between the Special Silver Committee and the Comex Board, and within the Board, about what actions to take, with decisions often altered within days.

Throughout the fall, Comex principally worried about the so-called Conti group's potential demand for deliveries on the December '79 contract. Especially puzzling had been ContiCommodity's ostentatious buying, which many Comex officials interpreted as an attempt to "bull" the silver market. At a meeting on October 22, the Special Silver Committee proposed a scale for reducing the Conti group's December '79 position by 500 contracts per week. On October 25, a representative of ContiCommodity proposed that its clients roll their positions into delivery months later than May '80 and this proposal was accepted. News of this agreement leaked, which Conti took as an opportunity to halt the rollovers.[15]

At first, Comex officials did not know about the Hunts' large positions. Only in late September, when the exchange asked its members for their customers' names, did the Hunts' positions emerge as larger and more worrisome than the Conti group's positions. (The CFTC, however, had possessed full information on the Hunts' positions all along, through the system of large trader reports.)[16] On November 6, the Special Silver Committee interviewed Herbert Hunt, who asserted that he had no connection with the Conti group, an assertion the Committee later confirmed to its

---

[15] The Conti group ultimately took delivery on 3,589 of its peak holding of 9,036 December '79 contracts.

[16] BPS resisted the CFTC's request for these reports, first made on September 7, 1979, until 1981. (McDonnell and Freund [1983] explain the large trader reporting system.)

satisfaction. As for his own positions, he stated that he did not plan to take delivery on them, but Comex's increases in original margin, which favored clearing members over outside customers,[17] were encouraging him to do so. But even as Herbert Hunt attempted to reassure Comex officials that he did not desire physical silver, his brother took an action that created the opposite impression. On November 28, just before the beginning of deliveries on the troubled December '79 contract, Bunker Hunt bought an additional 250 contracts.

Throughout the fall of 1979, officials at the CBOT likewise worried about its silver market, in which the largest positions were held by the Hunts (none was held by the Conti group). In general, the CBOT acted on its concerns by adopting Comex's decisions. Its main initiative was to contemplate restricting the trading on its silver market to liquidation of existing positions. Although the motion did not receive the necessary two-thirds vote at the close of discussions on October 17 and 18, a majority of the CBOT Directors favored it, an indication that many at the exchange remembered its difficulties with the Hunts in its soybean market in the spring of 1977 and simply did not want further dealings with them.[18] Later in October, the CBOT's Business Conduct Committee met with Herbert Hunt to discuss reducing the threat of his and his brother's large positions in silver. Herbert Hunt promised not to take delivery on his February '80 contracts if spreads were less than full carrying charges, a promise of which much was made at the trial.

By early October, if not earlier, market participants knew in general of the magnitude of the Hunts' positions.[19] At that time, the Comex Special Silver Committee detected no conditions for an immediate squeeze or corner and found, by surveying the largest shorts, that they were having no trouble finding bullion for delivery. What concerned exchange officials was the evidence that the silver futures market was functioning less well as a

---

[17] The Comex clearinghouse had increased much less the margin required of its own members than those clearing members were requiring their own customers to deposit.

[18] In April 1977, Bunker Hunt, Herbert Hunt, and several of Bunker Hunt's children collectively held far more soybean contracts than the 600 maximum for speculators, although each individually remained under the position limit. Because the 1976 soybean crop had been small, old-crop futures contracts traded at a 50 percent premium to new-crop delivery months. When the CBOT and CFTC asked the Hunts to reduce their positions in the old-crop contracts, they refused. A court battle was fought over whether the CFTC could pressure the Hunts to reduce their positions and over whether the Hunts had traded in concert. As part of a settlement, the Hunts agreed to respect position limits. (For more, see Markham [1987, pp. 94–7].)

[19] The CFTC did not publish for silver, as for other commodities, compilations from its large trader reports, and so did not provide information such as the aggregate positions of the four largest longs or the total positions of commercial dealers. Perhaps the CFTC viewed the information for silver too distorted by the presence of large tax-motivated straddles.

market. Figure 2.2 shows the problem by contrasting the Comex market's behavior in April 1979 with that in October 1979. As Figure 2.2(a) shows, the price of the nearby contract varied much more during October than during April. On four days in October, as Figure 2.2(b) shows, the futures market was "locked up (or down) the limit" the entire day. Because Comex's price-move limits did not apply to the nearest delivery month, trading persevered, but, as Figure 2.2(c) shows, October's volume declined to less than half that in April. From an individual trader's perspective, these problems added up to a distressing deterioration in liquidity.[20]

The deterioration in the liquidity of the silver futures market placed Comex officials on the horns of a dilemma: If they increased original margin in proportion to the increased volatility, as they should do to protect the contracts' integrity, they discouraged traders from taking on the new positions that would dampen the price swings. Their substantial increase in original margin for positions placed after September 18 also tended to lock in existing positions. Comex officials wanted the big, non-commercial players to exit the market, but the methods they chose made it more difficult for everyone to trade.

Several big players withdrew from the silver futures markets in early October with large "exchanges for physicals" (EFPs). An EFP cancels futures contracts in a private transaction off the exchange's floor, in trade for some of the physical commodity, often in a form or location other than that specified in the futures contract. Typically, EFPs occur between commercial dealers, who, while transferring ownership of coins (for example) also take the opportunity to offset their futures positions between themselves. Futures exchanges are ambivalent about EFPs, which, while offering a convenience to traders, deprive the floor of its life-blood of orders.

In two large EFPs registered on October 5, one of the parties was IMIC, while its counterparties were two principal shorts, Sharps, Pixley, Inc., and Mocatta Metals.[21] These EFPs seemed to confirm rumors that certain silver dealers were in financial trouble, for the two dealers relinquished to IMIC a sizable part of their working inventories. In its EFP, Sharps, Pixley agreed to deliver 5 million troy ounces of bullion promptly in London in exchange for IMIC's 1,000 (Comex) December '79 contracts (representing 5 million troy ounces of bullion in New York) at terms granting no advantage to either party. In exchange for IMIC's 4,583 futures contracts spanning

[20]   Comex officials had additional worries in the fall of 1979. Having found several traders with large positions in copper, the Comex Board held another series of emergency meetings and, in late November, restricted trading in the December '79 contract to liquidation only.

[21]   On October 12, IMIC also agreed to swap with J. Aron and Co. some 2 million troy ounces of silver by warehouse receipts deliverable on the CBOT for silver in London or Zurich. All was to be accomplished by November 16, with no cost to either party.

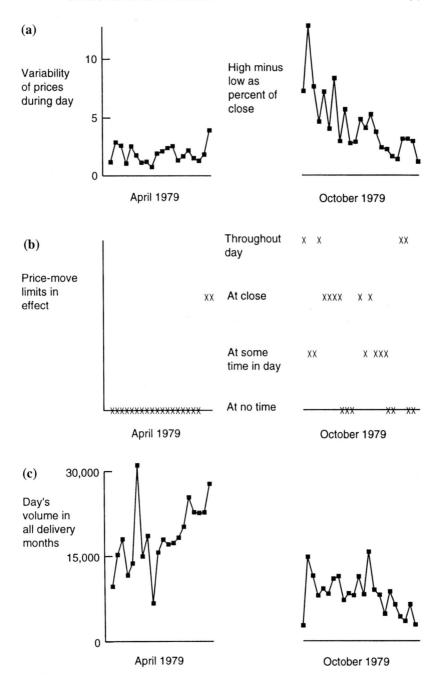

Figure 2.2. Comparison of liquidity within Comex silver market

December '79 through April '80, Mocatta Metals offered silver in various forms, locations, and times of deliveries. IMIC received no discount for bullion delivered at places or times other than the strict terms in its futures contracts, and for some coins, it paid more than their bullion equivalent.[22]

IMIC's EFPs, which supplanted most of its futures contracts, were perfectly consistent with its avowed business purpose of acquiring physical silver. Coupled with the deliveries already taken in September and October, IMIC had acquired 35.3 million troy ounces by mid-December, 27.8 million of that as bullion. Bunker and Herbert Hunt themselves took delivery of 6.425 million troy ounces during the fall of 1979. For the two Hunts, taking delivery afforded sizable tax advantages, given the increase in price since the summer. According to the U.S. tax laws then applicable, a liquidation of a futures position, including a rollover into a later month, triggered a taxable event, upon which any gain would be taxed. In contrast, deliveries taken were not a taxable event; the gain, if it still existed, would be taxed only when the silver was ultimately sold.

By standing for delivery on their futures contracts during the fall of 1979, the principal longs accumulated much of the silver in exchange-approved vaults. Their combined positions in the February '80, March '80, April '80, and May '80 contracts exceeded the free stocks as of mid-December by a multiple of 3.4. Whether they would squeeze the shorts committed to make delivery in the spring depended on both their intentions regarding taking delivery and on the amount of additional bullion that could be placed in the appropriate vaults. The exchanges' worries continued.

2.4   Silver dealers' worries during December 1979 and January 1980

December 1979 and January 1980 brought waves of price increases to the silver market. Having briefly passed $20 per troy ounce for the first time on the first business day of December, the spot price rose to $24.35 on

---

[22]   The minor issue of the conversion rate for coins within the EFP illustrates well the difficulty in taking anything in the silver market at face value, so to speak. According to a letter written by Henry Jarecki, Chairman, Mocatta Metals, to Herbert Hunt on January 15, 1980, the reason for converting coins at the rate of 0.720 troy ounces per $1.00 face value instead of the normal rate of 0.715 was that an option was involved, granted by banks who were keeping coins (in sealed bags) ostensibly as vault cash. Upon payment of a fee, ranging from 0.75 percent to 1.5 percent per annum, the "option" was to buy the silver coins at their face value (the minimum price the coins could ever have). The "option" was actually a means for the banks to earn some interest on otherwise non-interest-bearing required reserves and for metals dealers to avoid paying the full prevailing interest rate. Mr. Jarecki was disingenuous when he said IMIC should have paid for this arrangement. After all, IMIC could have bought coins on its own at the prevailing conversion of 0.715 and made these arrangements with the banks directly.

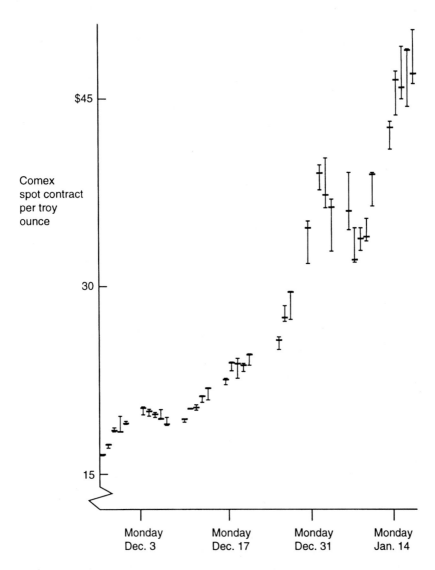

Figure 2.3. Daily Comex silver high, low, and close, November 26, 1979 through January 18, 1980

December 21, an increase of $8.40 since November 21. As can be seen in Figure 2.3, even that price spurt seemed small compared to the increase that followed. By January 2, the spot price had risen to $38.85.

With these substantial price surges, Comex officials felt the situation was slipping out of their control. Within the Special Silver Committee, limits on individual traders' positions were discussed at a meeting on December 18, and background papers were prepared. On Monday, January 7, the Special Silver Committee went to the full Board with a proposal to impose position limits, which Comex, unlike the CBOT, had never applied in any of its markets. The Board approved the proposal as Silver Rule 7.

The imposition of position limits was a reasonable response to the perception that large demands had been put on the futures market as a delivery mechanism. By continuing their informal pressure on major longs and shorts, Comex officials had enabled the December '79 contract to expire smoothly (in the sense that all shorts located deliverable bullion), but they could not countenance such incessant monitoring for every delivery month. Accordingly, Silver Rule 7 limited deliveries to 500 contracts per trader per month, with the restriction to begin in the January '80 delivery month already in progress. (A limit on the amount of deliveries taken had few, if any, precedents on any futures exchange.) In addition, Silver Rule 7 set for each trader a maximum aggregate position of 2,000 contracts (an approach with many precedents). This limit was to be effective from February 18, 1980, with the exception that traders with an existing position in excess of 2,000 contracts had until January 31, 1981 to comply, provided they reduced the excess at a rate of at least 10 percent per month.

Because Silver Rule 7 exempted commercial firms who could demonstrate that their futures positions, whatever their size, were tied to physical silver, whatever the form, the position limits fell disproportionately on the Hunts, as indeed they were meant to do. As of January 7, Bunker Hunt had 13,055 March '80 contracts alone. Allowed to take delivery on merely 500 by Silver Rule 7, Bunker Hunt had until late February to offset those contracts or to roll them into much more distant delivery months.[23]

Bunker Hunt's first response was to exploit a loophole in Silver Rule 7. Having a small position in the January '80 contract, on January 8, he "rolled back" 468 March '80 contracts into the earlier month, later to stand for delivery on all but 15. Despite the relatively small amount of silver involved, his rollback left many officials at Comex with the impression that he intended to flout the new regulations.[24] His many rollovers of the March '80 contract into much later delivery months (2,808 in the week of January 14 alone) seem to have gone unappreciated, although these were the actions Comex encouraged.

For several days following the Comex Board's decision about position

---

23   By February 25, Bunker Hunt had reduced his positions in the March '80 contract to the permissible 500 contracts. Herbert Hunt had similarly reduced his 1,248 contracts to the permissible 500 contracts, although with some prodding from the exchange.

24   Comex officials also concluded that Naji Nahas intended to avoid the position limits, when they learned that his friends and relatives were opening small accounts.

limits, the price of silver remained near $35. On Friday, January 11, however, the market closed at $38.75, 15 percent above the previous day's close. A week later, the market closed even higher at $46.80. The gain from December 11 equaled 134 percent and, since January 18 of the previous year, an incredible 646 percent. Many other metals also reached their all-time highs at this time. Copper was up 25 percent from December 11, platinum was up 60 percent, and gold up 80 percent. All these metals were reacting to political events, notably the Soviet invasion of Afghanistan.

During the price rise of January 1980, the futures markets in silver were failing in their primary responsibility of absorbing large orders with minimal changes in price. Whereas in the previous summer, the typical price change from one silver transaction to the next might have been $0.001 per troy ounce, by January 14, price changes of $0.25 or even $0.50 were frequent. As can be seen in Figure 2.3, the difference between a day's high and low price sometimes exceeded 10 percent of the closing price.[25] Because the silver market was perceived as too risky, the volume of trading decreased substantially. Those traders who arbitraged the Chicago and New York markets, fearing a significant price move while placing positions, often would not trade unless the differential exceeded $1 per troy ounce, previously an incredible profit opportunity. Many small speculators avoided the market. Those who employed silver futures for tax-motivated straddles turned to the gold futures market, whose liquidity remained as deep as previously. Those who used silver straddles as substitutes for interest-rate futures switched to the new interest-rate markets. These departures increasingly isolated the Hunts, the Conti group, and the large commercial shorts, any of whom would swamp the market in an attempt to exit.

In mid-January 1980, the major commercial shorts faced sizable prospective losses that were not necessarily offset by their inventories of silver coins and bullion. Not only did they face much higher interest rates and refining fees on their inventories but they had to pay interest on the substantial variation margin called for by the rising prices. In response to their problems, they took the initiative to arrange EFPs with the Hunts and to influence the regulatory environment.

A typical transaction that might have been made in July 1979 can illustrate the troubles for a commercial short. A dealer might have been offered bags of coins at an attractive $0.20 per troy ounce discount to bullion

---

[25] The limits on daily price moves in all but the nearest delivery month exacerbated the illiquidity. To trade the more distant contracts despite the price-move limits required a trade in the spot month and a straddle into the more distant month – a costlier method. In January 1980, the gold and copper markets were similarly affected by price-move limits, but because the limits were a higher percentage of the prevailing price than in silver, the more distant contracts traded freely for some part of each day. Silver futures "locked up the limit" for days on end.

because the seller was in a hurry. Buying the coins, the dealer might have sold the corresponding amount of bullion for delivery on March '80 contracts at the prevailing price of $10. By assuming that interest rates, refining fees, and margin expenses would remain relatively stable until March, the dealer could anticipate a profit of some $0.10 per troy ounce, which would amount to an attractive 17 percent annualized rate of return on the dealer's own capital.

Alas, by mid-January 1980, interest rates had increased from 10 to 15 percent, the refining fee for March service had surged from $0.10 to an incredible $4 per troy ounce (the refineries being pressed beyond rated capacity), and the March '80 contracts were trading at $48. This representative deal, with its implicit speculation that the interest rate and refining fee would remain stable, had done worse than could have been imagined. Also, the futures exchange, daily marking the March '80 contract price to market, had called on the dealer to pay the $38 difference in variation margin. Of course, the dealer would receive the much higher price upon making delivery in March. However, the variation margin was due prior to delivery and no provision had been made for the interest expense over the interim.[26] By March, this representative deal's cumulative interest expense on variation margin would approach $1.20 per troy ounce.

Given such unanticipated expenses for maintaining positions, the commercial short would be tempted to sell the coins and buy back the contract to deliver bullion, taking the losses with respect to interest rates and refining fees then and there. Yet because of the ever wider bid–ask spreads, such a hurried reversal of a trade in futures sacrificed not the $0.01 of the previous July but a minimum of $0.25 per troy ounce, while a similar hurried reversal in the coin market sacrificed not the previous $0.10 but several dollars per troy ounce, because other dealers, in the same bind, had little cash for buying coins. The loss on unwinding positions immediately would have exceeded the cost of persisting with them. Thus, as of mid-January 1980, a commercial short's typical trade of the previous July, made with the reasonable expectation of a profit of $0.10 per troy ounce, had developed into a $6 loss, $0.50 already realized because of interest paid on variation margin and $5.50 in prospect.

In mid-January 1980, those who owned bullion and had not previously sold it forward could realize extraordinarily high profits by selling at current prices. Owners of mines who had not yet committed their production could lock in high current prices by selling distant futures. (Occidental Petroleum purportedly sold 2.5 years' output of a mine entering produc-

---

[26]   Early in the development of futures markets, in the 1880s, the Liverpool Cotton Exchange adjusted variation margin for the time value of money, but decided that the small sums were not worth the administrative cost.

tion.) Those who owned refining capacity and had not committed that capacity in advance could enjoy years' worth of normal net revenue in just a few months. Those who had the financial reserves to buy coins could obtain them at a substantial discount, even allowing for the increased refining fees. Most commercial shorts, however, could only regret that they had committed to deliver bullion at prices much lower than were current – prices that did not cover their present expenses. They could take little solace from the thought that speculative shorts had lost even more.[27]

As silver prices became more volatile, the exchanges and their clearing-houses failed to increase the original margin they required of their members, which soon meant that most silver dealers were not sufficiently protecting their contracts. The Clearing Association for Comex, for example, had not raised the original margin required of its members since the early fall of 1979. Large dealers continued to post original margin of $1.50 per troy ounce, which had become an inconsequential protection because prices were moving that much within an hour. The variation margin, which, in principle, was adjusted daily to ensure that the contract price equaled the market price, was limited to $1.00 per troy ounce per day, and therefore, in mid-January, trailed behind the market price by as much as $9 per troy ounce. The system of original and variation margin is the first line of defense against default, in which case the clearinghouse, in principle, steps in to fulfill the contract. Because the Comex Clearing Association's guarantee of futures contracts depended on the collective backing of its members, who were predominately the commercial shorts in trouble, a single default would have closed Comex.

By mid-January, the principal shorts were approaching default, for they were running out of capacity to pay any more variation margin. Their situation made many bankers nervous, in some instances because the sums required by the shorts were approaching the limit a bank could lend to one customer. Engelhard Mineral & Chemical Corp., for example, had by mid-January paid some $1.3 billion in variation margin on its positions in silver.[28] A fundamentally sound company, it could probably have arranged

---

27 Minpeco itself had gotten into financial straights with the price surge of December. From mid-October through mid-November, it established short positions of 15.7 million troy ounces, half through London forwards, and all for relatively nearby delivery dates. Some 3.6 million troy ounces was backed by inventory (1 million in lead/silver concentrate); the remaining 12.1 million troy ounces was an "anticipatory hedge" of forecasted sales over the next year, in effect a bet that prices had peaked in the $16–17 range. At the higher prices of mid to late December, Minpeco closed out its short positions, losing on the 3.6 million troy ounces any appreciation of bullion for nearby delivery relative to lead/silver concentrate (perhaps $0.30 per troy ounce) and losing on the 12.1 troy ounces the full $6 to $7 per troy ounce.

28 As of December 31, 1979, its current liabilities (mostly short-term debt incurred by its Philipp Brothers affiliate) equaled $4.4 billion, up from $1.8 billion the year before.

credit with other banks, but hardly had time to do so. Engelhard was writing checks daily to the Comex and CBOT clearinghouses for some $54 million, with eight or nine such payments in prospect.

The solution for several of the commercial shorts was an exchange for physicals with the Hunts, the type of transaction Sharps, Pixley and Mocatta Metals had conducted with IMIC in October. From January 10 through January 22, Bunker and Herbert Hunt made EFPs with Engelhard's trading arm, Philipp Brothers, and also with Sharps, Pixley Inc., Bunker Hill Co., Swiss Bank Corp., and Westway Metals, which reduced Bunker Hunt's March '80 Comex position alone by 3,842 contracts. The EFPs with Engelhard reduced its futures positions by 5,700 contracts, or some 53 percent, allowing it to avoid paying over the next few days some $200 million in variation margin. All the EFPs called for the delivery of bullion, although mostly at locations other than exchange-approved vaults. The Hunts again offered generous terms to their counterparties, although they did enjoy some discounts for delayed delivery, in accordance with the carrying charges prevailing in the futures market.

Although the EFPs during mid-January had allowed the parties to reduce their futures positions without upsetting prices, and although the silver market on Friday, January 18, had closed several dollars below its high for the week, the sense of urgency among Comex officials did not abate. Raymond Nessim of Englehard, First Vice-Chairman of the Comex Board, set up an emergency meeting for Monday, January 21. That morning the Board delayed the opening of the silver market while it deliberated. It announced, effective that day, that trading in silver futures, regardless of the delivery month, would be limited to liquidation only.

The limitation of trading in all months to liquidation only was an extreme action. For practical purposes, it closed the Comex silver market, for only those with existing positions could trade and then only to close out their positions. Previously exchanges (including Comex itself for December '79 copper) had resorted to this restriction, but only for a single delivery month and usually in the last days before expiration. When the CBOT on January 22 imposed its own limitation of trading to liquidation only, an action already contemplated in October, it confined the restriction to its next two delivery months, February '80 and April '80.

With the limitation of trading to liquidation only, the price of silver for all delivery months fell precipitously. Although silver had passed $50 in London and Chicago as the Comex Board deliberated, it fell below $40 in the abbreviated session that followed, before closing at $44. After another Comex Board meeting that afternoon and the CBOT's decision to restrict trading, the spot price on Tuesday, January 22, closed at $34, down 27 percent from Friday's close. The price of gold also dropped, to 20 percent below its all-time high reached January 18. Because holders of short positions receive variation margin when prices fall, these declines greatly lessened the financial pressure on the principal commercial shorts.

2.5 The Hunts' worries during February and March 1980

As the pressure on the commercial shorts eased in late January, that on the Hunts increased, not only because the price fell but because the restriction of trading to liquidation only and the pervasive decline in liquidity fell disproportionately on them. With the position and delivery limits to become effective on February 18, Bunker and Herbert Hunt had to trade out of the nearby contracts while the commercial shorts did not.[29] Although they and the Conti group had still achieved enormous profits (as is evident in Figure 2.4(a)), it was increasingly obvious that prevailing prices of around $30 would not persist if they were to try to realize their gains.[30]

More insidious, the Hunts and the Conti group had become ever shorter of ready funds. When silver prices had been rising, the daily variation margin passing through the futures exchanges had converted the Hunts' and the Conti group's gains into billions of dollars of cash. For the most part, they had not used this cash to expand their positions,[31] but to take delivery of bullion, as the composition of their positions in Figure 2.4(b) shows. As the price fell, more and more of this cash had to be returned as variation margin on the remaining futures contracts. And, effective from February 4, the Hunts had to commit $12 per troy ounce as original margin on futures contracts – a substantial increase from $0.25 per troy ounce the summer before. Because large deliveries through the EFPs were scheduled for March 31, the drain on their ready funds promised only to increase.

Of course, the Hunts could use the bullion taken in delivery as collateral for loans. From January 21 until March 27, Bunker Hunt, Herbert Hunt, and IMIC added nearly $900 million of loans to the $500 million they had arranged previously (SEC, 1982, p. 34).[32] Yet these loans represented only

---

[29]   Furthermore, the Comex Board amended the rule restricting trading to liquidation only on January 24 to permit the establishment of short positions tied to commercial marketing, but did not allow new long positions even for commercial purposes.

[30]   Despite the lack of liquidity through February 14, when the restriction of trading to liquidation only was removed, Bunker and Herbert Hunt rolled 5,994 February '80, March '80, and May '80 contracts into more distant delivery months. They did not, however, take the occasion to reduce their positions outright.

[31]   An observer at the time, Angrist (1980) characterized the Hunts as pyramid builders, expanding their positions with profits, which would further increase the price. Only the trading by Lamar Hunt and by the Huddlestons (Bunker Hunt's daughter and son-in-law) looked much like a pyramid.

[32]   The affairs of those in the Conti group are less well documented; evidently, they too borrowed money to take delivery of silver.

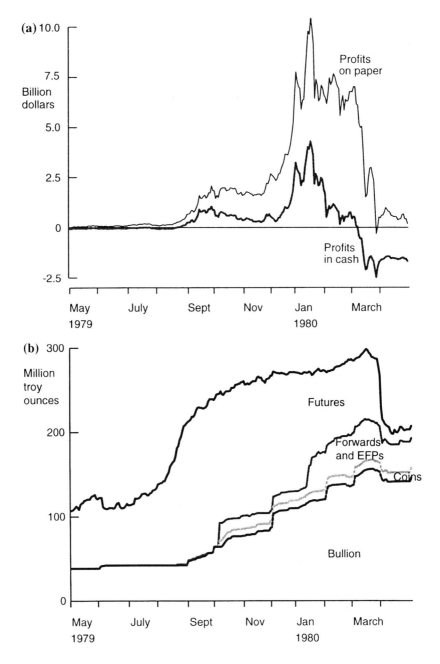

Figure 2.4. The Hunts' and Conti group's profits and composition of positions in silver from May 1979 through April 1980

65 to 75 percent of the value of the bullion, leaving them to finance $10 to $12 per troy ounce out of their own cash. The two Hunts had to work very hard to arrange the most recent loans, because a number of banks refused to increase their exposure or to lend at all (SEC, 1982, pp. 38–9). When, on March 14, a directive from the Federal Reserve officially discouraged U.S. banks from lending for speculation in commodities, Bunker Hunt himself flew to Europe to approach banks there.

Beginning on March 10, silver prices declined sharply from the previous level of $30 or so, falling to $17 on March 17–18, as can be seen for the settlement prices of the March '80 contract in Figure 2.5(a). Although other metals' prices declined too, perhaps in response to worsening symptoms of recession, silver's price fell the most, just as previously it had risen the most. The Hunts, as holders of long positions, were obliged to hand over variation margin of some $60 million daily because of the falling prices, as can be seen in Figure 2.5(b). Because the official settlement prices, such as that for the May '80 contract in Figure 2.5(a), again lagged behind market prices, more payments of variation margin were in prospect – on March 17, these payments would be more than $1 billion, if market prices did not change. Comex did not reduce the amount of original margin in proportion to the price decline, which would have released funds for variation margin. Worse, the loans backed by bullion required more cash to restore the 35 percent cushion.

On March 13, IMIC failed to provide $56 million in cash to Merrill Lynch to pay for deliveries just taken and variation margin due. On Monday, March 17, Bunker and Herbert Hunt notified Bache that they could not provide cash for variation margin due. In both cases, they instead offered bullion as security. Merrill Lynch and Bache chose to pay their own cash to the clearinghouses, in effect acquiescing to more loans to the Hunts.

Although by Tuesday, March 25, silver prices had recovered to just above $20, the variation margin calls to the Hunts, lagging behind the price fall because of the daily price-move limit of $1, had continued remorselessly at some $60 million each day. The fate narrowly avoided by the commercial dealers in January awaited the Hunts. On the evening of March 25, Herbert Hunt informed Bache that he and his brother would be unable to pay additional variation margin or supply collateral. The next night, at a formal meeting in New York City, Herbert Hunt informed the other brokerage houses.

Already by the afternoon of March 26, the Hunts' cash shortage had become public knowledge, unintentionally signaled by Bunker Hunt himself. From Paris, the last stop on his unsuccessful trip to arrange financing

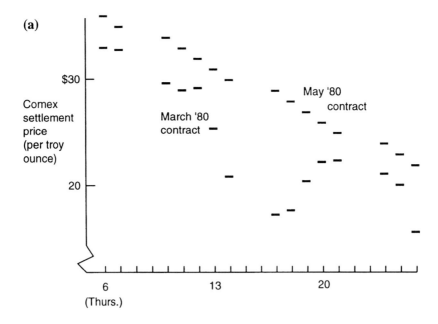

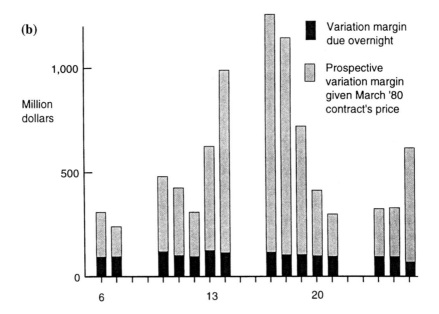

Figure 2.5. The price decline during March 1980 and the Hunts' and Conti group's variation margin payments

with banks outside the U.S.,[33] he announced an agreement among bullion owners to issue silver-backed bonds, to be "distributed through financial institutions in denominations small enough to attract a wide range of investors." According to his press release, the group of silver owners comprised Bunker Hunt, two Saudi associates, and Mahmoud Fustok and Naji Nahas, two of the Conti group. Bunker Hunt's announcement occurred while the silver markets in the U.S. remained open, upon which the price dropped to $15.80, adding to his need for cash to pay variation margin. The announcement of the silver-backed bonds was also damaging in the longer term, for it provided a strong suggestion of association between the Hunts and the Conti group.[34]

In response to the Hunts' failure to pay variation margin, their brokers began closing out their outstanding futures position and selling some of the bullion they held as collateral. Most of the selling took place on "Silver Thursday," March 27. The brokerage houses, not the Hunts, directed the selling, and other market participants were aware of the pressure to sell at any price.

Amid heavy volume and sharp price changes between transactions, the Comex silver market opened yet lower that Thursday, March 27, falling at one point to $10.40 per troy ounce, before recovering slightly the next day, but only to $12. Other metal prices, notably gold, also fell, but none so much as silver. The relationships among silver prices also changed. No longer was there a premium for immediate delivery of bullion, and the coin/bullion differential narrowed to the range of the previous summer.

A number of the commercial dealers took the opportunity to buy. Mocatta Metals had sold some 800 additional futures contracts over the previous week and repurchased the majority. Engelhard closed out a major part of its short position, some 1,800 contracts, for the first time since the EFPs with Bunker and Herbert Hunt in mid-January. (Mocatta Metals' and Engelhard's simultaneous trades in physicals are not known.) Occidental Petroleum also bought back the 1,250 contracts it had sold in mid-January, realizing a profit of $120 million.

The Hunts, their positions reduced by 47 million troy ounces,[35] continued their search for cash. Particularly troublesome was the more than $400

---

[33] The Hunts had millions of troy ounces in vaults in Europe that could have been used as collateral for loans, but they had not segregated these assets by prospective borrower, as European banks required.

[34] Another suggestion of association included that, when in New York in January 1980, Bunker Hunt stayed in the same hotel as Naji Nahas, who, it seems, made both reservations. In February, Bunker Hunt also agreed to buy some bullion from Mr. Nahas.

[35] Not all the Hunts' futures positions were immediately liquidated. Bache, its press notices to the contrary, rolled over some of the Hunts' positions into more distant delivery months in a complex series of transactions.

million due to Englehard on Monday, March 31. The Hunts offered to forgo taking delivery on the bullion as scheduled, to concede to Engelhard the bullion it held as security for performance of the EFPs, and to assign large oil rights in the Beaufort Sea (Bernstein, 1980). The Hunts also began borrowing against Placid Oil. Later, the Hunts used Placid as an umbrella to secure all their loans. With the Federal Reserve's tacit approval, a syndicate of thirteen banks lent Placid Oil $1.1 billion.[36] A recovery of the silver price to $15 in early April also eased the Hunts' finances. They paid all their outstanding balances with brokerage houses.[37]

On Thursday, March 27, Bache (and possibly Merrill Lynch) had substantively, although not technically, violated net capital requirements as a result of the Hunts' arrears. Many regulators were concerned that a failure of one such major brokerage house would trigger a cascade of similar failures. All financial markets were rattled on "Silver Thursday."

2.6   Recriminations and controversies

As events in the silver market receded from the front pages of newspapers, as the Hunts refinanced their remaining positions, and as silver prices stabilized, the sense that the financial system had been on the brink of a major failure induced some parties to call for investigations and others to cover their tracks as much as possible. Within a month, House and Senate subcommittees held hearings specifically on the silver crisis, at which the Hunts and exchange officials testified. Further Congressional hearings in May 1980 on re-authorizing the CFTC (House Committee on Agriculture, 1980) and on proposed changes in the Federal Reserve (House Committee on Banking, Finance, and Urban Affairs, 1980) became venues for investigating the silver market.

Over the next two years, several official reports were issued about the silver crisis. In preparation for testimony before Congress, Comex produced a chronology detailing its own and its clearinghouse's actions from September 1979, while the CBOT prepared a study of the silver and gold markets over the previous fifteen years. As a follow-up to its testimony before the House and Senate Committees on Agriculture, the CFTC produced a study on the silver market.[38] Originally, the Securities and Exchange Commission (SEC) was to have participated in this report, but it issued its own.

The first inquiry at the Congressional hearings was into the substantial

---

[36]   The loan agreement, which provided a line of credit, not all of which was called upon, did not specify a schedule for disposing of silver, but clearly it expected a reduction. The agreement explicitly restricted the Hunts from any speculation in commodities.

[37]   Naji Nahas, however, left substantial debts unpaid.

[38]   When submitted, the CFTC's report was the subject of additional hearings (Senate Committee on Agriculture, 1981, and House Committee on Agriculture, 1981).

loan negotiated by the Hunts at a time when the Federal Reserve's tight monetary policy made loans for others difficult to obtain. Accordingly, the Federal Reserve's Chairman was called to the hearings, where he spent much time emphasizing that the loan consolidated existing debts and so did not extend new credit (although most of the existing loans were only a few months old). In his view, the loan allowed the Hunts to dispose of their physical silver in an orderly fashion, although it was soon evident that the Hunts were not liquidating their hoard.[39]

Although the terms "manipulation," "excessive speculation," and "concentration" were used at the hearings in reference to the Hunts, even greater concern was expressed about whether the CFTC and the exchanges had overseen the silver market effectively. Both the CFTC, defending its jurisdiction of financial futures markets, and the exchanges, protecting their right to self-regulation, presented themselves as having been in control of the situation throughout. They could hardly claim that the Hunts had patently manipulated the silver market, for doing so would have indicted their own responses as inadequate. The Chairman of the CBOT testified that the silver price spike was attributable to economic and political events (Senate Committee on Agriculture, 1980, p. 251). Comex, which had taken most of the controversial actions, had to initiate a delicate public relations campaign, especially after several witnesses, self-appointed representatives of small longs, accused the commercial dealers on the Comex Board as having acted out of self-interest when restricting trading to liquidation only.

Taking up this theme of the exchanges' self-serving intervention, Bunker and Herbert Hunt asserted that the problems in the silver market should be ascribed to the decline in liquidity, which the exchanges' rules had exacerbated. They presented themselves as victims rather than causes of the price moves and categorically denied manipulating the market. Yet their evasiveness about their affairs and the emerging evidence of their huge positions increased suspicions about their role. They had not come to the hearings with compilations of their positions (they later provided them) and Bunker Hunt would not make an estimate, because "it would be a speculation and my lawyer tells me not to speculate" (Senate Committee on Agriculture, 1980, p. 194). Each claimed only the most general involvement in the mechanics of his trades and only a vague awareness of the other's trading.[40]

The SEC's report, published in 1982, focused on the price decline of March 1980 that culminated with "Silver Thursday." The report investigated not whether the Hunts affected the market,[41] only whether the various

---

[39] The loan remained outstanding a year and a half later, at which time the Hunts retained at least 63 million troy ounces of silver.
[40] Bunker Hunt freely acknowledged his friendship with Naji Nahas.
[41] Errors in investigative subpoenas and an injunction the Hunts obtained over the SEC's jurisdiction limited the scope of the report.

brokerage houses had followed procedures. While concluding that no rules had been broken, it castigated the brokerage houses for allowing bullion to be used as security for loans on bullion. It presented the brokerage houses as carrying such large positions for the Hunts that the price effect of a partial forced sale would obviously have jeopardized the value of the remaining positions. The report also questioned the brokers' practice of valuing positions by means of official prices constrained by the limit on daily price moves, because arrears could develop sufficient to threaten the solvency of the brokerage houses themselves.[42]

The SEC's criticisms were sensible yet narrow. It correctly questioned the use of silver as collateral to secure loans to purchase silver, but did not consider the overall valuation of an investor's collateral as the important issue. It pointed out the risks incurred by not fully marking to market during a price decline, yet did not recognize that such risks also applied during a price rise. The SEC seemed to be saying that a default during the price decline by Bache and Merrill Lynch would have greater repercussions than a default during the price rise by Engelhard, a clearing member owing billions of dollars to major banks.

In contrast to the SEC's report on the silver crisis, the CFTC's report, published in 1981, offered much less documentation and less specific analysis. It suggested, but did not conclude, that the Hunts' insistence on deliveries had contributed to the price spike, and it did not label the Hunts' effect a manipulation. It recounted the inconclusive meetings on silver held by the CFTC's Commissioners from September 1979 through March 1980, but made no judgment about the effectiveness of regulatory oversight, even though it could plausibly have argued that the few restrictive measures available to the CFTC might only have made matters worse.

Throughout the price spike, the principal regulators had been the two exchanges themselves, Comex more often than the CBOT. Although Comex's official report presented their many actions (recapitulated in Table 2.3) as disinterested, industry observers at the time questioned their fairness. Indeed, a strong case can be made that the interventions favored the large commercial shorts who dominated Comex's Board.[43] Comex's

---

[42]   The brokers' practice derived from the Comex Clearing Association's practice. Chastened by events in early 1980, the Clearing Association changed its rules to tie variation margin to changes in the spot contract's price should other delivery months be constrained by price-move limits.

[43]   Alan Trustman made this point the basis for an article in the September 1980 *Atlantic Monthly*, "The Silver Scam: How the Hunts Were Outfoxed." Roy Rowan also made this argument in the July 28, 1980 issue of *Fortune*, "Who Guards Whom at the Commodity Exchange." The SEC felt that there was the possibility of self-interest in Comex's restriction of trading to liquidation only, which is one reason why it broke with the CFTC over issuing a report together.

Table 2.3. *Major actions by exchanges in the silver market, September 1979 through April 1980*

Sep. 4–6	Comex and CBOT Boards increase original margin on new positions.
Sep. 17–18	Comex and CBOT Boards increase substantially original margin on new positions.
Oct. 3	Comex Board establishes a Special Silver Committee.
Oct. 18	CBOT and Comex delay opening silver market, while CBOT Board defeats proposal to require trading for liquidation only.
Oct. 25	Comex Special Silver Committee agrees with Conti group on plan for reduction of group's position in December '79 contract. It and CBOT Board raise original margin substantially to apply retroactively as of November 12. CBOT Board imposes position limits, effective February 1, 1980.
Nov. 6	Comex Special Silver Committee defers retroactive margin requirements to February 4, 1980; interviews Herbert Hunt about delivery intentions and connections with Conti group.
Nov. 7	CBOT Board defers position limits to April 1, 1980.
Dec. 6	CBOT Board reduces original margin on positions entered into after September 18, 1979.
Dec. 27	CBOT Board increases margin on all positions, including those predating September 18, 1979.
Jan. 7	Comex Board imposes position limits, effective February 18, 1980.
Jan. 18	CBOT Board raises original margin on all positions.
Jan. 21	Comex delays opening until 1.30 p.m. Its Board restricts trading to liquidation only in all months; disbands Special Silver Committee.
Jan. 22	CBOT Board retricts trading to liquidation only in nearby months.
Feb. 4	Comex Board raises original margin substantially on positions predating September 18, 1979.
Feb. 14	Comex Board terminates restriction of trading to liquidation only.
Mar. 6	CBOT Board reduces original margin on positions post-dating September 18, 1979.
Mar. 27	Comex Board reduces original margin.

President was certainly disingenuous when he stated (House Committee on Agriculture, 1980, p. 284) that Board members whose short futures positions equaled their physicals positions had nothing to gain or lose from the Board's decisions, because the typical commercial short faced prohibitive losses of $6 per troy ounce in mid-January 1980.

The specter of self-interest inevitably accompanies decisions by the board of a futures exchange when such boards are dominated by the exchange's own traders. In silver, as in other commodities, some board members had losing positions while others had winning positions (and often these losses or profits could be calculated only with reference to the member's positions in other commodities and on other exchanges). By and large, the boards of the CBOT and Comex avoided conflicts of interest during the turmoil in the silver market. The CBOT generally ensured that directors without positions in silver made decisions about that market. The boards of both exchanges considered the long-run viability of the silver futures market when they resisted the surprising proposals for forcibly closing out all positions at a previous price, made by Mr. Nessim of Engelhard in the fall of 1979 and by Bache with Herbert Hunt at the tumultuous end of March 1980.

Nonetheless, immediate self-interest was at the center of two decisions by the exchanges, each of which threatened the viability of the silver futures markets. The Comex Board's decision at its emergency meeting on January 21, 1980 to restrict all trading to "liquidation only" was, in my judgment, unduly influenced by the self-interest of a dominant commercial short (if not several others). Mr. Nessim of Engelhard, his firm at its capacity to pay variation margin, pressed for the emergency meeting and worked to take back the decision-making power delegated to the Special Silver Committee. The ostensible reason for the Board's hurried decision, made without back-ground papers, was that the position limits were not forcing the principal longs from the nearby contracts. Out-of-date evidence on the number of contracts outstanding was offered, which reflected neither the Hunts' siz-able EFPs nor Bunker Hunt's rollover of 2,500 March '80 contracts. If pressure on the nearby contracts constituted the problem, a trading restriction in just those delivery months should have sufficed.

The Comex Clearing Association's decision that increases in margin would apply to customers but not clearing members, and to new positions but not existing ones, was likewise dominated by the self-interest of the commercial shorts. Of course, had the Clearing Association required additional original margin from the commercial shorts, it might have brought the commercial shorts' cash needs in January 1980 beyond their capacity. But by exempting a significant group of traders from the smaller, *ex ante* adjustments that ensure the performance of contracts, the Clearing Association made a systemic crisis much more likely.[44]

The main problem with the exchanges' decisions during 1979 and 1980 was that they were so delayed. The increases in original margin and the tiering of margin with the size of positions were appropriate responses to the higher and more variable price of silver, yet they should have been applied sooner (and not left at $12 per troy ounce when the price fell to $12). The exchanges' position limits, although appropriate, were applied only after the Hunts had accumulated their large positions, mainly because the exchanges, with the CFTC's compliance, had not wanted to encumber tax-motivated straddles. More helpful would have been a limit, as was belatedly imposed, of deliveries to any one trader in any one month.

The exchanges' main failure was in not anticipating the possibility, however remote, of a price spike such as that of 1979–1980 or the possibility, however remote, of bullion going to a substantial premium over coins. Had the exchanges contemplated what would happen to those paying variation margin cumulating to several multiples of the original price, they might have redesigned the system to compensate for the interest expense until the delivery date. Had the exchanges focused on what would happen during unusual price relationships, they might have redesigned their contracts with safety valves. A (troy) ounce of prevention is worth a pound of cure.

2.7   Legal maneuvers

Somehow the tribulations of the silver market during 1979 and 1980 would have been incomplete without litigation. And lawsuits were quick to appear. The Hunts were among the first to approach legal counsel, the New York firm Hughes, Hubbard & Reed, about the possibility of suing Comex over its imposition of position limits and trading for liquidation only. (Hughes, Hubbard & Reed in turn approached Professor Ross for preliminary economic analysis of this complaint.)[45] The ACLI brokerage house sued its customer BPS. Mahmoud Fustok sued BPS; when that suit was dismissed for lack of jurisdiction, he sued ContiCommodity Services for assigning losing trades to his account and profitable ones to other customers. (This case went to trial in early 1986; Conti settled after the plaintiff's presentation.) The CFTC Division of Enforcement began an inquiry. Many of those

---

[44]   If the margin system of futures exchanges made trouble for commercial dealers, forward contracts offered no panacea. For instance, the forward contracts at some $37 per troy ounce, arranged with Engelhard as part of EFPs, were potential default for much more per troy ounce than the Hunts' futures accounts.

[45]   My own involvement began at that point, as a research assistant for Professor Ross.

who had lost money trading silver consulted lawyers.[46] Four class action suits were filed against the Hunts, the brokerage houses, and the exchanges,[47] although in only one of these suits was the class certified (two were dismissed for exceeding the statute of limitations), with Herbert Deutsch of the New York law firm Deutsch and Frey the enterprising attorney who accomplished the certification of the so-called Gordon class. Minpeco, which had been advised by its brokers, Merrill Lynch and Hutton, to sell short in October and November only to have the market move against it in December, consulted the small Washington-based law firm Cole and Corette, which the Peruvian government employed for trade matters. Minpeco filed suit in 1981 (registered as No. 81 Civ. 7619 (MEL)) for $750 million against its brokers, the Hunts, the Hunts' brokers, the CBOT, and Comex. These and a number of other silver-related suits were consolidated under Judge Morris E. Lasker, U.S. District Court, Southern District of New York.

When, in early 1982, the U.S. Supreme Court removed an uncertainty about the right of private action in Federal courts for damages under the Commodity Exchange Act,[48] Minpeco's suit became much more credible. On behalf of the Hunts, Hughes, Hubbard & Reed directed Professor Ross to explore a defense. He and his associates commenced with a laborious reconstruction of daily trades from the Hunts' poorly kept records, a compilation of other metals' prices for comparison, and time lines of political and economic events, thus establishing the types of economic analysis used much later at the trial.

The Hunts, however, changed strategies again. The economic analysis was stopped, Hughes, Hubbard & Reed was dismissed, and the Dallas-based firm Shank, Irwin, Conant, Williamson & Grevelle, which the Hunts had used as counsel for their Congressional testimony, took over. The new strategy became one the Hunts had used to advantage before: the attritional war of seeking every delay in the scheduling of a trial and fighting every request for documents and depositions. Because the loser does not pay the winner's legal costs under U.S. civil law, a defendant with deep pockets can

---

[46] Even some who profited during this period found themselves in acrimony. Occidental Petroleum and its partners in the mine whose production had been sold forward in January 1980 sparred over the large profits from buying back the contracts in March.

[47] *Zeltzer v. Hunt* (S.D.N.Y., No. 80 Civ. 4009 (MEL)) proposed a class of all who traded silver in commercial quantities from January 1979 through March 1980; *Gordon v. Hunt* (No. 82 Civ. 1318 (MEL)) proposed a class of those who sold short during July and August 1979; *Korwek v. Hunt* (No. 84 Civ. 7934 (MEL)) proposed a class of nearly anyone who traded silver during 1979–1980; and *Grosser v. Comex* (No. 84 Civ. 412 (MEL)) proposed a class of those on the long side of the market from January through March 1980.

[48] *Merrill Lynch v. Curran*, 456 U.S. 353 (1982), involving the allegation of manipulation of the May '76 potato contract on NYMEX.

often exhaust a plaintiff.[49] For example, the Hunts' attorneys attempted, according to Judge Lasker, to prolong prohibitively the deposition taken of the class representative Ronald Gordon, with the result that Judge Lasker had to take the rare step of ordering the deposition to be taken in the courthouse where he could rule forthwith on any objections.

By 1987, the Hunts' attritional strategy for the lawsuits concerning silver was in trouble, for five mutually reinforcing reasons. First, the Hunts, niggardly restricting Shank, Irwin's staffing and expenditures, had left the initiative to Minpeco and other plaintiffs. Shank, Irwin pursued only minimally Minpeco's own records, most important of which concerned Minpeco's relationship with silver mines also owned by the Peruvian government. Instead, the great majority of the documents produced (more than 1.5 million) and the depositions taken (more than two hundred) were at the plaintiff's request. Cumulatively, the documents and depositions, many of underprepared witnesses, had locked the Hunts into a factual record, while Minpeco had lost little flexibility, even in the nature of the legal arguments.

Second, the Hunts' own pockets were no longer so deep. The collapse in oil prices in 1986, from $30 per barrel to $15, severely affected both Placid Oil, which had major holdings in undeveloped leases, and Penrod Drilling, which saw the bookings for its exploratory rigs all but cease.

Third, the Internal Revenue Service was disputing the tax accounting of many of Bunker Hunt's and Herbert Hunt's trades, from their straddles of June 1979 to the transactions among family members in the aftermath of "Silver Thursday." The IRS claimed more than $600 million in back taxes, even a fraction of which would strap the Hunts. The IRS's contesting of the straddles prevented the Hunts from using a persuasive defense in the silver manipulation litigation: namely that the straddles were placed during the summer of 1979 to minimize taxes.

Fourth, the CFTC Division of Enforcement, which had finally filed manipulation charges against the Hunts in 1985, itself had the deep pocket of the U.S. government behind it. Indeed, the very length of time taken by the Division of Enforcement worked against the Hunts. The charges had been so long expected by others in the CFTC that the Division of Enforcement could vindicate itself only with a vigorous prosecution.

Fifth, Minpeco's financial resources increased. Its attorneys at Cole and Corette, with the help of their economist expert, Professor Houthakker, had pieced together the details of the Hunts' trading and had established the Hunts' contacts with the Conti group. In 1985, two lawyers new to the firm, Mark Cymrot and Thomas Gorman, took over the case, stepped up the schedule of discovery and depositions, and pursued several new legal arguments. By combining the Hunts' and the Conti group's holdings, they

---

[49] Total legal fees in all the silver litigation surely exceeded $50 million.

made tenable a charge of antitrust violations, with the prospect of treble damages.[50] Also, at the suggestion of Professor Houthakker, they advanced the notion that those brokerage houses who had dealt with the Hunts and then Minpeco had breached their fiduciary responsibility by not informing Minpeco of the dangers from their other clients.[51] These arguments made Minpeco's lawsuits much more threatening to the brokers, from the perspective of bad publicity as well as damages. And contrary to the brokers' expectations, Judge Lasker denied their motion for summary judgment, although he had previously dismissed the exchanges as defendants.[52] First, ContiCommodity settled, then BPS, then Hutton, ACLI, Bache, and Merrill Lynch. By the fall of 1987, Minpeco had received $64 million, enough to fund a long war with the Hunts. In Peru, the officials who had presided over Minpeco's losses were viewed with suspicion until the much-publicized announcement of settlements, which gave instant credibility to the view that Minpeco had indeed been abused and so justified the Peruvian government's continued expenditures for Cole and Corette's fees.

In the spring of 1987, while the legal vise tightened on the Hunts, their lead attorney at Shank, Irwin left for another firm in Dallas, one that could not represent the Hunts because of a client conflict. The Hunts transferred their defense to a firm in New York with considerable experience in complex civil litigation, Kaye, Scholer, Fierman, Hays, and Handler. (Robert Wolin, who at Shank, Irwin had done much of the work and who had managed to hold the litigation together despite the uncooperative clients, continued to work on the case.) Kaye, Scholer worked with the other law firms who represented IMIC, Mr. Fustok, and other defendants (not all of whom chose to defend themselves).

Also in the spring of 1987, the defense attorneys sought out Professor Ross and his associates for the first time in four and a half years, with the news that formal, lengthy responses to the CFTC Division of Enforcement's experts would be due in just a few months and depositions by Minpeco's lawyers were imminent. Little time remained for the economists to pursue any detailed investigations other than those begun years before or

---

50   The decision in another case deriving from the default on the May '76 potato contract, *Strobl v. New York Mercantile Exchange*, 768 F. 2d 22 (2d Cir., 1985), cert. denied, 106 S. Ct. 527 (1985), opened up the antitrust perspective, for which the precedents were conflicting (Danovitch, 1986, and Schacter, 1986). In the district covering the Chicago futures markets, the precedents would probably have precluded a claim under the Sherman Act (Kern, 1987). (Actually, one of the first manipulation cases, *Peto v. Howell*, 101 F.2d 353 (7th. Cir., 1938), was brought solely under the Sherman Act.)

51   Judge Lasker had previously ruled that Minpeco could pursue its claim of common law fraud against the Hunts and the brokers, 552 F.Supp. 332 (S.D.N.Y., 1982).

52   673 F.Supp. 684 (S.D.N.Y., 1987), reiterating 552 F.Supp. 327 (S.D.N.Y., 1982). See Klejna and Meyer (1990) for the implications of Judge Lasker's ruling for brokerage houses embroiled in manipulation cases.

for Kaye, Scholer to consider afresh the strategies to be used in the case. Indeed, given the complexity of the case and the time constraints, it is impressive that Kaye, Scholer could orchestrate a coherent defense at all.

In motions filed with Judge Lasker, the Hunts' attorneys at Kaye, Scholer concentrated on reducing the $250 million ($750 million once trebled) that Minpeco claimed as damages. Kaye, Scholer was most successful against the so-called lost-profits claim – Minpeco argued that when it entered into its short positions, having sensed that the price of $17 per troy ounce was unnaturally high, it would have made some $8 per troy ounce upon the price returning to its unmanipulated level. Kaye, Scholer replied that, had there been no manipulation, Minpeco would not have entered into the positions; Judge Lasker essentially agreed that Minpeco could not make this lost-profits claim in addition to a claim for its out-of-pocket losses resulting from the price rising above $17.[53] Kaye, Scholer argued that the appreciation on the physical silver Minpeco itself held should offset any losses on its futures positions; Judge Lasker agreed as a matter of law.[54] Pursuing this theme, Kaye, Scholer argued that the silver holdings of Minpeco's owner, the government of Peru, should also offset Minpeco's losses on futures positions (what with Peru producing much of the world's silver, Minpeco's lawsuit would terminate); Judge Lasker ruled that the defendants had not established that Peru treated its mining and merchandising operations as a single entity.[55] Together, Kaye, Scholer's arguments reduced the maximum damage claim Minpeco put before the jury to $150 million (before trebling). Had Minpeco's been the only litigation against the Hunts, Kaye, Scholer might well have advised such a strategy of damage limitation for the trial itself, to the point of conceding that the Hunts bore some responsibility for Minpeco's losses. Any such concession was precluded, however, by the CFTC Division of Enforcement's investigation, because even a tiny distortion of futures prices would incur a large fine on each of the Hunts' many futures contracts.

The hearing before a CFTC administrative law judge opened in November 1987 and in early 1988 the pace of legal proceedings accelerated further. Judge Lasker, by announcing that Minpeco's case would commence in February, intended to spur negotiations for a settlement. And the case nearly settled, with the Hunts proposing $20 million and Minpeco $40 million.[56] The Hunts, unwilling to add to their offer and predisposed to gamble,

---

[53]   676 F.Supp. 486 (S.D.N.Y., 1987).

[54]   686 F.Supp. 420 (S.D.N.Y., 1988).

[55]   686 F.Supp. 427 (S.D.N.Y., 1988). The single-entity defense had been raised very early, Judge Lasker first ruling on it in 1982, 549 F.Supp. 857 (S.D.N.Y., 1982).

[56]   Recollections differ about the amounts in this offer and counteroffer (another attempt was made while the jury deliberated), but all agree the amounts were on the order of tens of millions of dollars.

opted for the uncertainties of a trial.

Minpeco v. Hunt opened on February 24, 1988 and lasted until August 20. Unable to sustain two trials simultaneously, counsel for the Hunts asked that the CFTC's hearing be suspended, a Federal District Court case having precedent. To deal with the burden of information for presentation and cross-examination, Minpeco's attorneys, principally Mr. Cymrot and Mr. Gorman, pursued a strategy of total immersion, moving themselves and support staff from Washington to New York, while at Kaye, Scholer, under the direction of Aaron Rubinstein, different attorneys became specialists in different aspects of the case. Lasting twice as long as forecast, the trial was nearly as complicated as the events of 1979–1980 that had given rise to it.

2.8   Ambiguities and complications

Inevitably any chronicle, let alone one covering a period as tumultuous as 1979–1980, must emphasize some particulars over others. If anything, the chronicle here has overemphasized the Hunts, no doubt because their actions are well documented and their idiosyncrasies so noticeable. (Table 2.4 recapitulates their major actions.) The stories of the silver price spike, notably the more journalistic accounts by Davis, Fay, Hurt, and Trustman, have emphasized the human-interest slant, whether about the Hunts, the CFTC Commissioners, or the Senators at the hearings. Personalities matter, but so do tax laws, margin rules, delivery procedures, refining capacity, and dealers' bid–ask spreads. Moreover, the sequence of changes in these mundane factors over the course of 1979–1980 matters, especially as evidence of whether the personalities were influencing or reacting to events.

Much more so than in the trial, the chronicle here has covered the actions of the principal silver dealers and the exchanges. The actions of the commercial dealers demonstrate that the Hunts were not the only big players in the market. Moreover, many of the commercial dealers were important members of the exchanges, placed to monitor the web of silver prices and to alter trading rules. If a chronicle must emphasize personalities, it should dramatize 1979–1980 as a Homeric battle between dominant longs and dominant shorts, all with the flaw of imagining themselves outside the control of the Fates.

A problem with the chronicle here is its *ex post* organization of the period. The phases of silver prices from May 1979 through April 1980, shown earlier in Figure 2.1, are apparent only with hindsight, for they were hardly evident as events unfolded. Amid the price run-ups in September 1979 and in January 1980, the exchanges had little notion of the effect of their actions on the price of silver. Similarly, the Hunts and the commercial

Table 2.4. *Major actions in the silver market by Bunker Hunt, Herbert Hunt, and the Conti group, May 1979 through April 1980*

Mid-May – mid-June	Hunts expand considerably their already substantial futures positions.
Early June	Herbert Hunt takes delivery of bullion through futures.
Late June	Hunts place substantial straddles.
Late July	Hunts incorporate IMIC, which begins nearly daily purchases of futures through early September.
August	Conti group makes its major purchases of futures.
Early Sep.	IMIC and Conti group take delivery on futures.
Early Oct.	IMIC takes delivery on futures and participates in large EFPs with two commercial dealers.
Mid-Oct.	Conti group agrees to roll over futures for December delivery into later delivery months.
Late Oct. – early Nov.	Hunts meet with CFTC, Comex, and CBOT officials overseeing silver market.
Early Dec.	Bunker Hunt and especially Conti group take delivery on futures.
Mid-Jan.	Hunts participate in large EFPs with several dealers.
Late Jan. – mid-Feb.	Hunts roll over large number of futures contracts into more distant delivery months.
Early Feb.	Herbert Hunt takes delivery on futures.
Early March	Bunker Hunt takes delivery on futures.
Mid-March	Some members of the Conti group begin to reduce remaining futures positions and establish short positions to make delivery.
Late March	Bunker Hunt broaches silver-backed bonds.
Late March	Hunts and IMIC fail to meet calls for variation margin; brokers forcibly liquidate their remaining futures positions and some bullion.
Early April	Hunts consolidate bank financing to retain their holdings of bullion.

shorts arranged large exchanges for physicals in reaction to recent changes in silver prices rather than in anticipation of future changes. At least the chronicle here avoids the extreme found in some versions, which attribute such foresight to the Hunts that every change in the silver market up until the price collapse of March 1980 was planned or anticipated by them.

The chronicle here offers many instances of ambiguity, both in the Hunts' actions and in the silver market's response. The many ambiguities were the reason why the trial was needed and by extension why the economist experts were needed. Examples of these ambiguities can be found in the subjects of the next four chapters. As regards evidence of a corner, the coin/bullion differential certainly widened to a record – which is consistent with untoward pressure having been placed on deliveries of bullion – but a major scrap refinery was also on strike, and the dealers who were the normal purchasers of coins were under financial constraints. As regards the direct causes of the price changes, the forced sale of the Hunts' remaining futures positions certainly contributed to the price decline of late March, but the timing of their purchases was not so closely associated with the price rises as was the timing of the major political events. As regards what might have been the price of silver without the Hunts, futures contracts for delivery two years ahead, which provided ample time for the location of bullion, revealed very high prices, but because of the departure of those using the silver futures market for tax minimization or for synthetic versions of interest-rate futures, those prices could not be said to represent the opinions of very many traders. Finally, as regards the evidence of the Hunts' intent from their own actions, Bunker Hunt's rollback of March '80 contracts into the January '80 contract upon Comex's imposition of position limits could well be a clever effort to avoid the spirit of Comex's rule, but it could be merely his display of petulance at the less-than-impartial design of that rule.

Some sense of chronology is the first step in disentangling the competing explanations of the turmoil in the silver market. The importance of a day-by-day sequence is most obvious as regards the timing of price changes relative to the Hunts' trading or to political events, for a supposed cause cannot logically occur after the jump in price. A day-by-day sequence also helps expose internal inconsistencies in justifications for actions, as when someone claims to have done something based on circumstances that only emerged months later. Although the jury greatly needed a clear, concise chronology of May 1979 through April 1980, the trial was not organized to provide it; indeed, some aspects of the trial intentionally muddied it.

The economists' familiarity with the technical vocabulary, their experience with ambiguities in other commodity markets, and their training in the use of statistics to disentangle competing interpretations, made them necessary intercessors for the jury. Yet, the economists organized their testimony around topics such as delivery patterns, refining charges, or the correlation of the Hunts' trading with the Conti group's. By emphasizing topics, they further reduced any sense of chronology the jury could have obtained.

Without a sense of chronology, the very complexity of the many exchange actions, trading styles, and price changes makes the whole period of May 1979 through April 1980 seem hopelessly confusing. In that confusion, only two facts are likely to stand out: the price of silver reached an extraordinary high and the Hunts had very large positions.

3   Identifying a manipulation

Because the Hunts protested that they had not manipulated the silver market and because no incriminating documents were found, the economist expert witnesses (and, more fundamentally, the jurors) needed to infer from the Hunts' actions and the circumstantial evidence whether a manipulation had occurred. Presumably, a manipulation of a particular type has an easily identified effect; if that effect is observed (and no other explanation readily found), the evidence of a manipulation having occurred is strengthened. Regarding a classic corner, for example, had the price of bullion for immediate delivery in New York and Chicago vaults soared to $50 per troy ounce while prices for coins, for bullion at other locations, and for the bullion for delivery two years hence remained near $8, such a situation would have provided nearly unassailable circumstantial evidence of the Hunts' liability; had these other prices soared as high as bullion for immediate delivery in exchange-approved vaults, those facts would have provided nearly unassailable evidence of the Hunts' not having cornered the market. Regarding a manipulation of investors' expectations, had a flood of new orders for distant futures contracts followed the Hunts' own trading, with a small spillover into other precious metals markets, that situation would have provided strong evidence of the Hunts' involvement in such a manipulation; had prices and trading volumes in other precious metals markets increased much more than silver, those facts would have provided strong evidence of non-manipulative causes.

The exercise in identifying a manipulation from circumstantial evidence presupposes that the manipulation falls into some broad class. Likewise, any alternative explanation for that circumstantial evidence, such as geopolitical uncertainty, ought to be part of a category visible and measurable on other occasions. Of course, events in the silver market may not all accord with those expected under either the broad class of manipulations or the broad class of the alternative explanation; the identification of manipulation requires a judgment about which explanation fits more of the evidence.

64

At the trial, however, statements of the class into which the Hunts' manipulation fell were conspicuous by their absence. Repeatedly, the plaintiff stated that the Hunts had manipulated the silver market, while the defense asserted the opposite, yet no one made clear the nature of the logical exercise of identifying a specified type of manipulation from circumstantial evidence.

Indeed, during all their days of testimony in *Minpeco v. Hunt,* not one expert even defined "manipulation" clearly. For example, the plaintiff's economist defined manipulation "as an effort to move a price in a desired direction" (Trial Transcript, p. 8519), which is too vague to identify anything. Testifying for the defense, Professor Ross defined an artificial price as one that "comes about because of some misadjustment in supply and demand and the ordinary workings that usually determine a competitive price" (Trial Transcript, p. 13277), which offers no method for discerning an artificial price. He disagreed with the plaintiff's expert's opinion that the silver market had been manipulated, but offered no definition of what he meant by manipulation (Trial Transcript, p. 13382), nor did the other defense experts.[1]

By sidestepping the definition of manipulation, the expert witnesses did no worse than the statute and previous case law, which, as many commentators have criticized, leave the term undefined. Perhaps some imprecision must be accepted in a term meant to encompass corners, rumors, feigned investor interest, and so on, in a variety of markets. In a specific case, however, the type of alleged manipulation ought to be defined precisely. If the alleged manipulation is *sui generis*, the reasoning about whether it occurred becomes circular. The definition of manipulation is needed not to describe a violation of the law but to determine whether the law was violated.

As part of the exercise in identifying a manipulation, the economists examined a variety of evidence from the silver market. This evidence included statistics on bullion stocks, coin refining, silver prices in several market centers, intertemporal price spreads, the coin/bullion differential, and the gold/silver ratio – a long list, which encompasses the types of market evidence considered in almost all other manipulation cases. Indeed, the CFTC Division of Enforcement made much of the length of the list, implying that the longer the list, the surer the identification of manipulation.

Yet the economists' analysis of the market-based evidence should not have commenced without a clear statement of the type of the Hunts' alleged manipulation. Were the alleged manipulation an across-the-board price effect, the discussions of the coin/bullion differential and the market's geographic extent were irrelevant, for they spoke to the existence of a corner. Without a

---

[1] Here and elsewhere, in the interest of succinctness, I write that the experts offered opinions about whether a manipulation or a monopolization occurred. The defense experts fastidiously avoided such direct statements, in line with the concurrent decision, in *United States v. Scop*, 846 F.2d 135 (2nd Cir., 1988), that expert witnesses must not offer opinions in terminology embodying legal conclusions.

clear concept of manipulation, the economists did not appreciate that their topics of intertemporal spreads, the coin/bullion differential, and the gold/silver ratio were merely different manifestations of a single phenomenon. Without identification of the alleged manipulation, the expert witnesses worked at cross purposes. The defense experts prepared charts about a delivery squeeze, because before the trial, the plaintiff's expert had "concluded that the Hunt and Conti groups were operating a corner of the silver futures markets" (Minpeco's Answers to Expert Interrogatories, p. 21). At the trial, the plaintiff instead emphasized the Hunts as attempting a price-effect manipulation, and discounted during cross-examination the defense experts' testimony regarding a corner. Had the defense experts recognized the change in the plaintiff's identification, they might have countered with evidence such as the frequency of large positions in futures markets.[2]

This chapter reviews the market-based evidence and the economists' analysis of it. Section 3.1 describes how the economists compiled statistics on the bullion available to satisfy the Hunts' futures contracts. Section 3.2 computes the prospective manipulative profits implied by the economists' analysis of this "deliverable supply." Section 3.3 describes the analysis by which the economists looked at bullion prices in several locations to determine the geographic extent of the market. Sections 3.4 through 3.6 report on the intertemporal price spreads, the coin/bullion differential, and the gold/silver ratio as studied by the economists.

In the various sections of this chapter, the concept of a web of prices, previously used in Chapter 2, will be used to clarify why the economists examined particular evidence and to determine whether their implicit classification of the Hunts' alleged manipulation made sense. Thus, this chapter will attempt an inductive reconstruction of the various economists' classifications from the variety of evidence each emphasized. What should be a report of the economists' deliberate and conscientious identification in the circumstantial evidence of a specified type of manipulation must instead be its own exercise in identification.

2   The differences in the various experts' conceptions of the Hunts' manipulation continue. Both Professor Kolb and Professor Edwards have included a few pages on the Hunt case in textbooks they have each written on futures markets. Professor Kolb (1991), presenting the existence of a manipulation as self-evident, graphs the spot price of silver over 1979–1980 (as in Figure 2.1 here); Professor Edwards (Edwards and Ma, 1992), presenting a manipulation as doubtful, adds to the same plot the prices for distant futures contracts. In short, Professor Kolb continues to believe the dominant evidence is in the level of prices (evidence relevant to a price-effect manipulation), while Professor Edwards continues to emphasize the price relationships (evidence relevant to a corner).

3.1   The perspective of deliverable supply

In the course of the handful of manipulation cases, the courts and the CFTC
have evolved the concept "deliverable supply." The concept of deliverable
supply centers attention on the bullion available in exchange-approved vaults
to satisfy the Hunts' futures contracts. The concept of deliverable supply also
leads to consideration of the amount of bullion that could be moved to
exchange-approved vaults at a minor expense, should the amount already on
hand (and not already held by the Hunts) be insufficient. Stocks in position
combined with stocks that could easily be made "deliverable" determine
whether someone with a large share of those stocks could squeeze the shorts
committed to deliver or could achieve a short-term monopoly over bullion.
Thus, any economist in the Hunt case taking the perspective of deliverable
supply was connecting the accusation of manipulation to the accusation of
monopoly.

Deliverable supply accounts for the quantities that could be transported to
the specific location or transformed into the specific grade called for in a
futures contract. For example, deliverable supply reflects the amount of #2
corn that could move to Chicago at a $0.01 per bushel premium over usual
price relationships, the amount at a $0.02 premium, a $0.03 premium, and so
forth. Similarly, deliverable supply encompasses the dimension of time; for
example, it reflects the amount of corn that could move (at a premium of,
say, $0.02) in one day, one week, one month, and so forth.[3]

When used properly, the concept of deliverable supply across the continua
of space, time, and grade provides an insightful analytical tool. It does not
prejudge whether a manipulation occurred. It does, however, prejudge the
type of manipulation, for it is relevant in the instance of a corner.

Because the defense experts used the concept of deliverable supply to
organize much of their testimony, it is evident that the defense conceived of
the Hunt case in terms of a classic corner. The plaintiff's expert, in contrast,
conspicuously avoided the term "deliverable supply" and the associated
analysis, seemingly identifying the Hunts' manipulation as other than a corner. Yet, in testifying about the defendants' monopoly power over bullion,
the plaintiff's expert revealed that a corner was to remain central to his identification of the Hunts' alleged manipulation despite the plaintiff's change in
emphasis to a price-effect manipulation.

The plaintiff's separate charge of monopolization arose from the strategic
perspective of the treble damages under the antitrust statutes and the tactical
perspective of the Hunts' large positions. In antitrust proceedings, a market

---

[3]   The concept can also encompass flexibility on the demand side, measuring in effect
"excess supply." Corn moving to Chicago must be bid away from uses elsewhere. If
feedlots, say, have other types of feed handy, they would cease (temporarily) bidding
for corn at a small premium, but if not, they might bid very high.

share of 70 percent (or more) had come to be a nearly incontrovertible indication of market power. Professor Houthakker has noted recently that he
ceased his search for conspirators once his list of the Hunts' allies reached a
70 percent share over at least one plausible set of futures delivery months.
When speaking of the Hunts, he regularly used the vocabulary of antitrust,
with terms such as "market power" and "control." The plaintiff's counsel,
Mr. Gorman, has noted recently that the antitrust perspective of controlling
price fits with the plaintiff's emphasis on a price-effect manipulation.[4]

To make the Hunts' share of physical silver appear as large as possible for
the sake of an antitrust argument, the plaintiff restricted consideration to bullion already in exchange-approved vaults. To make the Hunts' share of outstanding futures contracts appear as large as possible, the plaintiff restricted
the delivery months to those before June '80, claiming that the Hunts
"targeted" the December '79, February '80, and March '80 futures contracts.
The plaintiff's restrictions make sense if the main allegation is that the Hunts
attempted a corner of bullion in exchange-approved vaults over that four-
month period. That is to say, even though the plaintiff's conception of antitrust and manipulation as price effects may have fitted, the evidence the
plaintiff chose to emphasize did not.

The plaintiff presented its arguments about monopolization with graphs
similar to those in Figures 3.1 and 3.2. These eye-catching graphs convey a
strong impression of market dominance. Figure 3.1(a), by late 1979 shows
that the Hunts and their alleged allies held more than 60 percent of the bullion
in Comex- and CBOT-approved vaults. Similarly, Figure 3.2 shows the
increasingly large share of the futures contracts outstanding held by the
Hunts and their alleged allies. The plaintiff's most effective chart, which it
referred to as the "overhang" diagram, was Figure 3.1(b), which shows that
the Hunts had a call on two to three times more silver than the exchange-
certificated bullion that they did not already own.

The defense experts did not directly counter the plaintiff's expert's charts
and the implicit conception of monopolization as control over certified stocks.
Instead, the defense experts, Professors Ross and Edwards in particular,
emphasized a chart similar to Figure 3.3, which shows bullion in exchange-
approved vaults compared to bullion elsewhere in the world. The defense
experts' point was that the total supply of silver exceeded the demands the
Hunts controlled through their futures contracts. Yet they did not drive home
their point by dwelling on their pie chart or presenting the information in
other ways, such as how much bullion could have been available day by day

---

[4]   On direct examination (Trial Transcript, p. 8703), the plaintiff's expert, observing that
      the Hunts' accountants had hesitated to use the prevailing price to value inventory
      because it would drop if they liquidated all their holdings at once, said "this is, of
      course, the definition of market power, namely, that an action by the particular traders
      involved would have moved the price in a certain direction."

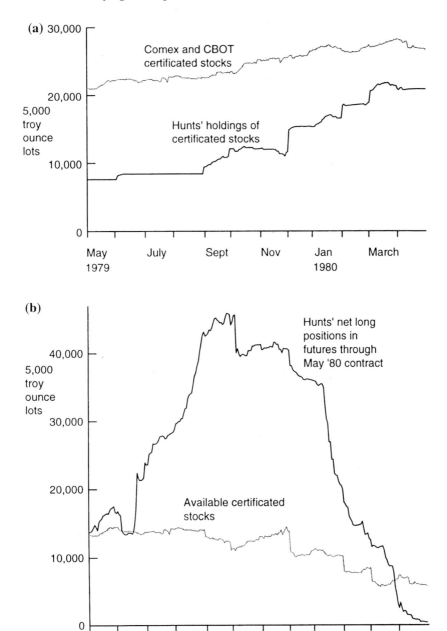

Figure 3.1. The Hunts' (and Conti group's) call on deliverable stocks of silver

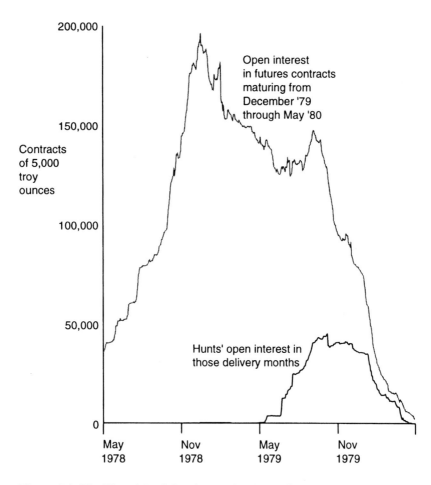

Figure 3.2. The Hunts' (and Conti group's) share of open interest in the "target" contracts

given the time needed to place it in exchange-approved vaults from its present locations. That is, they did not convert Figure 3.3 into the equivalent of the daily "overhang" Figure 3.1(b) showing the Hunts' call on exchange-certificated stocks. More important, the defense failed to recognize that even in the context of the world's silver bullion, the Hunts' call on bullion looked large. The defense thought it sufficed to show that all the Hunts' demands could have been satisfied – hence their potential demands could not have distorted prices. Yet, by conventional definitions of monopolization, the

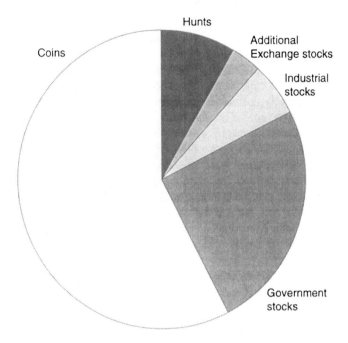

Figure 3.3. Bullion stocks as of December 31, 1979

Hunts would still have appeared to have had "market power," and hence control over certificated stocks as the plaintiff claimed.

Several arguments were available to the defense, however, to confront the plaintiff's evidence in Figure 3.1. As regards Figure 3.1(a), had the Hunts removed the bullion they owned from the exchange-approved vaults, which was their legal right, their share of the bullion would have looked correspondingly smaller.[5] Where the Hunts held their bullion should not influence the impression of their market dominance, or the measure of market dominance is suspect. As regards Figure 3.1(b) – the crucial picture of an "overhang" several times the bullion not already in the Hunts' hands – large "overhangs" happen to be common in futures markets. In the wheat, corn, and soybean markets, the positions of the four largest traders combined (although they are not necessarily acting in concert) as of a few days before a

---

[5] The Hunts very likely refrained from removing bullion for two reasons. First, any movement to Texas would have subjected them to sales tax (House Committee on Government Operations, 1980, pp. 113–16). Second, the warehouse receipts of exchange-approved vaults were required as security for any loans from brokers.

delivery period more often than not exceed stocks in exchange-approved elevators (Peck and Williams, 1991). These data for wheat, corn, and soybeans were not publicly available at the time of the trial, but figures covering all delivery months, not just expiring contracts, were published for many commodities. These, too, show that traders commonly hold futures positions large in comparison to supplies in approved delivery locations. The point of such evidence about the prevalence of large futures positions would not be that large positions never lead to trouble but that an "overhang" not be taken as convincing evidence of market power. The defense viewed this condition as so obvious that it did not present the relevant comparisons, although, of course, the jury did not know these facts about commodity markets.

The defense experts took the Hunt's proportion of futures contracts in Figure 3.2 to be nearly as irrelevant as in Figure 3.1 and so made little effort to refute it. The defense experts did emphasize that anyone could enter the futures market at any time, merely by paying the small brokerage fee. By implication, the Hunts' share of those silver futures contracts that were outstanding was immaterial.[6] As a futures delivery month approaches the end of its natural life, the last remaining long and the last remaining short must comprise 100 percent of the futures market, without, of course, having any market power. By implication, the Hunts' share of the outstanding contracts during the delivery period was immaterial.

The defense's arguments all revolved around the idea of potential entry, namely that others could enter into a futures contract, that others could move bullion into an exchange-approved vault, that others could transform other forms of silver into bullion. Yet potential entry is not an easy concept to define, explain, or measure.

In conventional antitrust disputes, the concept of potential entry is often central. Those alleging monopoly attempt to draw the relevant market's boundaries tightly, claiming no one else can produce a comparable good or can overcome the transport costs; those defending the alleged monopolist strive to draw the boundaries widely, claiming that others can easily enter the market. Many commentators (for example, Fisher et al., 1983, Chapter 3) have castigated antitrust proceedings for drawing sharp boundaries to calculate the alleged monopolist's share within that "market." Rather, they have argued that the analysis should view the market as a continuum, with some suppliers being potential entrants at small differentials in price, others at larger differences, and still others potential entrants only at a substantial differential. Their recommended approach corresponds to "deliverable supply."

---

6   This argument ignores that a long can enter only if a short simultaneously enters. Presumably, a short would enter only if he held the commodity to deliver or anticipated a liquid market for offsetting the contract.

"Deliverable supply" is the concept that the defense experts used in preparing Figure 3.3. Through Figure 3.3, they implicitly argued that most, if not all, silver bullion in private hands could be transported to exchange-approved vaults at a negligible expense. The defense experts' emphasis on the abundance of coins likewise presented an implicit argument about the price differential that would elicit the speedy melting of coins.

The defense did not, however, calculate deliverable supply systematically, by surveying mines, coin dealers, and industrial bullion holders about the differentials at which they could temporarily supply more bullion or temporarily cease using bullion. Nor did the defense try to compile evidence from other periods about the degree of flexibility implied by the response of silver suppliers and users to those differentials. As a result, the arguments of the defense were less convincing than they might have been.

Much of the opposing expert testimony about the Hunts' control over bullion in exchange-approved vaults simply passed in the dark, in large part because no expert acknowledged employing the concept of deliverable supply. The plaintiff's expert, without ever justifying the style of analysis, emphasized the Hunts' futures contracts compared to the bullion then in exchange-approved vaults that they did not already own. The defense experts, also without justifying the style of analysis, emphasized the additional bullion that could be brought to the vaults to satisfy the Hunts should they stand for delivery. To all of these points, the evidence offered by the other experts was not wrong; it was irrelevant. Moreover, the very style of the various experts' analyses tended to lead to their conclusions. It is not that the experts deliberately avoided a style of analysis detrimental to their arguments. Rather, it is that each expert's initial choice of analytical style, made in good faith and made consistent with previous analysis, led to particular conclusions, given the specifics of the Hunts' positions and the specifics of the worldwide silver market.

3.2   Potential profits from a manipulation

Alone among the economists involved with the Hunt case, the CFTC Division of Enforcement's expert Dr. Burrows attempted to calculate deliverable supply with a systematic survey of users and holders of silver. The specificity of his calculation is interesting for its bearing on the monopolization charge, more interesting for the insight it offers into Dr. Burrows's implicit classification of the alleged manipulation, and most interesting for what it reveals about the possible profits from a manipulation of the silver market.

The Hunts' paper profits as of January 1980 exceeded $5 billion (recall Figure 2.4). Not surprisingly, Minpeco and the CFTC Division of Enforcement made much of them. The relevant number, however, is the plausible profit *ex ante*, for the Hunts are alleged to have planned the manipulation.

The *ex ante* profits reflect the reasonable estimates of how users and holders of silver would respond to the increased demand for bullion.

Using Charles River Associates' model of worldwide silver supply and demand, developed with the Silver Institute, Dr. Burrows computed the bullion that would come available at different prices and over different periods, given the model's engineering-based estimates of the price responsiveness of mines and industrial consumers. His computations are reported in Table 3.1 for the situation in late November 1979, showing the bullion that could become available over the six months through May 1980 depending on the prevailing price. (He presumes a balance at $8 per troy ounce.) His figures, although showing more bullion available than do the plaintiff's computations (and also larger futures positions for the Hunts), imply that the Hunts' "overhang" could only be satisfied at a substantial increase in price.[7] Reasonable projections from his figures place the price at which all the Hunts' call on bullion could be satisfied at about $21 per troy ounce, as in Figure 3.4.

Dr. Burrows implicitly treated "manipulation" as an across-the-board increase within the web of silver prices. Dr. Burrows sought to determine what additional production would arrive from mines and what cutback in consumption would be made by industrial users if silver prices went *permanently* to $14. Yet, these numbers he compared to a *temporary* demand, because the Hunts would not require another 215 million troy ounces over the six months June 1980 through November 1980, the six months December 1980 through May 1981, and so on. Without permanent demand from the Hunts, industrial production and consumption would balance at $8 for later periods. Thus, Dr. Burrows also implicitly imagined a corner's steep backwardation in prices – that is, a change in price relationships.

Presumably, mines, scrap refineries, industrial consumers, and dealers with working inventories respond differently to a permanent increase to $14 than to an increase they know will persist merely for six months. Mines have an incentive to use higher grade ores, scrap refineries to delay maintenance, consumers to reschedule production runs, dealers to reduce working inventories. These responses may not be large, but unfortunately, Dr. Burrows did not (and could not) calculate them. Thus, even the most detailed calculations made by an expert did not determine deliverable supply.

According to Dr. Burrows's main point, if the Hunts stood for delivery on all their futures contracts, they would acquire a large proportion of available bullion. This complete insistence on delivery is an odd idea of how a manipulation would work, however, because the Hunts could not make any

---

7   The key line in Table 3.1 shows the difference in industrial production and consumption at various prices. The total flow of silver is much larger, however – some 170 million troy ounces. Thus, from the perspective of antitrust, the Hunts' share of the total deliverable supply is smaller.

Table 3.1. *Bullion forthcoming from December 1979 through May 1980 according to estimates by Charles River Associates (million troy ounces)*

	Price (per troy ounce)			
	$8	$10	$14	Actual 1979–1980
New supplies through May 1980 in excess of industrial consumption	0	18	42	110
As of late November, stocks held by others	149	149	149	149
As of late November, principal longs' call on bullion through futures, forwards, and EFPs	215	215	215	215
Excess of total available over principal longs' positions	–66	–48	–24	44

"New supplies" includes secondary refining. The "principal longs' positions" include all contracts with delivery by May 1980; this figure is higher than the comparable one according to Minpeco.
Source: Burrows CFTC Report, Chapter 6, p. 12.

profits from those shorts desperately buying back their futures contracts. If the Hunts released some shorts from their obligations they would not acquire so much bullion nor drive the price as high as $21.

The optimal strategy for a cornerer would be to release the number of shorts that would maximize the revenue from the number released (that is, the amount not taken in delivery multiplied by the price increase caused by taking delivery on the remainder). Following the general theoretical model of Fackler (1993), these computations are attempted for silver in Figure 3.4 (using percentage overhang, because of discrepancies in absolute amounts).[8] According to Dr. Burrows's own figures, the optimal amount to release would be around 41 percent, not 100 percent, and the price would be around $13, not $21. Actually, the Hunts released even more, some 56 percent of their overhang (using deliveries taken on futures and EFPs through March 7,

---

[8] Unlike in Table 3.1, not all stocks of bullion are assumed to be available at a price of $8, but only 25 million troy ounces. At a price of $25, all private stockholders would release their stocks. This more plausible reformulation, besides making the behavior smoother, leads to an optimal manipulation with a higher price and more profits, a bias against the points made with Figure 3.4.

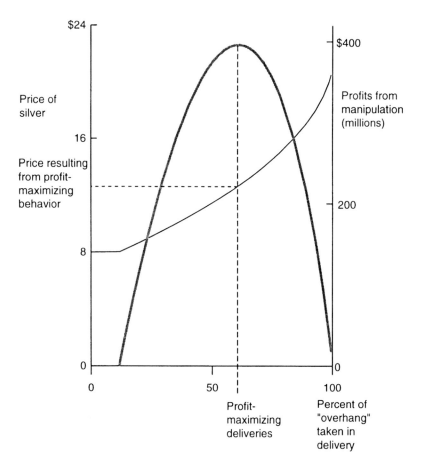

Figure 3.4. Profits depending on the amount of "overhang" taken in delivery (interpolating the price response reported in Table 3.1)

1980, as the amount not released), an amount according to Dr. Burrows that would have a much smaller price effect, perhaps $3 per troy ounce above the balance price of $8. (Of course, prices did not peak at $11, or even $21, but $50. Something else must have been happening in silver besides the Hunts' demand for the physical metal, or else Dr. Burrows's whole set of calculations is wrong.)

As cornerers, the Hunts need not have made the precise calculation of the amount of their futures contracts to offset. Yet, they surely would have planned to offset a large fraction of their overhang, otherwise they would not have profited from the discomfort to which they put the shorts. Dr.

Burrows's Table 3.1 and Minpeco's dramatic "overhang" chart (Figure 3.1(b)) dramatize an implausible course of action: that the Hunts would insist on taking delivery on all their futures contracts.

Manipulators wishing to spread a rumor would not attempt to claim, for example, that the U.S. President, the German Chancellor, the Japanese Prime Minister, and the Saudi King had just been assassinated simultaneously, for other traders would be suspicious of such extreme claims. Manipulators feigning investor interest would not attempt (through wash sales and cross trades) to inflate volume by a factor of ten to twenty, both because of the expensive transaction fees and because of the implausibility of the increase. Manipulators aiming at a price effect would know not to trade at the time of day or on a day when the market is particularly liquid because the price effect would be smallest. More relevant, no one analyzing an alleged manipulation of these types would take such extremes seriously. In the instance of alleged corners, however, an inherently implausible action becomes the focus of the analysis.

Figure 3.4 gives the profits the Hunts might have earned had they followed the optimal strategy of releasing some of the shorts, given Dr. Burrows's estimates of the price-responsiveness of others in the silver market. These profits at most amount to some $400 million, before expenses (brokerage fees, interest costs, lawyers, expert witnesses, etc.). This *ex ante* profit, as large as it is, seems small given the Hunts' investment and risk – too small to have induced them to attempt to corner silver.

None of the economist expert witnesses made computations in the style of Figure 3.4, even though the result of such computations was central to the inference of whether the Hunts had manipulated the silver market. Unfortunately, economists have not developed an analytical structure for such problems, and in actual cases have not even used the rudimentary analysis represented in Figure 3.4. (That analysis ignores the obvious complications of different price responsiveness given the degree of manipulative "surprise," anticipation of interventions by exchanges, and financial constraints on the manipulator.) Unfortunately, economists do not have the required knowledge of price responsiveness. For many commodities, it is difficult to obtain even crude estimates about quantities, such as the amount in commercial channels, when what is needed is the extent to which that amount changes with price and not just with price but with price relationships.

3.3   Extent of the bullion market

One reason no one conducted a comprehensive study of deliverable supply is that interviews with all those involved with silver bullion would have been prohibitively expensive. Under such circumstances, it is natural to look for some analytical shortcut. An obvious place to look is in the web of prices itself. By their nature, prices compress the information about all involved with the commodity and are much more visible than the quantities to which they correspond.

If the prices for the same grade of a commodity at two locations or for different grades at the same location move in parallel, the distinctions must be, for practical purposes, irrelevant. How users make as much use of one grade as the other or why they can move the commodity between locations at negligible expense or even how much they move need not be investigated. Thus emerges a test for the extent of the market for silver bullion: Should prices at several locations move in parallel, the bullion at those locations will be interchangeable and in the same effective market.[9]

Table 3.2 provides such a test among four easily obtainable bullion prices for different locations for 247 business days over May 1979 through April 1980. The price in Chicago is the daily closing price of the expiring futures contract on the CBOT, the so-called spot (or prompt) contract. The Comex price is the equivalent, but for New York, and represents the silver over which the Hunts' futures positions had their principal "overhang." The third entry is the spot price, converted to dollars using the afternoon dollar/sterling exchange rate, recorded at the afternoon session on the LME, approximately the opening time on Comex. The fourth entry is Handy & Harman's quotation, the most widely disseminated quotation for bullion among the major dealers in the New York area and given daily just before noon.

According to the upper panel of Table 3.2, the correlations among these four daily price series are as close to 1.0 as one could imagine. Comparable correlations are observed in periods before and after that of 1979–1980.[10] More to the point, the price moves are virtually one for one even when measured day by day, as can be seen in the lower panel.[11] (Discrepancies on individual days are most likely attributable to the prices not being measured at the same instant; correlations between day-by-day changes whose underlying series are less nearly synchronous are lower.) Therefore, even in the

---

9   A high correlation between prices need not prove that two markets are integrated, as has been pointed out by those studying staples in developing countries (e.g., Harriss, 1979). Common weather might account for a high correlation even though two markets never trade because of high transport costs. In the case of silver bullion, these worries about interpreting correlation coefficients do not apply. Independent evidence places the transport costs at under $0.10 per troy ounce, traders are known to monitor the price differences, and traders are known to send shipments between locations.

10   Stigler and Sherwin (1985, p. 559), finding a similar correlation between Comex and CBOT silver prices in 1982, conclude that the "example does not pose an interesting question about whether the two centers are in the same market: They clearly are."

11   As Simons and Williams (1993) observe concerning market definition for antitrust, the magnitude of price movements matter more than correlations. Price changes at the various locations for silver were $1 for $1.

Table 3.2. *Correlations among bullion prices at four locations, May 1, 1979 through April 30, 1980*

Correlations among daily prices			
Quotation	CBOT	LME	Handy & Harman
Comex expiring contract's close	.999	.993	.997
CBOT expiring contract's close		.992	.997
LME afternoon session			.982

Correlations among day-by-day changes in prices			
Quotation	CBOT	LME	Handy & Harman
Comex expiring contract's close	.956	.540	.757
CBOT expiring contract's close		.500	.768
LME afternoon session			.752

unsettled conditions of mid-January 1980, silver bullion in commercial channels, wherever it was located, bore the same price.

Many economists who examined the silver market instinctively conducted the correlation analysis contained in Table 3.2 and came to the same conclusion. The CBOT itself, in its testimony before the U.S. Senate Committee on Agriculture (1980), was the first to do so. "These correlations demonstrate that futures and cash [prices] did move together. Further, they suggest that the information affecting silver prices was the same in major world silver markets" (pp. 292–3). The defense experts as early as 1982 studied the various public quotations for bullion and concluded that Chicago, New York, and London were effectively the same market. The CFTC Division of Enforcement treated London as part of the market that the Hunts were alleged to have manipulated. According to their expert (Kyle CFTC Report, p. 11), the behavior of prices in London "indicates that the increased demand for silver bullion was an increase in the worldwide demand for bullion generally, not just Comex stocks."

In contrast, the plaintiff's expert did not study the correlations among New York, Chicago, and London; he simply stated that they were not necessary for determining whether the Hunts had manipulated the silver market (Trial Transcript, p. 8752). The one-for-one price moves among bullion at various locations presented the plaintiff's expert with several logical difficulties, however. Prices in those markets in which the Hunts had few positions, especially London, could not reflect the fundamentals of supply and demand, or the price in New York would seem sensible. So the plaintiff's expert simply asserted that the price on the LME did not reflect fundamentals (Trial Transcript, pp. 8513–14). Faced with a comparable price decline on all exchanges when Comex restricted trading to liquidation only on January 21, 1980, he took the price decline as proof that Comex was a distinct market, for if bullion in Comex-designated vaults were part of a larger market, restrictions involving it alone would not affect the rest of the market (Trial Transcript, pp. 8679–80). (His argument implicitly imagines a part of a market to be an insignificant part.) To explain the obvious connections among bullion centers worldwide, the plaintiff's expert proposed the idea of "indirect monopolization" (Trial Transcript, p. 8776), which resulted from the Hunts' control of a narrow "antitrust market."

Instead of a correlation analysis, the plaintiff's expert proposed to concentrate on what he called an "antitrust market," which he defined as "the smallest complex of economic activities in which it is possible to exercise market power" (Trial Transcript, p. 8664). An "economic market" is broader, and reflects the possibilities of substitution within demand and supply (Trial Transcript, p. 8749). "To control the whole silver market, it is enough to control certain parts of the futures market together with deliverable stocks" (Trial Transcript, pp. 8666–7).

The plaintiff's expert's distinction between an "economic market" and an "antitrust market" derived from the *Department of Justice Merger Guidelines,* as revised in 1984, and more specifically from a paper by his collaborator Professor Spiller (Scheffman and Spiller, 1987), discussing the *Guidelines'* definition of a geographic market.[12] In the context of a regional cartel, an antitrust market might be larger than an economic market, as when the price difference between two regions is just beneath the transport cost but, were a cartel to raise price even slightly, supplies would pour in from the other region. Or an antitrust market might be smaller than an economic market, as when some of a region's suppliers would be unable to increase their quantities were some other suppliers to form a cartel to raise prices.

---

[12] Determination of the extent of a market for analysis of mergers is itself problematic and contentious (Pitofsky, 1990; Morris and Mosteller, 1991), especially when statistical techniques are used to infer market power (Scheffman, 1992).

The distinction between an economic market and an antitrust market allows an analytical shortcut. Instead of studying everything about a commodity, an expert can examine just the key area of possible monopoly power. In the instance of futures markets, the key area is what Pirrong (1993) calls the "end game," namely the last few days (or even hours) of a delivery month when a dominant long who insists on delivery leaves the shorts with only the stocks already on hand.

Thus to the plaintiff's expert, it sufficed to examine the Hunt's positions relative to just those stocks already in exchange-approved vaults. He maintained that once a contract entered its month-long delivery period, it was essentially a distinct antitrust market (Trial Transcript, pp. 8790, 8755–8). The practical advantage of his analytical shortcut was the easy measurement of silver that could be delivered, for the exchanges publish statistics on the bullion held in vaults.

Fundamental to the plaintiff's shortcut was whether or not there were tight limits on the bullion that could be placed in exchange-approved vaults. The plaintiff's expert testified that silver bullion newly brought to an exchange-approved vault could not be deliverable on futures contracts until it had been re-assayed, a process usually taking three weeks.[13] The defense countered with testimony of Chase Manhattan Bank's vault manager, who explained that the mark on the silver bar was sufficient proof of quality; thus silver bullion could be delivered on a futures contract within a day or two, the time it took to prepare a warehouse receipt.[14]

The actual speed of bullion becoming eligible for delivery should have complicated the plaintiff's analysis considerably. The relevant silver for a month-long antitrust market should have included any bullion that could have been moved to the exchange-approved vaults, namely virtually all bullion in the world. Moreover, the Hunts' influence was alleged to have lasted for a matter of months and market participants knew of the Hunts' large positions long before the last days of a contract expiration – more than enough time for a short to bring bullion to an exchange-approved vault.

Given the actual provisions for placing bullion in exchange-approved vaults and the actual geographic connections in the silver market, the defense's analytical shortcut made sense and the plaintiff's did not. The idea of an analytical shortcut is not ill advised, however. Sensible analysis should begin with both a narrowly defined market and a broadly defined market. If

[13] The classification of the whole delivery month as the "end game" was essential to the plaintiff for another reason. Most deliveries to the Hunts were made early in the month (principally because the clearinghouses allocated each day's delivery notice to the oldest outstanding long position, which was frequently the Hunts). By the last few days of the delivery period, the Hunts had small futures positions relative to stocks.

[14] Professor Houthakker seems to have confused the registration procedures for silver with that for gold, for which re-assaying is required.

the defendants did not have a substantial presence in even the most narrowly defined market, it is unreasonable to conclude that they had market power. If the defendants did have a significant presence in even the most broadly defined market, it is unreasonable to conclude that they could not have had market power. Of course, these limits may leave a substantial gray area, but they possibly exclude one of the two conclusions without the need for a lengthy investigation.

Problems arose because the defendants' experts used the broad definition of a market and the plaintiff's expert the narrow definition, whereas their arguments logically required the reverse. Moreover, each set of experts confused the limiting arguments with a description of the market for silver bullion. If it was necessary for the plaintiff's expert to show that the Hunts dominated the most narrowly defined market, it was also necessary for the plaintiff's expert to demonstrate that the possible substitutes for bullion in exchange-approved vaults were not close ones. If it was necessary for the defense experts to show that the Hunts did not dominate the most broadly defined market, it was also necessary for the defense experts to show that all the silver within that market was treated as much the same commodity.

Objectively, a distinction among silver bullion in various trading centers was irrelevant. The plaintiff, by distinguishing as finely as Comex-designated silver for December '79 delivery, substantially underestimated its definition of the relevant market and overstated the Hunts' share of physical silver and the "overhang" represented by their futures contracts.

Unfortunately for the defendants, an expansion of the universe of silver that was equivalent in practice to the specific conditions of silver deliverable on Comex or CBOT futures contracts did not bring that much more silver into the count. Vaults in London, Zurich, and at commercial dealers held some 70 million troy ounces, an amount equal to the bullion in Comex and CBOT vaults not already owned by the alleged manipulators. Yet the alleged manipulators' potential demand through futures contracts exceeded even this expanded pool of bullion. According to price correlations and relationships, the expansion of ready bullion beyond two times the free stocks in exchange-approved vaults, whether through refining or delay in taking delivery, involved more than merely nominal costs.

3.4   Distortion of intertemporal price relationships

The CFTC Division of Enforcement's expert Professor Kyle conceived of the Hunts' alleged manipulation as one that would affect price relationships. "A monopolist exploits the fact that the supply and demand for assets is not perfectly elastic, i.e., small changes in price do not result in large adjustments in quantities supplied and demanded. Because the short-term elasticities of supply for commodities tend to be less than the corresponding long-term elasticities, the exploitation of monopoly power in a manipulation is likely to be temporary. This implies that during a manipulation, prices for nearby delivery of the commodity tend to be high relative to prices for deferred delivery" (Kyle CFTC Report, p. 47). Given this perspective on the definition of manipulation, which is essentially that of a corner, Professor Kyle devoted much of his analysis to intertemporal spreads because they record any premium for the immediate delivery of bullion by the extent that intertemporal spreads are below the "full carrying charges" of vault fees and interest expenses. Thus, should the spreads among the silver futures prices for various delivery dates have displayed full carrying charges throughout 1979–1980, no claim of a corner could be supported.

Professor Kyle examined spreads on both Comex and the LME, for the extended period of 1973 through 1982. Given that vault fees are small, he computed the extent to which the observed spreads in silver were below the interest rate.[15] According to his calculations, shown in Figure 3.5(a) for the LME, silver spreads were nearly always at full carrying charges except for two sustained periods, late 1973 through early 1974 and late 1979 through early 1980. Deviations from full carrying charges were greatest during this later period, with spreads typically falling 6 percent below full carry (at an annualized rate) and in late January 1980 to 10 percent below full carry. Professor Kyle concluded that this behavior for spreads was at least consistent with manipulation. He was careful to say only "consistent with manipulation" because there are many natural non-manipulative reasons why spreads might be below full carrying charges.

Yet Professor Kyle ultimately concluded that a manipulation had occurred, because he proceeded to put silver in a context that makes spreads below full carrying charges seem most unnatural. He compared silver solely to gold. Compared to gold spreads, which have only rarely been below full carrying charges, silver spreads over 1979–1980 look abnormal.

Intertemporal spreads in other metals tell a very different story, however, and so they became a central subject for the defense. More broadly, the spreads in other metals reveal the problem with relying on circumstantial evidence. To which metals and to which period should silver during 1979–1980 be compared for signs of unusual price behavior?

Figure 3.5, which is much like the graph the defense presented to the jury, displays intertemporal spreads for five additional metals: platinum, palladium, copper, lead, and zinc. Platinum and its relative palladium are both precious metals, while silver is often a by-product of copper, lead, and zinc

---

[15] He computed the spreads as percents of the price of silver; he could also have presented them as dollars per troy ounce, with the interest expense converted similarly.

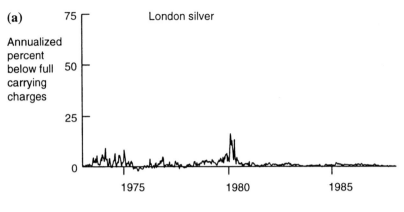

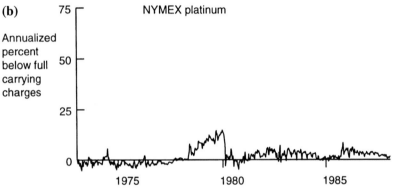

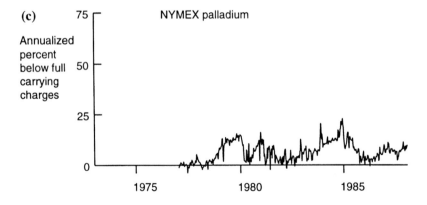

Figure 3.5. Comparison of three-month spreads below full carrying charges for six metals

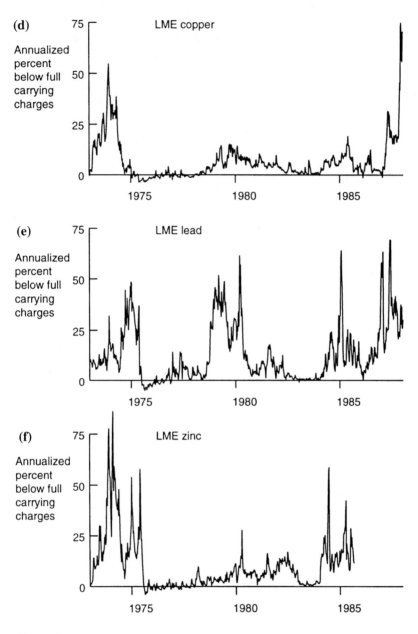

Figure 3.5. (cont.)

mining.[16] All six series show the extent to which the near-term intertemporal spread is below the standard of full carrying charges, expressed at an annual rate and plotted on the same scale.[17]

Two main facts emerge from these time series of the carrying charges in other metals. One is that spreads below full carrying charges are common in other metals, including precious metals like platinum and palladium. Gold is the exception, not the rule. Moreover, the amount below full carrying charges (that is, the premium for immediate delivery) in these other metals was at times far higher than anything observed for silver. Lead and zinc for delivery three months later has been known to sell at half the price of the metal for immediate delivery. Although one can point to days in late 1979 and early 1980 when the spreads in silver were more below full carrying charges than the spreads in these other five metals,[18] these other spreads were all more "consistent with manipulation," in Professor Kyle's words, than were spreads in silver.

The second main fact from Figure 3.5 is the similar timing of the outbreaks of spreads below full carrying charges, which were clustered in mid-1973 through 1974 and mid-1979 to mid-1980. It would seem that something was influencing all the metals in both these periods. Both periods marked the end of long economic expansions, a point made by Fama and French (1988) and Bailey and Chan (1993).[19]

These intertemporal spreads concern relationships within the web of a metal's prices as of one moment in time. It is a common mistake to confuse the relationship between the spot price at one time and the spot price at a later time with the relationship at one time between the spot price and the price for delivery at that later date. The CFTC made this mistake in its original analysis (1981, pp. 111–14) of the turmoil in the silver market. Observing that the price of silver was high from late 1979 to early 1980 (when the Hunts took deliveries) and that the price was low in April and May 1980 (when the

---

16   The prices for platinum and palladium are from NYMEX while those for silver, copper, lead, and zinc are from the LME. The palladium market, which began in 1977, is the least active among these markets. Trading in zinc on the LME was suspended in late August 1985.

17   The standard of full carrying charges is the Eurodollar interest rate for dollar-denominated contracts and the three-month interest rate for the pound for the others, along with a series for the typical fees among LME-licensed warehouses for the base metals. To minimize the effect of extreme observations, the median in each group of five successive observations is plotted.

18   Silver spreads reached their extreme just after the exchanges' restriction of trading to liquidation only.

19   Metals again showed such price patterns in 1988–1989, again prefiguring an economic downtown. The only exception was silver, whose spreads remained at full carrying charges. This exception weakens the argument the defense made about the situation in 1979–1980.

Hunts took no deliveries), the CFTC concluded that the Hunts' insistence on delivery resulted in a price premium of as much as $40 per troy ounce.

Properly considered, the actual evidence from intertemporal silver spreads only weakly suggests a corner. Rather than silver spreads in late 1979 and early 1980 displaying marked backwardation (with the prices for delivery by May 1980 commanding something like a $20 premium over delivery dates later in 1980), the spreads were only slightly below full carrying charges, in the range observed for other metals at the time. Yet, whatever the evidence from intertemporal price relationships, the evidence should have been examined only if the Hunts' alleged manipulation was a corner.

3.5 Distortion of the coin/bullion differential

The economists examined a third area of relations within the web of silver prices for evidence of manipulation: the differential between coins and bullion. Depending on the wear the coins have experienced, one dollar in face value of U.S. silver dimes and quarters yields 0.715 troy ounces of .999 bullion. The refining technology for converting coins (and other silver scrap) into ingots of bullion is quite simple and usually inexpensive. In the late 1970s, secondary refineries processed tens of millions of troy ounces annually, out of the hundreds of millions of troy ounces of coins still available. In the summer of 1979, refineries were quoting $0.10 per troy ounce for the service. Such direct pricing is known as "toll" refining, as the refiner does not own the silver. Whenever refiners buy coins on their own account and sell bullion, the difference between their bid price for the coins and their ask price for bullion becomes an implicit price for refining.

The coin/bullion differential, or equivalently, the secondary refining margin, corresponds in other manipulation cases to grade distinctions, such as #3 wheat separated from the deliverable #2 grade by cleaning and drying. As in other manipulation cases, there are a series of questions regarding grade differentials, which are best kept distinct, even though that seems never to be done in practice. What should happen to grade differentials when the demand for the grade deliverable on futures contracts is artificially boosted? Were the grade differentials abnormal during the alleged manipulation? If so, how did the alleged manipulator respond to them? Could there possibly be some innocent explanation for any abnormal differential?

The discussion of the coin/bullion differential at the trial and in the reports to the CFTC tended to muddle the logical chain of questions. For example, the defense experts offered evidence about the secondary refining margin in copper during 1979–1980 without explaining why this evidence was relevant to a manipulation of the silver market. The plaintiff's expert argued that the flood of bullion from scrap refineries is what overwhelmed the Hunts in March 1980 while ignoring the contradiction with his other argument that deliverable supply was restricted to bullion already in exchange-approved vaults. The CFTC Division of Enforcement's expert Dr. Burrows did not reconcile the obvious responsiveness of coin prices to his assumption in calculating deliverable supply that refiners had an absolute capacity beyond which they would not bid for coins.

Of more interest now than the muddled presentation of the evidence about coins is another argument made by those alleging the Hunts to have been manipulators. They offered the coin/bullion differential as a distinct indicator of manipulation. The plaintiff's expert said that the abnormal coin/bullion differential was "a further indication of the existence of manipulation in the silver futures market" (Trial Transcript, p. 8559). Similarly, the CFTC Division of Enforcement included the coin/bullion differential on its list of supposedly separate evidence of manipulation.

Although the plaintiff's expert testified about coins, Professor Kyle for the CFTC Division of Enforcement devoted much more attention to them. (Reflecting on the case recently, he ranked the coin/bullion differential among the most important evidence for his conclusion of manipulation.) He examined the quotations from a principal dealer in coins, Mocatta Metals. His series for the differential between Mocatta Metals' bid for coins and its ask for bullion is plotted in Figure 3.6. From this series, he concluded that "during many days in January 1980, the Mocatta coin prices were extraordinarily distorted relative to bullion prices" (Kyle CFTC Report, p. 41). Whereas before the fall of 1979 the implicit refining margin had been on the order of $0.10 per troy ounce, "between January 16 and January 25, the differential was approximately ten dollars per ounce!" He took this behavior as another piece of evidence that the demand behind the price spike was for bullion for immediate delivery rather than for hoarding silver generally. He went further to say this coin/bullion differential was sufficiently attractive that any long-term investor would have exchanged his bullion (or rights to bullion) for coins, implying that the Hunts, since they did not follow this strategy, must have been manipulators.[20]

The defense experts (led by me on this subject) responded with several arguments. First, I observed that the Hunts had taken coins in lieu of bullion (although mostly through the EFP with Mocatta Metals in October 1979). Second, I observed that there could be some non-manipulative explanations: a strike at a major refinery in the fall of 1979 and whatever was concurrently increasing refining margins for base metals.

Third, I argued that the series constructed from Mocatta Metals' coin quotations overstates the implicit refining margin in the crucial days of mid-January 1980. Mocatta Metals, it seems, effectively withdrew from the wholesale

[20]   Professor Kyle glosses over the fact that the Hunts took so few coins at these differentials, which is surely far from a manipulator's profit-maximizing number.

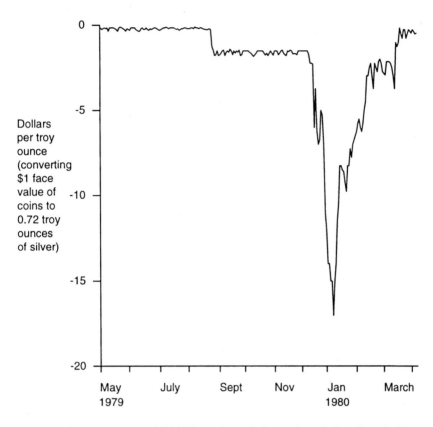

Figure 3.6. Mocotta Metals' bid for coins relative to its ask for silver bullion

market, buying little from those retail dealers who were themselves deluged with small lots of coins appearing from the backs of dresser drawers.[21] That is to say, Mocatta Metals' bid quotations in mid-January were probably no more than nominal, and probably overstated the differential by $5 to $6. Other public quotations for coins at the time implied a smaller coin/bullion differential.[22] Also, Mocatta Metals' coin/bullion differential is far above toll

---

[21] Explaining to Herbert Hunt in a letter dated January 15, 1980 why the discount on coins had risen to the range of $1.25 per troy ounce, Henry Jarecki, Chairman of Mocatta Metals, writes: "The main coin buyers were ourselves and one New York firm, but that firm bought only the quantity they could put in their own in-house pipeline. We, for our part, were reluctant to buy more…"

[22] These coin prices, given in the *Wall Street Journal* and quoted on the American Board of Trade are as suspect as those of Mocatta Metals' due to little volume but the point is that they imply less abnormal coin/bullion differentials than $10.

prices for refining. Many market participants have commented that in these weeks refining charges had risen far above the previous level, but none mentioned a charge above $4 per troy ounce.[23]

Altogether, these variously observed coin/bullion differentials seem very fragile. The bid–ask spreads, which were on the order of several dollars in any case, were probably for much smaller quantities than previously. In effect, few if any dealers, were actually "making a market" in coins. Any investor trying to buy silver coins in quantities approaching millions of troy ounces might have found the bargain disappearing. This argument the defense experts omitted, however. (This argument leaves unanswered why the Hunts took few coins when the coin/bullion differential was widest.)

The defense experts accepted the unstated proposition that a manipulation would manifest itself in the coin/bullion differential, precisely because it accorded with their own conception of the Hunts' alleged manipulation. By not deriving this proposition for the jury, they missed the opportunity of making clear that the plaintiff and the CFTC Division of Enforcement accepted that the Hunts' alleged manipulation was a corner, for an investor-interest manipulation or a price-effect manipulation would not be expected to manifest itself in a wider coin/bullion differential.

The defense experts also failed to make clear that the CFTC Division of Enforcement's expert and the plaintiff's expert were saying nothing new with the evidence of the coin/bullion differential. The evidence about the coin/bullion differential, abnormal or not, is the same evidence as that about intertemporal spreads in futures prices, just looked at from another perspective. The CFTC Division of Enforcement and the plaintiff were double counting their indications of distorted prices.

A proof of this proposition takes some development, but the proof is important. Consider the implications for the spot coin/bullion differential of three conditions: (1) Enormous quantities of coins and other silver scrap are available; no one would ever need to pay a premium for the immediate delivery of coin over deferred delivery. This implies that futures prices for coins—if such a market were active—would accord with full carrying charges. (2) The usual refining margin is $0.10 per troy ounce. (3) Bullion for immediate delivery commands a premium over bullion for delivery one year later, that is, bullion spreads are below full carrying charges. The second and third of these conditions are Professor Kyle's observations about the actual state of the silver market. The first is reasonable; if coins were showing a premium for immediate delivery, it would only further reduce the estimate of the spot coin/bullion differential.

---

[23]   A level of $3–4 is in fact Professor Kyle's estimate for days in January and early February other than the period January 16–25.

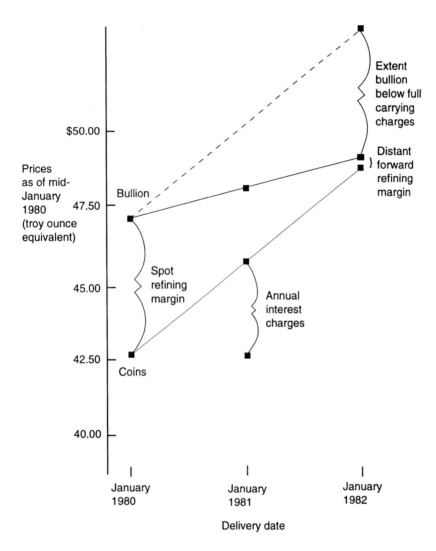

Figure 3.7. Algebraic relationship between coin refining margin and carrying charges for bullion

Applying these assumptions and analysis to mid-January 1980, as in Figure 3.7, one finds a coin/bullion differential of about $3.75 per troy ounce. All observers agree that the refining margin for execution for say March '81 remained the usual charge of $0.10. Professor Kyle concludes that bullion prices were, for delivery just more than a year ahead, on the order of 8 percent below full carrying charges during the week of January 14 when the spot bullion price averaged $46, which would imply a premium for immediate delivery over delivery one year later of $3.75. This $3.75 accords with explicit refining charges noted by market participants.[24]

All this is not sophistry, but the equilibrium relations that must hold among coins and bullion by the simplest of arbitrage. Given that coins are at full carrying charges because they are so abundant, if there is a premium for the immediate delivery of bullion, there must be a similar premium in the spot coin/bullion differential. By the same reasoning, if there is a substantial premium in the spot coin/bullion differential over the contractual price of refining for later execution, there must be a similar premium for immediate delivery of bullion. Consequently, a rise in the price of spot bullion relative to spot coins and a rise in the price of spot bullion relative to bullion delivered much later are the same phenomenon. They do not separately indicate the presence of a manipulation.

3.6   Distortion of the gold/silver ratio

In many manipulation cases, the economists involved have compared the supposedly manipulated commodity to one of its close substitutes. For example, if hard wheat prices increased along with soft wheat prices, so that the relationship changed much less than the prices themselves, the explanation of a sudden increase in the soft wheat price as a surge in export demand seems more reasonable. If aluminum prices fell while copper prices rose, so that the relationship diverged from typical patterns, the explanation of copper prices as an upswing in fabricating demand seems less reasonable.

By being called a "precious metal," silver invites comparison to gold. This comparison, namely the ratio of the price of gold bullion to the price of silver bullion, became a major area of expert testimony in the Hunt case. The course of the gold/silver ratio for twenty years can be seen in Figure 3.8. By no means has it been constant.[25] The gold/silver ratio was especially variable during 1979 and 1980. On May 1, 1979 (and for much of the summer), it stood at around 31:1; in September it fell to 24:1; in mid-January 1980, it reached a low of 16:1, before rising to 40:1 by April. (This progression in the gold/silver ratio is simply another way of saying that during 1979 and 1980 silver's price first rose more than gold's and then fell faster.)

Examining the equivalent of Figure 3.8 (the figure placed before the jury only went back as far as 1976), the plaintiff's expert pronounced the

---

[24]   Here one has more confidence in the prices in the futures market than the quotations for silver coins. Therefore, the best method for determining the premium in the spot refining margin is to deduce it from futures spreads. It can be taken as established, by Professor Kyle himself, that the coin/bullion differential peaked at $4 per troy ounce.

[25]   Jastram (1981) documents the variability back to the thirteenth century.

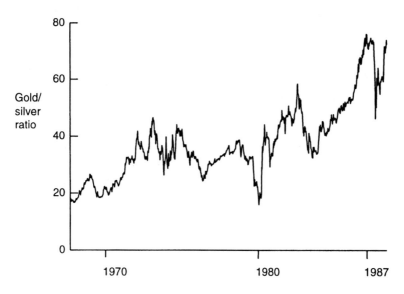

Figure 3.8. Gold/silver ratio, 1968 through 1987

gold/silver ratio of 16:1 during early January 1980 to be "abnormal by any standard" (Trial Transcript, p. 8528) and added it to his list of evidence indicating a manipulation. Quite apart from whether the ratio during January 1980 looks unusual over the whole twenty-year period of Figure 3.8 (let alone the fact that the U.S. kept an official ratio of 16:1 during the nineteenth century through coinage laws), such a focus on the gold/silver ratio exemplifies the analytical problems caused by the absence of a precise identification of the Hunts' alleged manipulation. If "manipulation" means a corner, it is difficult to represent the gold/silver ratio as new evidence. If "manipulation" means to fool other investors about long-term price relationships, it is difficult to reconcile the timing of the movements in the gold/silver ratio with the behavior of the alleged manipulators. If "manipulation" means the cumulative circumstantial evidence of abnormalities, it is difficult not to conclude that gold was also a manipulated market.

The reason why the gold/silver ratio is redundant as evidence about a corner is the same as for the coin/bullion differential. Again, the concept of the web of prices clarifies the issue. A corner raises the price of silver bullion for immediate delivery relative to the price of silver bullion for delivery years later. The silver price for delivery, say, two years later is determined by long-term mining costs and so forth, as is the price of gold for delivery so far ahead. Because the price of gold for immediate delivery shows none of the premium for immediate delivery due to a corner, it corresponds to the price of gold for later delivery and hence remains in its normal ratio with silver for delivery in two years. The decrease in the spot gold/silver ratio thus reflects nothing more that the premium from the corner.

A specific numerical example, as in Figure 3.9, might elucidate the point. Suppose the ratio between two-year-ahead gold futures and two-year-ahead silver futures is 30:1. Suppose, because of a corner, silver bullion for immediate delivery stands at a 50 percent premium (apart from interest expenses) to silver for delivery in two years. By algebra (and more deeply by the storage arbitrage in gold), the spot gold/spot silver ratio must be 20:1.

This numerical example does not demonstrate that no corner could conceivably occur in silver nor that the gold/silver ratio would not reveal the corner. The point is rather that the gold/silver ratio reveals nothing that has not already been revealed by the carrying charge in silver futures, or by the coin/bullion differential. If all of these relationships appear unusual, the evidence of manipulation is not three times as strong; it is the same evidence.[26]

In discussing other aspects of the comparison of silver to gold, the plaintiff's expert was less than careful with his implicit classification of the Hunts' manipulation. He noted how ContiCommodity's Norton Waltuch ostentatiously purchased silver futures contracts in August 1979. Taken alone that might support the idea of a manipulation of investor interest, encouraging others to jump on the bandwagon of precious metals, gold included. Yet the plaintiff's expert glossed over the fact that, although the investors were being fooled by the ostentatious purchases in August, the main part of the price spike in all precious metals occurred from late December to early January. In response to the defense's explanation of the rise in the price of silver as being due to investors desiring silver (and gold) because of political uncertainty, the plaintiff's expert pointed to the decline during late 1979 of the number of futures contracts outstanding, especially in silver. But, in contradicting the defense's explanation, he was conveniently forgetting his own argument elsewhere that the Hunts' purpose with many accounts and allies was to fool others into supposing widespread investor interest existed.

On several occasions, the plaintiff argued that the Conti group's purchases, ostentatious or not, and the Hunts' purchases, anonymous or not, moved the price of silver because of the sheer quantities. From that perspective, what happened within the web of silver prices mattered less than the movement of the entire web relative to gold. Yet Professor Pindyck, conducting his analysis as an expert for the various brokerage houses sued by Minpeco, concluded that there was no manipulation, whether or not the

---

[26] If silver coins, like silver bullion, were in temporarily short supply, or if gold bullion, like silver bullion, were in temporarily short supply, the three relationships need not move together. Yet both silver coins and gold bullion were abundant; hence they offered the same evidence of the temporary demand for silver bullion.

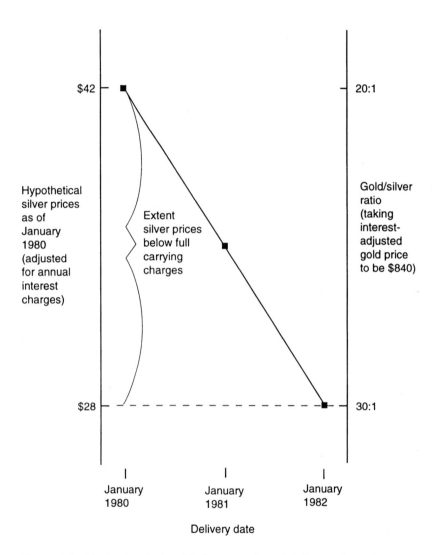

Figure 3.9. Algebraic relationship between the gold/silver ratio and carrying charges for silver

Hunts moved all silver prices relative to gold, for to him "manipulation" concerned the relationship within the web of silver prices, that is, a corner.

Finally, a broader comparison of silver with gold reveals problems with the exercise of inferring manipulation from circumstantial evidence. According to the plaintiff's expert, "gold was not manipulated whereas silver was"

(Trial Transcript, p. 8542). Yet over 1979–1980, gold rose 250 percent to its highest-ever price, showed considerable day-by-day variability in prices, hit price-move limits in futures a record number of times, had dealers' bid–ask spreads for bullion and coins widen, appreciated through January 1980 relative to platinum before falling to the previous ratio. To the plaintiff's expert, these very patterns in silver indicated manipulation, however. Of course, these patterns were more pronounced in silver. Yet if manipulation reveals itself only in the degree of such patterns, it becomes all the more imperative to have some recognized standard, that is, an *ex ante* definition of manipulation. Otherwise, the *ex post* patterns identify the manipulation, and the whole exercise of inferring the presence of a specified type of manipulation becomes a foregone conclusion.

In one aspect the silver market differed from the gold market not just in degree but in kind. Spreads in silver fell below full carrying charges while those in gold did not. The plaintiff's expert, classifying silver as manipulated and gold as not, thus placed substantial weight on the evidence from intertemporal spreads. Quite apart from whether silver spreads were unusual compared to those in metals besides gold, the emphasis on intertemporal spreads reveals the plaintiff's expert's principal conception of the supposed manipulation: a conventional corner of the shorts who must scramble for deliverable supplies. Had that been the plaintiff's definition from the outset, the evidence about the gold/silver ratio would have been superfluous.

3.7   Consistency in the manipulation identified

The lack of any identification of the Hunts' alleged manipulation profoundly affected the trial, especially the experts' testimony. In a trial overlong for other reasons, the economists analyzed evidence either irrelevant or redundant. In a trial needing a sharper focus, the economists often did not bring to bear the relevant evidence. In a trial which was itself the culmination of much short-term tactical legal maneuvering, the economists introduced further internal inconsistencies into the arguments.

A plaintiff, by initiating a legal proceeding, has the principal burden of making an internally consistent complaint. As plaintiff, Minpeco argued that the price rise in silver came when the shorts, apprehensive about needing to deliver regardless of the delivery date, covered their positions with purchases of futures (Trial Transcript, pp. 8715–16, also p. 8962). That argument is plausible, but the plaintiff's expert offered no specific evidence of the shorts covering, instead offering evidence of the intertemporal price spreads and the coin/bullion differential, which did not address the manipulation identified. Another example of inconsistency is how the plaintiff presented the Conti group's trading in August 1979 as ostentatiously impressing other investors (in accord with an investor-interest manipulation), while presenting the Hunts as attempting to hide their connections, which would seem to fit better with the idea of a corner.

Also, the plaintiff dramatized the Hunts' taking so much bullion in delivery and having a call on even more. Where were the Hunts to have made their profits? Presumably by selling their silver at inflated prices (which, because they did not do so, led the plaintiff to characterize their behavior as "uneconomic"), or by taking coins at a discount (which, again because they did not do so, apparently indicated their involvement in a manipulation).

The lack of pressure to identify a class of manipulation permitted the plaintiff to present a monopolization charge at variance with many of its own arguments about manipulation. The plaintiff argued that the decline in open interest, namely the number of futures contracts outstanding, indicated that investors were not interested in silver. Quite apart from whether open interest measures investor sentiment, the plaintiff's argument presupposes that others could freely enter into or exit from futures contracts. Yet under the monopolization charge, the plaintiff suggested that the Hunts controlled the futures market. According to the plaintiff's account of May 1979 through 1980, the supply of new bullion by March of 1980 overwhelmed the Hunts' finances. But how then was the deliverable supply in the "antitrust market" only the amount of bullion already in exchange-approved vaults?

The CFTC Division of Enforcement offered two experts: Professor Kyle, who concentrated on price relationships, and Dr. Burrows, who concentrated on the quantities of silver mined, refined, and consumed, at various price levels. Seemingly, these two experts complemented each other. Actually, they contradicted each other. If Dr. Burrows's computations of the amount of silver that would flow from mines and industrial consumers were correct, the implied price relationships should have approximated Professor Kyle's observations. Dr. Burrows conducted his experiments by changing the level of silver prices across the board, not the relationships within the web of silver prices. Dr. Burrows investigated a price-effect manipulation while Professor Kyle investigated a corner.

The defense likewise failed the test of internal consistency. It asserted that silver bullion throughout the world could easily be moved into exchange-approved vaults and was in sufficient quantity to satisfy any demand from the Hunts. Yet, the amount of bullion that actually moved into exchange-approved vaults during the silver crisis was relatively small compared to the bullion supposedly available, even though the price of bullion for immediate delivery rose to a premium of several dollars per troy ounce over bullion for delivery a year later. The defense stressed that the large number of coins could be converted into bullion relatively easily; however, the coin/bullion differential fell because coins could not be melted quickly enough.

The defense's explanation of the premium for immediate delivery was inconsistent with its view on the scope of the bullion market. The defense explained away the spreads below full carrying charges as part of the pattern seen in other metals markets. Explanations of spreads below full carrying charges in the copper market, say, hinge on a temporary supply disruption or a demand for copper during the present only; either way, some component of supply or demand is inflexible. Thus, according to the defense, the silver bullion market was distinguished both by flexibility and the lack of it.

The inconsistencies within the arguments of the plaintiff, the CFTC Division of Enforcement, and the defense arose in part because the economist expert witnesses failed to put forth a model of the Hunts' manipulation and of the alternative explanation of the price spike.[27] Although "model" may invoke the highly mathematical formulations in vogue in economics journals (and inapplicable in legal settings, as noted by Flynn [1988]), the term also means any abstraction that permits careful scrutiny of the chain of reasoning, of the internal consistency of arguments, and of ancillary implications. One helpful analytical structure is the concept of a web of prices, for which explicit prices exist for every type of silver, at every location, for every delivery date. Had the concept of the web of prices been applied throughout the trial, it would have been recognized that some of what was presented as distinct evidence of manipulation was actually other evidence repackaged. It would also have been recognized that the supposedly fresh subject of monopolization overlapped with the subject of manipulation and essentially classified the type of manipulation the Hunts were alleged to have committed. Instead, the frequent use of the approximation "the price of silver" discouraged systematic reflection on the connections among the evidence.

The inconsistencies resulting from a lack of precise identification of the Hunts' alleged manipulation affected many other aspects of the economists' testimony. Most obvious is the topic of inferring manipulative intent, the subject of Chapter 6. Also, the classification of the manipulation mattered to tests of the causes of the price spike, the subject of Chapter 4. Were the manipulation a corner, the price moves should have coincided with the trap of the corner being revealed, whether through the Hunts' insistence on deliveries or public statements by regulators about the Hunts, and not at the time the positions were put in place. Were instead the manipulation to fool other investors or were it to affect prices through excessively large purchases, the price moves should have occurred near the time of the manipulators' trading. Needless to say, this reasoning was not made explicit at the trial. Finally, the type of manipulation concerned the calculation of damages, or more broadly, the calculation of what the price of silver would have been without the Hunts, the subject of Chapter 5. The experts' preferred style of analysis for the

---

[27]   Professor Kyle alone had a formal model of manipulation (Kyle, 1984, extended by Pirrong, 1993). Professor Kyle used this model implicitly in his report to the CFTC, but he did not model formally the alternative theories of the price spike.

Hunts' price effect did not necessarily coincide with the implicit picture of manipulation they drew using their choice of evidence about whether a manipulation had taken place.

The absence of a precise identification of the Hunts' manipulation ultimately worked to the detriment of the defense. Why did the defense not try to raise the analytical level, why did it not attack the plaintiff's vagueness about "manipulation," why did it not make clear the nature of the inferential exercise? In part, the defense, like the plaintiff, felt that the jury would not understand some of the finer points of commodity market economics such as the redundancy between intertemporal spreads and the coin/bullion differential. In part, the defense believed that the vagueness of "manipulation" would keep the plaintiff from pulling its case together. Yet the defense left the jurors to construct their own definitions of manipulation and to reason about the evidence according to those unarticulated definitions.

More fundamentally, the Hunts' legal strategy prior to the trial – when they resisted inspection of their trading records and denied connections even among their own trading – was a poor basis on which to lay the arguments developed by their experts. At a very early stage, the Hunts had conceded a major advantage to the plaintiff. The economists' testimony would have complemented much better a legal strategy in which the Hunts admitted having accumulated large positions and having spoken to others about silver, for neither action is the offense of manipulation. Mr. Gorman, Minpeco's counsel, and Mr. Rubinstein, the Hunts' counsel, both believe such an approach may have won the case for the Hunts, because it would have kept the Hunts from denying the obvious connections within their affairs and would have forced Minpeco to identify the manipulation.

To the jury, the economists' testimony must have seemed like a conversation only half overheard, because the central issues of the definition of "manipulation" and the identification of the type of manipulation the Hunts were alleged to have committed were never spoken about. Yet more confusing, the economists clearly disagreed about the type, even though none of them explained the possible types nor made clear how particular topics within the evidence related to particular types of manipulation. All the while the legal professionals, when before the jury, treated the definition of manipulation and the relevance of the evidence as self evident. Before Judge Lasker alone, the defense attorneys argued for a definition developed by the CFTC emphasizing the cornered shorts needing to come hat in hand to the dominant long. In his Charge to the Jury, Judge Lasker, following previous manipulation cases, used a definition of manipulation so broad as to encompass all possible types. Judge Lasker's Charge did not suggest that the jurors identify the type of the Hunts' alleged manipulation before proceeding to infer whether the Hunts had committed it.

At its most basic level, the Hunt case concerned the assigning of a cause to the unprecedented rise in the price of silver between May 1979 and January 1980. The Hunts trading received the attention it did, not because of the unusual spreads between delivery dates and the uncharacteristic coin/bullion differential, but because of the extraordinary course of the spot price. As the jury was instructed by Judge Lasker, the plaintiff had to prove that the defendants played a substantial part in causing the price rise. Ultimately, the plaintiff came close to identifying the Hunts' alleged manipulation as the impact on the price itself.

In most legal disputes a central event must be explained. Even in previous manipulation cases, there was a central event, which took the form of a suspicious price rise over the last days or hours of a particular futures contract. The alleged manipulator's behavior could be described as a single action: usually a long position established days or weeks earlier and held unchanged through the price rise. Also, the alleged manipulator was the principal actor: usually, few other longs remained in the expiring contract and no new longs entered. Under such circumstances, the question to be resolved is whether the alleged manipulator's action proved sufficient to have caused the price rise (and whether that action was illegal).

The Hunt case, in contrast, dealt with multiple actions causing many events over many months. Because the defendants allegedly manipulated the silver market over a period of at least nine months, they could not reasonably be said to have performed just one manipulative act. The price rise ostensibly caused by them comprised thousands of individual price changes, which took place amid the activity of hundreds of silver traders. News of the Hunts' positions could well have persuaded those traders to buy and sell at prices higher than previously, but a host of other factors could have done so as well. Under such circumstances, the question to be answered is not whether the Hunts caused the price of silver to rise, but rather how much of that rise in price was due directly or indirectly to them (and whether that effect was illegal).[1]

In previous manipulation cases, the statistical analysis had concentrated on the historical range of price relationships. In the Hunt case, the analysis also attempted to determine the extent to which the alleged manipulators' actions had directly or indirectly influenced the price. This appeal to statistical analysis in turn raised an issue new to manipulation cases, namely the proper way to test for causality.

To disentangle from multiple events the systematic effects of several factors, while others remain unknown or unmeasured, economists utilize multiple regression analysis. This is the core of the field of econometrics, and it determines the association between a "dependent variable" and an "independent variable," while holding other measured factors constant. A classic example is a regression relating yields on a number of plots of land to fertilizer applied and to rainfall, in the presence of less easily measured factors such as variations in soil quality and sunlight. The association between yields and the variables fertilizer and rainfall is systematic and plausibly interpreted as causality (more fertilizer increases yields). Ideally, variation in unknown factors – collectively, the "error term" – is minor. The unknown factors, however, sometimes align so as to disguise the true relationship between yields and fertilizer, so econometricians speak of the degree of "statistical significance."

All the economist expert witnesses in the Hunt case relied on some form of regression analysis in testing for the causes of the price rise in silver during 1979 and 1980. Through regression techniques, Professor Kyle (expert for the CFTC Division of Enforcement) examined the connection between silver and gold to show the effect of the Hunts' presence. Dr. Burrows (also for the Division of Enforcement) conducted so-called Granger causality tests, based on regression methodology, to determine whether the trading in silver influenced gold, an analysis later duplicated by the plaintiff's experts. The defense experts used multiple regression analysis to distinguish the Hunts' trading from other possible influences on silver by relating the daily changes in their positions to the daily changes in the price of silver. The plaintiff's experts developed a regression technique to define the effect of the Hunts' trading, in which they examined the relationship between the daily price levels of silver and the levels of the Hunts' positions. (Also see Rudzitis [1987].)

With regard to the more specific tests for causality, however, there was little consensus. The experts disagreed as to whether a factor's effect should be

---

[1] The legal concept of causality is quite general and involves an analysis of the relationships between individuals and the impact of their actions on each other and on other parties. As Crane (1981) notes regarding securities law, the concept includes both a corporate insider's duty to shareholders and the impact on prices of any of her trading. This "price impact" idea of causality is the relevant one for this chapter.

measured directly in silver prices, indirectly in terms of what remains after effects from other factors have been accounted for, or indirectly in terms of how it manifests itself in other markets such as gold. The experts also disagreed as to whether a causal factor should explain the level of a price or the change in the price, and whether an effect on a price should be found hours and days, or months and years after the causal event.

The tests for causality yielded disconcertingly different results. Professor Kyle concluded that the Hunts must have affected the price of silver because silver was less influenced by the price of gold than normally. Yet Dr. Burrows concluded that, because price changes in silver tended to precede those in gold, the Hunts caused silver to rise in price more than gold. The defense experts found no statistically or substantively significant relationship between daily price changes in silver and changes in the Hunts' positions. In contrast, the plaintiff's experts concluded that the Hunts had clearly caused the cumulative price rise.

Considering that the economists all accepted regression analysis as an appropriate analytical tool, why did their specific tests differ so greatly? The answer forms the subject of this chapter. The differences among the experts' approaches are not mere technical details; rather, they fundamentally determined the experts' conclusions about the Hunts' effect on the price of silver.

Regression analysis entered the trial itself largely because of Professor Ross who, years before the CFTC Division of Enforcement or Minpeco made specific allegations, had compared the Hunts' trading to changes in silver prices. Professor Ross's studies, done with my help, became prominent in the written responses to the CFTC Division of Enforcement, and later assumed a central role when the defense lawyers began to work on their economic arguments for the trial. In contrast, Minpeco's expert witness, Professor Houthakker, the editor of a leading econometrics journal, hesitated to introduce regression analysis, believing the jury would not follow the discussion of it. Only reluctantly (after Professors Kolb and Spiller had undertaken the analysis) did he testify about regression results in anticipation of the statistical arguments to be offered by the defense.

In the end, the presentation of regression results at the trial did little to enhance the jurors' understanding of the issues at stake, but not necessarily because they were unable to understand statistics. They gave every indication of following a description of a "scatter diagram," which is the heart of regression analysis, and they were probably capable of understanding the purpose of the econometrics if explained well. Regrettably, the relevant statistical testimony was never presented thoroughly. The lawyers and economists compressed it on direct examination to a matter of minutes, making it impossible for the jury to compare the various approaches. The opaque terminology of econometrics surely kept the jury from following the substantive arguments. It may have kept the plaintiff's lawyers from recognizing that some assertions were flawed – flaws that, if exposed, would have weakened the plaintiff's case. It certainly prevented the defense experts from communicating with the defense lawyers, with the result that important segments of the defense testimony were left unconnected.

In this chapter, I explain the statistical approaches used in the case: first, the measurement of the Hunts' effect by relating their daily trading to the price of silver; second, the calculation of the time it took for the Hunts' trading to manifest itself in prices; third, the measurement of political and economic events on silver prices; fourth, the determination of an effect of silver itself on other metals, primarily gold; and fifth, the analysis of the Hunts' effect together with that of political events. This sequence proceeds from relatively simple to more complex, with individual experts' results interspersed throughout. In the sixth section of this chapter, I reflect upon the limitations of the statistical tests for causality used by the various economists. The final section concerns strategies used at the trial, in which I consider how the statistical analysis played before the jury and how the adversarial nature of the trial affected the presentation of the econometric tests. The results were quite different from what might have been produced in an academic setting.

4.1   Measurement of the Hunts' effect on daily price changes

The most straightforward way to determine whether the Hunts had an effect on the price of silver is to measure that price shortly before and after they made their trades. The strongest possible statistical evidence for the plaintiff would be if each of the additions that the Hunts made to their positions in the fall of 1979 were accompanied by a sharp jump in price that day or the very next one, followed by a plateau until the next Hunt action. Ideally (from the plaintiff's perspective), the Hunts' decisions to stand for delivery would have sparked price rises as soon as those intentions became known; and the days on which they made substantial purchases would be the days of the largest percentage increases in price, while the days on which the Hunts made substantial sales would be those of the largest percentage decreases in price.

The strongest statistical evidence for the plaintiff, then, would be offered by a substantively and statistically significant coefficient in a regression of the percentage change in the price of silver from one day to the next on the change in the Hunts' position over that interval, with the Hunts' trading explaining most of the variation in the dependent variable.[2] It would still need to be determined that the Hunts provoked those changes and had not simply traded in response to the price changes. Association alone would not neces-

---

2   Such regression analysis corresponds to an "event study" as commonly used in analysis of securities prices, except that the additional information on the size of the trade is also employed.

sarily imply causality, although the reverse would hold – that is, the absence of an association would imply an absence of causality.

For reasons that remain unclear, neither the experts for the CFTC Division of Enforcement nor those for the plaintiff tested the Hunts' direct effect on day-by-day changes in the price of silver, even though those tests might have produced the statistical equivalent of a smoking gun. Those tests were conducted instead by the experts for the defense.

In reference to the classic application of regression analysis mentioned above, the percentage change in the price of silver took the place of wheat yields, the Hunts' trading that day stood for the amount of fertilizer, and the idiosyncratic factors behind traders' decisions replaced sunlight and soil quality. The results of the simplest version of the test, using the Hunts' trading aggregated across all types of silver including futures contracts, are presented in the top panel of Table 4.1. (Although it was formally submitted into evidence, the jury did not see this table during testimony. Instead, they saw the corresponding scatter diagram, Figure 4.1.)

Far from the plaintiff's ideal of a strong causal connection, according to regression in Table 4.1, prices did not change day by day in proportion to the Hunts' trading. Specifically, according to the coefficient –0.00028 in the top panel of Table 4.1, for every 5,000 troy ounce lot the Hunts purchased on any one day from May 1, 1979 through April 30, 1980, whether bullion, coins, or futures contracts, the price fell 0.00028 percent. Of course, a price fall as the result of a purchase is nonsensical. Effectively, the coefficient is zero, which is the message from the t-statistic of –0.59, which is "insignificant" by conventional standards. (Statistical significance for a one-sided test at the conventional 95 percent level would require a t-statistic greater than 1.66 and for 99 percent, 2.36.) The same message is delivered by the R^2, which at 0.001 says that merely 0.1 percent of the variation in the dependent variable, namely the daily percentage changes in the price of silver, was associated with the Hunts' trading. From the plaintiff's perspective, the R^2 should have approached its maximum of 1.00, the coefficient should have been positive and large, and the t-statistic should have been far beyond 2.36.

Thus, it does not seem that those days on which the Hunts added to their positions coincided with days of above-average price rises in silver. Yet it is possible that the full effect of their trading did not emerge on the days they traded. By this argument, the price change on a particular day would be statistically related to the Hunts' trading on that and previous days. The regression reported in the middle panel of Table 4.1 tests this proposition, which the results again fail to support. None of the coefficients on the Hunts' previous trading is statistically significant, either individually or together.[3]

---

[3]   The conclusion remains the same with even more lags or with changes measured week to week.

Table 4.1. *Changes in the price of silver related to the Hunts' daily trading*

Price changes related to the Hunts' aggregate trading

Dependent variable: Percent change in Comex close from previous day

$R^2 = 0.001$
Durbin–Watson statistic = 1.49

Independent variable	Coefficient	t-statistic
Change in Hunts' position from previous day	–0.00028	–0.59

Price changes related to Hunts' trading on previous days

Dependent variable: Percent change in Comex close from previous day

$R^2 = 0.023$
Durbin–Watson statistic = 1.51
F-statistic for the five coefficients = 1.16

Independent variable	Coefficient	t-statistic
Change in Hunts' position from previous day	0.00014	0.27
Change in position one day previously	–0.00089	–1.47
Change in position two days previously	–0.00012	–0.20
Change in position three days previously	–0.00049	–0.81
Change in position four days previously	0.00086	1.56

Price changes related to the composition of the Hunts' trading

Dependent variable: Percent change in Comex close from previous day

$R^2 = 0.023$
Durbin–Watson statistic = 1.52

Independent variable	Coefficient	t-statistic
Change in bullion from previous day	0.00032	0.30
Change in coins from previous day	–0.00399	–0.74
Change in futures (net) from previous day	0.00002	0.04
Change in EFPs from previous day	0.00257	1.65
Change in forwards from previous day	–0.00348	–1.49

The regression uses daily observations from May 1, 1979 through April 30, 1980, a total of 253 observations. It includes a constant term. The variable "Hunts' position" comprises all accounts alleged to be part of the manipulation, including those of the so-called Conti group, and is measured in units of 5,000 troy ounces.

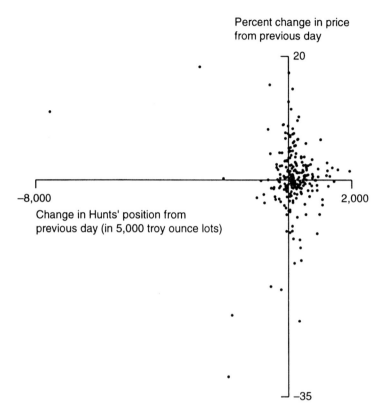

Figure 4.1. Day-by-day changes in the Hunts' positions related to day-by-day changes in the price of silver (Comex close), May 1, 1979 through April 30, 1980

Of course, the other traders in the silver market may have sent the price higher when they understood the Hunts to be in a position to corner the market. That proposition could be tested directly, if only it were possible to measure their combined expectations about the Hunts. Presumably traders would be influenced by knowledge of the Hunts' positions or by signals made by the Hunts or the Conti group through their particular actions, such as taking deliveries or arranging EFPs.[4]

4   The idea that the Hunts and the so-called Conti group worked in concert arose several years later. Quite apart from whether they did conspire to manipulate the silver market, other traders' changing expectations about conspiracy could not have caused the price rise.

This form of the proposition about other traders' delayed expectations can be tested with a regression disaggregating the Hunts' position into components such as bullion, futures, EFPs, London forwards, and coins, as shown in the bottom panel of Table 4.1.[5] Presumably, if the Hunts purchased silver in any form, its price would rise, but especially if it were bullion rather than distant futures contracts – a pattern that would be expected particularly during a corner. In such a case, we would expect to find a hierarchy among the coefficients in the bottom regression in Table 4.1; the largest would be bullion, followed by EFPs for bullion, London forwards, futures, and coins.[6] But this pattern does not in fact happen among the estimated coefficients in Table 4.1. Not only is bullion not the most important variable, as predicted, but not all the coefficients are positive. In any case, they are not statistically significant as a group.[7] Thus, a closer analysis of the Hunts' trading fails to reveal any statistical association with the day-to-day price changes in silver prices.

4.2   Measurement of the Hunts' effect over time

When Minpeco and the CFTC Division of Enforcement charged the Hunts with causing the price of silver to rise, the principal evidence they offered was the relationship between the daily price of silver and the Hunts' daily holdings over 1979–1980. In so doing, Minpeco and the Division of Enforcement related the level of prices to the level of the Hunts' positions. The Division of Enforcement's expert, Dr. Burrows, drew attention to the similarity between the plot of the price of silver and the plot of the Hunts' holdings. His implicit analysis can be shown here by the scatter diagram in Figure 4.2, which sets the daily price of silver from May 1979 through April 1980 against the Hunts' daily positions. Each business day during that year corresponds to a point on the scatter diagram. From Figure 4.2, it is obvious why Dr. Burrows performed no formal statistical analysis, for a relationship between the Hunts' holdings and the price of silver is apparent even visually. The top panel of Table 4.2 shows the corresponding formal regression analysis. The coefficient on the variable "Hunts' position" is statistically and substantively significant by any standard.

As can be seen from the contrasting scatter diagrams in Figure 4.1 and Figure 4.2, the analysis relating the daily changes in the Hunts' position to daily changes in the price of silver and the analysis relating the daily level of the Hunts' position to the daily price level of silver represent two approaches whose conclusions cannot be more different. Even though the underlying

---

[5]   The EFP variable measures that part of the agreement that did not result in immediate delivery of bullion or coins.

[6]   A delivery on a futures contract would cause an increase in the price equal to the differential in the coefficients.

[7]   Lags of the various types of positions do not add to the statistical association.

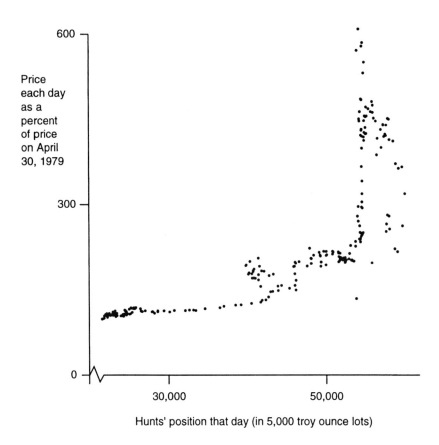

Figure 4.2. The Hunts' position related to the price of silver (Comex close), daily, May 1, 1979 through April 30, 1980

data are identical, the first seemingly confirms that the Hunts had no discernible effect on the price of silver; the second that they seemingly had an important effect. Clearly, both conclusions cannot be correct. As it happens, the analysis relating levels to levels is subtly yet seriously flawed and therefore deserves some further scrutiny here.

Because the Hunts were accused of causing the price of silver to rise, their actions should have resulted in a change in the price of silver. Hence, the appropriate test for causality relates changes to changes, which Minpeco and the CFTC Division of Enforcement implicitly accepted when they alleged that the Hunts, by adding to their silver holdings in 1979, changed the price of silver from what it had been in 1978. Yet, as was emphasized in the plaintiff's expert testimony and closing arguments, the full change in price need

Table 4.2. *Relationship between the Hunts' trading and the price of silver*

Levels related to levels

Dependent variable: Comex close as a percent of close on April 30, 1979

$R^2 = 0.513$
Durbin–Watson statistic = 0.04

Independent variable	Coefficient	t-statistic
Hunts' position	0.00583	16.26

Correction for serial correlation (using AR(1))

Dependent variable: Comex close as a percent of close on April 30, 1979

$R^2 = 0.981$

Independent variable	Coefficient	t-statistic
Hunts' position	0.00132	0.98
First-order serial correlation	0.987	100.12

Changes related to changes (using Ordinary Least Squares)

Dependent variable: Percent change in Comex close from previous day

$R^2 = 0.001$
Durbin–Watson statistic = 1.49

Independent variable	Coefficient	t-statistic
Change in Hunts' position from previous day	–0.00028	–0.59

The regressions use daily observations from May 1, 1979 through April 30, 1980, a total of 253 observations. All include a constant term. The variable "Hunts' position" comprises all accounts alleged to be part of the manipulation, including those of the so-called Conti group, and is measured in units of 5,000 troy ounces.

not be worked out in a matter of a few days, nor need the interval, whether days or months, always be the same. An extended delay would indeed be plausible were other traders to recognize the size of the Hunts' positions only long after they were placed, perhaps only when the Hunts stood for delivery. Also, traders might anticipate future actions, such as the demand for physical delivery, well before those actions take place. For either reason, although causality implies change, it is not obvious over what interval of time the change would occur.[8]

Even though the Hunts' daily trading did not appear to move the price of silver on those days, a pattern of sharp price increases as soon as information about the Hunts' positions or trading intentions became public would have provided the plaintiff with evidence almost as strong. The plaintiff did not point to any such pattern, however. No sharp price increases occurred at the time of the Hunts' meetings with exchange officials or at the time of the meetings of Comex's Special Silver Committee (meetings that might have suggested an emergency to outside observers).

Of course, the plaintiff could have offered the testimony of many traders about the times when they learned of the Hunts' positions and the effect that knowledge had on their decisions to buy or sell.[9] Instead of reconstructing traders' reactions through their own testimony, the plaintiff implicitly argued that the price of silver itself measured traders' reactions to the Hunts. Should, in an extreme case, a very long interval be necessary for all effects on silver prices to occur, it would be appropriate to consider the price on a particular day as having been influenced by all the Hunts' trading to date; that is, to relate the price level on a particular day to the level of the Hunts' position on that day.

Although the defense experts were inclined to dismiss out of hand regressions relating levels to levels in favor of regressions relating changes to changes, practice in other areas of economics suggests that either style can be appropriate. Many econometric studies of commodities, such as the U.S. Department of Agriculture's analysis of farmers' responses to crop programs, employ the price level. In many other studies, day-by-day changes are employed as a matter of course. A particularly relevant example is the large literature testing the effect of the Federal Reserve's discount rate, because the Federal Reserve is a large player in the money markets. Believing it so obvious as to need no justification, economists tend to relate changes in the Federal Reserve's discount to changes in other economic variables such as the interest rates of major commercial banks.[10] Clearly, each style of analysis finds its appropriate application in different circumstances.

In the Hunt case, the statistical evidence itself casts doubt on the appropriateness of the style of analysis in which the price level is related to the level

8   Securities traders seem to recognize quickly when some insider is trading illegally; the price response over a few days is out of proportion to the insider's quantity (Meulbroek, 1992).
9   Actually, the defense experts compiled newspaper reports on the silver market during the fall of 1979, which often quoted prominent traders' explanations of price changes, to show that the Hunts were rarely mentioned.
10   See Waud (1970), Baker and Meyer (1980), Roley and Troll (1984), Smirlock and Yawitz (1985), Cook and Hahn (1988), Wagster (1993), and Thornton (1994).

of silver held. The corresponding regression reported in the top panel of Table 4.2 has a very low Durbin–Watson statistic compared to the desired value of 2.0. The Durbin–Watson statistic measures the degree of serial correlation in the regression's error term, in this instance a very high degree of serial correlation. That is, the element of the silver price not "explained" by the Hunts' position tends to be the same day after day. This might seem to be a mere technicality – after all the relationship in Figure 4.1 is obvious – but to a specialist in time series, a low Durbin–Watson statistic makes it very probable that the observed relationship is spurious.[11]

The defense experts tried to expose the problem in the style of statistical analysis that relates levels to levels by replacing the Hunts' positions with a time series that could not possibly have caused the price of silver to rise and fall over 1979–1980, namely the morning temperature in Buenos Aires. Of course, in a series stretching over more than one year, the temperature in Buenos Aires cycles annually, in no pattern with the price of silver. Over a single year, however, it reaches its peak in January, just as the price of silver did in 1979–1980. A scatter diagram relating the temperature in Buenos Aires daily over 1979–1980 to the Comex silver close the same days, shown in Figure 4.3, reveals a relationship as strong as the one between the Hunts' position on a particular day and the price of silver. Indeed, the formal regression analysis of the relationship between the temperature and the price of silver in Buenos Aires, shown in the upper half of Table 4.3, indicates a statistically significant coefficient and an R^2 comparable to that for the Hunts. According to the statistical technique relating levels to levels, therefore, the temperature in Buenos Aires could just as well have been the cause of the rise in the price of silver. If the regression analysis is conducted relating the change in the temperature to the change in the price of silver, as in the lower half of Table 4.3, the coefficient is not statistically significant, which is the sensible conclusion and which demonstrates that the proper statistical technique is to relate changes to changes (though not necessarily daily changes). More generally, if a particular econometric technique indicates that the morning temperature in Buenos Aires caused the price of silver to rise, the technique ought to be dismissed as inappropriate. This point the defense experts tried to make at the trial, but without placing Figure 4.3 and Table 4.3 before the jury.[12]

---

[11] This problem was first diagnosed by Granger and Newbold (1974). (The phrase "spurious regression" is theirs.) Many other specialists in time-series statistics have extended their criticism, which is now prominent in textbooks for practitioners.

[12] Petzel (1981) also demonstrates the importance of statistical technique in his retrospective analysis of the controversial price decline in wheat in 1925. The Grain Futures Administration, by relating levels to levels, had concluded that large speculators had caused the price decline. Using a more modern statistical technique, Petzel uncovers no such connection.

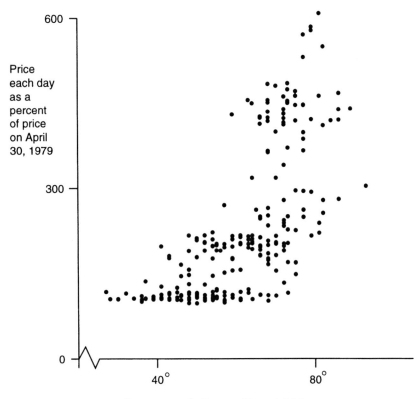

Figure 4.3. Weather in Buenos Aires related to the price of silver (Comex close), daily, May 1, 1979 through April 30, 1980

The plaintiff's experts had recognized to some extent the statistical problem from relating the daily price of silver to the daily level of the Hunts' positions. Rather than relate daily price changes to daily trading, however, they made a correction for the degree of "autocorrelation" in the regression's error term. Their style of regression analysis is shown in the middle panel of Table 4.1. Although their correction for autocorrelation reduces the estimate of the connection between the Hunts' positions and the price of silver, the coefficient remains statistically significant. The plaintiff's experts emphasized the statistically significant coefficient as evidence of the Hunts' causing the price of silver to rise.

Actually, as can be seen in Table 4.2, the degree of autocorrelation in the error term is indistinguishable from 1.0. An autocorrelation coefficient of 1.0

Table 4.3. *Weather in Buenos Aires and the price of silver*

Levels related to levels (using Ordinary Least Squares)

Dependent variable: Comex close as a percent of close on April 30, 1979

$R^2 = 0.468$
Durbin–Watson statistic = 0.41

Independent variable	*Coefficient*	*t-statistic*
Buenos Aires temperature	6.52	14.85

Changes related to changes (using Ordinary Least Squares)

Dependent variable: Percent change in Comex close from previous day

$R^2 = 0.001$
Durbin–Watson statistic = 1.50

Independent variable	*Coefficient*	*t-statistic*
Change in temperature from previous day	–0.00080	–0.02

The regressions use observations on business days from May 1, 1979 through April 30, 1980, a total of 253 observations. All include a constant term. The temperature, reported in *The New York Times*, is measured at 8.00 a.m. local time.

implies that the proper correction is to take the first differences of the variables, namely to relate the daily change in the price of silver and the daily change in the Hunts' position. Thus, the proper regression specification is that advocated by the defense experts, one that reveals no significant relationship between the Hunts' trading and the price of silver.

4.3   Measurement of the effect of political news

As the defense observed, the economic and political situation in late 1979 and early 1980 at least plausibly contributed to the increase in the price of silver. Precious metals generally become most desirable as investments during periods of inflation and political instability, both of which increased during these months. In late 1979 and early 1980, inflation figures in the U.S. were much higher than expected. In November, the seizure of the American Embassy in Tehran and the storming of the Grand Mosque in Mecca created the perception of a dangerous instability in global politics. Soon afterward, in late December 1979, the Soviet military intervention in Afghanistan overshadowed all other stories on the front pages of newspapers; indeed, the business section of *The New York Times* represented news of the war in Afghanistan as the driving force in the precious metals markets.

To prove that these troubling occurrences caused the price of silver to rise, it would be necessary to compare the timing of events with the corresponding price changes. The situation providing the simplest and strongest statistical evidence for the defense's argument would be for silver to have rallied sharply and nearly synchronously with the unwelcome economic and political news. Ideally (from the defense's perspective), following a late afternoon release of unexpectedly high inflation figures, the silver market would have opened the next morning substantially above the previous close and would have remained near that price for several days. As the news services were reporting an unsettling political event, the price of silver would have jumped within minutes. Ideally, too, the Hunts would not have traded on the days on which such political events occurred.

The political and economic events did not, however, align perfectly with changes in the price of silver. The course of silver prices during the first week of the Afghanistan crisis (see Figure 4.4) illustrates the discrepancy all too well. Just before the Comex close on Wednesday, December 26, 1979, President Carter rebuked the Soviets for a build-up of troops on its Afghan border. Late the next day, a coup in Afghanistan was reported and by Friday morning, December 28, it was found to be led by the Soviets, in their largest military intervention since World War II. Over the weekend President Carter forcefully told the Soviets to pull out their troops. Monday, December 31, began with reports of the Soviets deploying troops in rebellious areas of Afghanistan, reports that continued on January 2, 1980. Had the silver market moved unambiguously in response to the Afghan crisis, the timing and magnitude of the price changes would correspond to the timing and importance of the breaking news. Silver prices would have rallied just before the close on December 26 in response to President Carter's remarks, and a large price move would have taken place from the close of trading on December 27 to the opening on December 28. Silver prices would have opened substantially higher on December 31 and remained there through January 2. On the contrary, as Figure 4.4 shows, the rally just before the close on December 26 was minor and the price of silver moved only a small amount on December 27, the day of the coup. Although the price opened higher on December 31, it rose the same amount again between 10.30 and 11.00 a.m., and closed substantially below what became the opening price on January 2.

Even though the price of silver did not move synchronously with the reports from Afghanistan, it is inconceivable that the Soviet intervention, which nearly ruptured relations between the two superpowers, had no influence on silver traders. The price of silver rose 50 percent in a week and, at that time, traders spoke of these events as influencing precious metals prices.

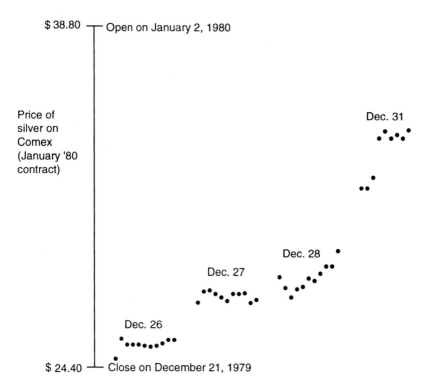

Figure 4.4. Reaction of silver to the Soviet invasion of Afghanistan (price observed every half hour)

The lack of synchrony could have various explanations, ranging from traders' failure to realize immediately the full ramifications of the coup to their anticipation of some of the American responses.

If sense can be made of the silver market's response to the Soviet invasion of Afghanistan only by presuming lags in some instances and leads in others, the reason behind the price moves is not observed, but assigned. That is, reactions to changing prices are deduced from the timing and magnitude of the price moves themselves, just as when the price moves are used to construct traders' supposed expectations about the Hunts.

One idea may help break the circularity of such assignment of causality. The idea, pursued by the CFTC Division of Enforcement's Professor Kyle, is simply that general political and economic events may influence other metals markets, especially gold, at much the same time and in much the same way as silver, and hence may reveal the timing of the silver market's reaction. The idea presumes not that traders of other metals comprehend immediately the ramifications of political events, only that they think much like silver traders. Professor Kyle chose gold as representative of what was happening in other markets, "because it is the most widely traded and actively watched precious metal, and many firms that deal in silver also deal in gold" (Kyle CFTC Report, p. 16). By this reasoning, gold's price changes may be used as a "proxy" for general political and economic events. This approach might be called an indirect measurement of such events.

This indirect measurement through other metals' prices helps to make sense of the timing of silver's reaction to the Afghan crisis. The price changes in gold every half hour from the opening of silver on Comex on December 26 through the close of silver on December 31 correlated at 0.79 with the contemporaneous changes in silver. The leads and lags of changes in gold, however, were uncorrelated with the half hourly changes in the price of silver. Much of what affected silver affected gold at the same time.

Gold moved along with silver throughout 1979 and 1980. Gold reached its all-time peak price in January 1980, as measured by Comex closing prices, on January 21, 1980 at $825.50 per troy ounce – up from $247 on April 30, 1979 and above the low on March 27, 1980 of $463.00. This spike in the price of gold was one of the main points of the defense. Indeed, the defense expert witnesses compiled the prices of many other commodities whose prices rose substantially in late 1979 and early 1980. Figure 4.5 displays four of them: gold, platinum, copper, and the three-month interest rate. In all of them a price spike is visible, although not as dramatic as in the one in silver.

Individually and collectively, the contemporaneous price moves in these other commodities are correlated with those in silver. Over May 1, 1979 through April 30, 1980, the day-to-day percentage change in the price of silver (as represented by the Comex close) is correlated at 0.72 with the day-to-day percentage changes in gold (the Comex close); 0.69 with platinum (the NYMEX close); 0.40 with copper (the Comex close); and –0.13 with the day-to-day change in the three-month Eurodollar rate (at 4.00 p.m., New York time).[13] Thus, a substantial part of the movements in silver prices over this year can be "explained" by the general political and economic events as manifested in these four series.

Strangely, Professor Kyle used the connection between gold and silver prices in 1979 and 1980 to produce an argument that was nearly the opposite of that of the defense experts. "Events that affected silver prices but not gold prices between September 1979 and March 1980 were somewhat more important than was typical during the period from the beginning of 1978 to the middle of 1980" (Kyle CFTC Report, p. 17). Because the Hunts confined themselves to silver and could have affected its price but not that of

---

13   The multiple correlation is 0.76, with the gold change and the platinum change the two statistically significant variables.

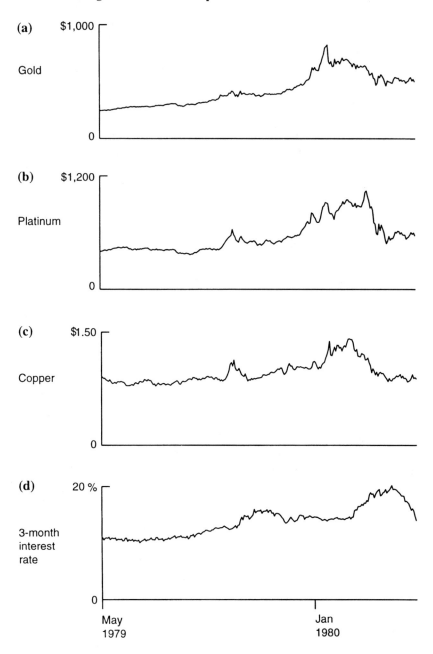

Figure 4.5. Price movements of four commodities from May 1979 through April 1980

gold, he reasoned, their trading must therefore have contributed to the rise in the price of silver.

In his statistical analysis, Professor Kyle correlated day-to-day changes in the price of silver with day-to-day changes in the price of gold. He computed the squared correlation of the contemporaneous price changes – the R^2 in a regression of silver on gold – over intervals of three months from 1975 through 1982. His estimate of the proportion of the event as unique to silver was 1.0 minus these squared correlation coefficients. His computations are duplicated in Figure 4.6 . The statistical connection between price changes in gold and silver is weaker in 1979–1980 than immediately before and after that interval. In the longer period from 1973 through 1987, however, the segment of 1979–1980 does not look out of character. More important, silver's correlation with changes in gold's price must be a minimum estimate of events in silver in common with other markets. Thus, when the set of markets is extended, as in Figure 4.6, to include platinum, copper, lead, and zinc, the squared (multiple) correlation for the segment September 1979– March 1980 looks no different from previous and subsequent intervals.[14]

Professor Kyle's procedures inadvertently reveal a more fundamental problem with using gold (and other metals) as a proxy for more direct measurement of the effect of political and economic news. Nothing constrains silver to react to every piece of news to the precise extent that gold reacts. Silver might be more sensitive than gold to particular types of events and less sensitive to others. Indeed, that silver does not move in perfect correlation with gold (or all metals collectively) in periods outside of 1979–1980 proves that silver is sometimes more, sometimes less, sensitive. The correlation over any one period, such as 1979–1980, merely indicates the average sensitivity of silver compared to gold over the many events.

Thus, some factors clearly were influencing all metals prices in 1979 and 1980. Nevertheless, the effect on silver can be measured only indirectly, as those factors manifest themselves through other commodities, and as a result, can be measured with less than perfect accuracy. The interpretation of silver prices would be much more straightforward had the connections been direct and obvious, but they were not.

4.4   Measurement of silver's effect on other metals

In 1979–1980, as in earlier periods, the price changes in silver were highly correlated with the price changes in gold, although the correlation does not

---

[14]   In passing, it is worth noting that a direct test of the Hunts' effect would have been more convincing than this indirect one. Yet had Professor Kyle included the Hunts' trading explicitly in the regression style he used for gold, he would have replicated the analysis of the defense experts, which showed no direct connection between the Hunts' trading and the price changes in silver.

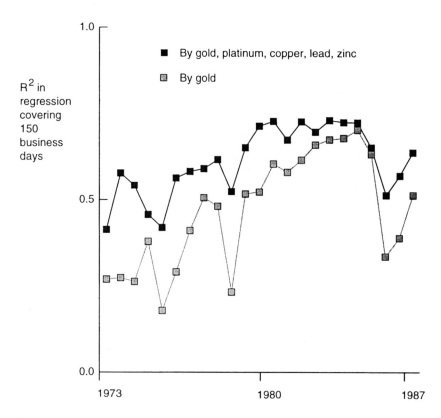

Figure 4.6. Price movements in silver "explained" by price movements in other metals

necessarily indicate causality in either direction. Many political and economic events that influence gold also influence silver, yet some events must be specific to the gold market, and, if they spill over to the silver market, can reasonably be said to cause the price change in silver. Likewise, some events specific to the silver market may spill over into the gold market. When the price of gold is employed as a proxy for general political and economic events, some part of the general events measured by gold may instead be attributed to silver.

Complicating the analysis of causality, silver may well have influenced gold in 1979–1980. The price of gold dropped much as did silver on January 22, 1980, following the imposition on January 21 of trading for liquidation only in the silver market. And on March 27, 1980 – the day the Hunts' missed their margin call and the price of silver fell 32 percent – the price of gold fell 7 percent, an uncharacteristically large move. Why gold reacted to these events is less important than that gold did react.[15]

From the proposition that events in the silver market influence the gold market arose the far stronger proposition that the Hunts may have been responsible for the increase in the price of gold as well. The plaintiff's experts made this proposition the center of their analysis. Of course, the Hunts traded no gold over 1979–1980 and so their effect, if any, was indirect. If the Hunts were responsible for the increase in gold prices, it becomes more plausible that the price of silver would have been low except for their trading. The plaintiff's experts tried to test for this connection, first, by showing a reverse connection from silver to gold, then by adjusting gold for that reverse effect. In actual application, however, they made a mistake at each stage, which together resulted in the attribution of a strong effect on silver to the Hunts.

The idea that the Hunts' trading of silver may have regularly influenced the price of gold originated with the CFTC Division of Enforcement's expert Dr. Burrows, whose argument and statistical procedures were presented at the trial by the plaintiff. To test his proposition rigorously, Dr. Burrows performed a so-called Granger causality study. His results suggested that in 1979 and 1980, the price moves in silver tended to precede those of gold; he interpreted this finding as events in silver to some degree causing the changes in the price of gold. He concluded that the price of gold would not have increased so much had the Hunts not been present in the silver market.

So-called Granger causality tests begin from two assumptions: "(i) The future cannot cause the past. Strict causality can only occur with the past causing the present or future.[16] (ii) A cause contains unique information about an effect that is not available elsewhere" (Granger and Newbold, 1986, p. 220). Time is prominent in these assumptions, because Granger causality tests concern the relationships between two time series. If one series, call it Y, never moves before the movement in series X, series Y cannot "cause" series X. Series X could cause series Y, provided no other series, call it Z, contains the same information. One complication is that series X and series Y may move simultaneously, in which case additional information is required to determine causality. Thus, according to Granger, only if series X precedes series Y without duplicating any possible series such as Z, can series X be said to cause series Y.

---

[15] Professor Spiller has said recently that to him these price drops were the most important economic evidence in the case, next to the size of the Hunts' positions.

[16] But this assumption does not allow for the effects of anticipation. For example, some effects of a tax law may occur before the law is passed.

Table 4.4. *Granger causality tests between silver and gold*

Using Handy & Harman prices

Dependent variable: Percent change in gold price from previous day
$R^2 = 0.056$

Independent variable	Coefficient	t-statistic
Silver percent change lagged once	0.137	3.84
Silver percent change lagged twice	−0.034	−0.95

Dependent variable: Percent change in silver price from previous day
$R^2 = 0.001$

Independent variable	Coefficient	t-statistic
Gold percent change lagged once	−0.031	−0.28
Gold percent change lagged twice	0.055	0.50

Using closing prices on futures markets

Dependent variable: Percent change in gold price from previous day
$R^2 = 0.009$

Independent variable	Coefficient	t-statistic
Silver percent change lagged once	0.052	1.40
Silver percent change lagged twice	0.009	0.25

Dependent variable: Percent change in silver price from previous day
$R^2 = 0.015$

Independent variable	Coefficient	t-statistic
Gold percent change lagged once	0.208	1.88
Gold percent change lagged twice	0.058	0.52

The regressions use observations on business days from May 1, 1979 through April 30, 1980, a total of 253 observations. All include a constant term.

Dr. Burrows's Granger causality tests can be seen, in abbreviated form, in the top half of Table 4.4. Using observations for 1979–1980, he related the change from the previous day in the price of gold according to Handy & Harman (a widely noted spot price) to changes in the Handy & Harman silver price one and two days previously. In a second regression, he related the change in the price of silver to the change in the price of gold one and two days previously.[17] According to this second regression, previous changes in the price of gold did not anticipate changes in the price of silver. In the first regression, however, his results were statistically significant. With this indication of silver moving first, he concluded that silver "caused" gold.

Dr. Burrows intended to apply the Granger causality tests appropriately, yet he did not for three reasons. First, something (such as changes in the Federal Reserve's monetary policy) could have influenced both silver and gold, but have manifested itself first in silver. Although his actual tests included variables on exchange rates and interest rates as other possible influences, the list was, inevitably, far from inclusive. (However, a series that consistently first influences silver is not easy to name and so this criticism is not very telling.)

Second, Dr. Burrows should never have used the Granger causality tests on gold and silver because the procedures are problematic where two time series are contemporaneously correlated. Such is the case with the gold and silver markets. For 1979–1980, the contemporaneous correlation between the two Handy & Harman series is 0.66.

Third, and most important, Dr. Burrows should have made sure that the gold and silver prices he used were observed at the same time, as the Granger causality tests require. The Handy & Harman prices for gold are quoted earlier in the day than those for silver prices. The gold price is essentially the afternoon London "fix" among bullion dealers, usually announced between 10.15 a.m. to 10.30 a.m., New York time, while the silver price derives from the Comex silver market minutes before 12.00 noon, one and a half hours later.

The effect of the later quotations for silver can be seen with reference to Figure 4.7, which adds Comex gold to the detailed series for silver during the first week of the Afghan crisis. The price change that occurred between, say, 11.00 a.m. and 11.30 a.m. on Thursday, December 27 is credited by Dr. Burrows to the Thursday-to-Friday change in the gold market and the Wednesday-to-Thursday change in the silver market. Because gold and silver price changes are contemporaneously correlated, statistical tests will show the previous day's silver price change "explaining" the current change in the gold price.[18]

When gold and silver prices are measured simultaneously, the appearance of silver "causing" gold disappears. The bottom half of Table 4.4 reports regressions using the Comex gold close and the CBOT silver close, prices merely five minutes apart. These regressions show no hint of silver

---

17   Actually, as many as five lags were used. In all cases the first lag was the crucial variable for the outcome of the test.

18   Indeed, the R^2 in the top half of Table 3.4 accords closely to an hour and a half's share of the total price change.

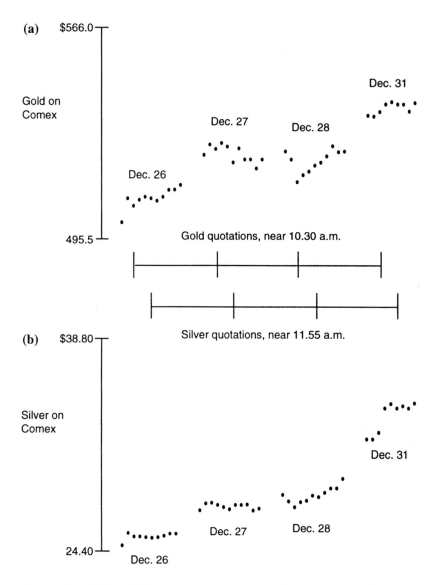

Figure 4.7. Gold and silver price movements on Comex (observed every half hour) and the timing of Handy & Harman's gold and silver quotations

preceding gold. By implication, according to this test, neither did the Hunts' trading have such an indirect effect on the gold market. (These points I made to the jury, using a large chart similar to Figure 4.7.)

Minpeco's three experts duplicated Dr. Burrows's Granger causality test, and Professor Houthakker testified at the trial about it. The plaintiff's experts used the conclusion that silver moved before gold to justify an expansion of their statistical analysis of the Hunts' supposed direct effect on the price of silver. They argued that the Hunts' effect on silver accounted for the price of gold. So, before gold could be used as a proxy for general political and economic events, an adjustment needed to be made for the reverse flow of events in the silver market, specifically the Hunts' trading. This reasoning led them to estimate through regression analysis the effect of the Hunts' trading on gold and to construct a purged gold variable, which they called RESID. They included this RESID variable, otherwise "gold unrelated to the Hunts," as a second explanatory factor along with the Hunts' position in a regression with the price of silver as the dependent variable. With a correction for autocorrelation in the error term, this regression formed, in essence, the plaintiff's principal presentation of the statistical relationship between the Hunts' trading and the price of silver. It is shown here in the bottom half of Table 4.5. The regression in the upper half of the table, using gold without adjustments, shows how important the adjustment was to the plaintiff's conclusion that the Hunts' trading contributed significantly to the rise in the price of silver.[19]

Although it became the central evidence for this conclusion, the regression in which the price of silver was related to the Hunts' trading and to the adjusted price of gold is nonetheless erroneous. The intermediate step, adjusting gold to reflect the Hunts' trading in silver, employs a regression relating the level of the price of gold to the level of the Hunts trading – the style of regression criticized in Section 4.2 and avoided by the plaintiff's experts otherwise. That intermediate regression assigns far too much of the price rise of gold to the Hunts. Consequently, what should have been the normal relationship between gold and silver is misattributed to them.

Proof of the problems with the plaintiff's adjustment to gold can be found in a replication of the procedure using the morning temperatures in Buenos Aires (see Table 4.6). As expected, if silver is related to the temperature and unadjusted gold, the temperature makes no contribution, as can be seen in the top of the three panels of Table 4.6. In the middle panel, gold is "explained" by the temperature in Buenos Aires, the strong connection being spurious (the result of relating levels to levels).[20] The effect of the temperature is

---

19   In Table 4.5 it is not a misprint that the coefficient and statistical significance on the gold price variable are identical in the two regressions. It is the constant term that alters. In effect, the average percentage change in the price of gold is misattributed to the Hunts.

20   The Durbin–Watson statistic again should alert the econometrician to the danger.

Table 4.5. *The plaintiff's correction for the Hunts' influence on the price of gold*

Silver related to the Hunts with no adjustment to gold (using AR(1))

Dependent variable: Comex close as a percent of close on April 30, 1979

$R^2 = 0.991$

Independent variable	Coefficient	t-statistic
Hunts' position	0.00227	2.70
Gold (percent increase from April 30, 1979)	1.75	17.52
First-order serial correlation	0.972	66.14

Silver related to the Hunts with adjustment made to gold (using AR(1))

Dependent variable: Comex close as a percent of close on April 30, 1979

$R^2 = 0.991$

Independent variable	Coefficient	t-statistic
Hunts' position	0.00662	7.53
Gold unrelated to the Hunts	1.75	17.52
First-order serial correlation	0.972	66.14

The regressions use observations on business days from May 1, 1979 through April 30, 1980, a total of 253 observations. All include a constant term. The gold price is the close on Comex.

subtracted from the percentage increase of gold from April 30, 1979 to create the RESID variable, that is, the "adjusted" price of gold, which is used in the bottom and most important regression. Hey presto! The Buenos Aires temperature becomes a major factor in silver's price rise. On just such statistical procedures did the plaintiff's experts come to their portrayal of the Hunts' trading as causing price rise in silver.

Although a reconstruction of the RESID variable using the temperature in Buenos Aires should have exposed the problems with the plaintiff's statistical arguments, there is perhaps one reason why the RESID procedure was not discredited. Granted that the Hunts influenced the silver market, it is at least conceivable that the silver market in turn influenced gold, in which case treating gold as independent of the Hunts would understate the Hunts' effect in silver. But here is the real puzzle about the RESID procedure. It was

Table 4.6. *The plaintiff's technique applied to the weather in Buenos Aires*

Silver explained with no adjustment to gold (using AR(1))

Dependent variable: Silver close as a percent of close on April 30, 1979

$R^2 = 0.991$

Independent variable	Coefficient	t-statistic
Buenos Aires temperature	0.0239	0.27
Gold (percent increase from April 30, 1979)	1.73	16.78
First-order serial correlation	0.982	61.82

Gold's relationship to the weather (using Ordinary Least Squares)

Dependent variable: Gold close as a percent of close on April 30, 1979

$R^2 = 0.537$
Durbin–Watson statistic = 0.53

Independent variable	Coefficient	t-statistic
Buenos Aires temperature	3.15	17.05

Silver explained with adjustment made to gold (using AR(1))

Dependent variable: Silver close as a percent of close on April 30, 1979

$R^2 = 0.991$

Independent variable	Coefficient	t-statistic
Buenos Aires temperature	5.49	16.47
Gold unrelated to the weather	1.73	16.78
First-order serial correlation	0.982	61.82

The regressions use observations on business days from May 1, 1979 through April 30, 1980, a total of 253 observations. All include a constant term. The temperature, reported in *The New York Times*, is measured at 8.00 a.m. local time.

unnecessary. Even elementary econometrics textbooks instruct that if a particular independent variable has a direct effect on the dependent variable and an indirect effect by way of its influence on another independent variable which in turn affects the dependent variable, the first variable's "total effect" would be the coefficient with the first variable the only independent variable in the regression. In other words, the total effect of the Hunts, supposing that they influenced gold to some extent, would be the estimate in the middle panel of Table 4.2, which involved no RESID variable at all. Accordingly, the plaintiff could have argued that, depending on the weight given to an indirect effect through gold, the Hunts' effect on silver was in the range from the top panel in Table 4.5 to the middle panel of Table 4.2, either of which shows a statistically significant relationship.[21] The defense experts would have had no obvious counter to this argument. [22]

4.5   Measurement of simultaneous causes

Despite the inadequacies of gold as a proxy for political and economic news, the most reasonable statistical analysis of the causes of the price rise in silver relates the daily percentage change in the price of silver to both the Hunts' trading and to the changes in the price of gold. As listed in the upper panel of Table 4.7, the estimated coefficient for each variable shows the effect of that variable holding the other variable constant. Unlike the regression using the Hunts' trading alone (Table 4.1 previously), with the effect of gold included, the coefficient for the Hunts' trading is positive. This is the first econometrically sound indication of any connection between the Hunts and the daily price moves. Of course, the measured effect remains small: If the Hunts had purchased an additional 1,000 futures contracts, the price would have risen merely 0.52 percent.

If this finding of some connection between the Hunts' trading and silver prices changes is substantive, there should also be a sensible pattern among the coefficients when the Hunts' aggregate position is broken down into components. Bullion should have a larger positive effect than futures, futures a larger effect than London forwards, and so on. This proposition is tested by the regression reported in the lower panel of Table 4.7. The explanatory variables are expanded to include other proxies for political and economic news, specifically platinum and copper. Also, to reduce the reverse effects on the three metals, three special days are singled out.[23]

---

21   But both show first-order serial correlation in the error term of a magnitude so close to 1.0 that first differences would be a better technique.

22   Another reason why the RESID technique was not discredited may have been that the temperature in Buenos Aires just seemed silly as a variable. The plaintiff's experts, for example, concluded that the defense experts must have searched every imaginable series to find one to discredit their RESID technique and that the temperature in Buenos Aires was the only one that made the RESID technique look bad. Actually, it was the first and only series the defense experts considered, and it was picked because it sounded so ludicrous.

23   In effect, these three days are not used to determine the coefficients of the other variables.

Table 4.7. *The Hunts' trading in relation to gold and changes in the price of silver*

Few explanatory variables (using Ordinary Least Squares)

Dependent variable: Percent change in Comex close from previous day

$R^2 = 0.517$
Durbin–Watson statistic = 1.79

Independent variable	Coefficient	t-statistic
Change in Hunts' position from previous day	0.00052	1.52
Percent change in gold from previous day	1.208	16.34

Many explanatory variables (using Ordinary Least Squares)

Dependent variable: Percent change in Comex close from previous day

$R^2 = 0.652$
Durbin–Watson statistic = 1.96
F-statistic on the five coefficients for the Hunts = 0.59

Independent variable	Coefficient	t-statistic
Hunts' trading		
Change in bullion from previous day	–0.00062	–0.96
Change in coins from previous day	–0.00023	–0.07
Change in futures (net) from previous day	0.00017	0.47
Change in EFPs from previous day	0.00085	0.89
Change in forwards from previous day	0.00052	0.36
Other metals		
Percent change in gold from previous day	0.706	7.18
Percent change in platinum from previous day	0.504	6.36
Percent change in copper from previous day	–0.071	–0.85
Unusual days		
Imposition of position limits	–4.016	–1.48
Imposition of trading for liquidation only	–5.384	–1.91
Silver Thursday	–21.718	–6.38

The regressions use daily observations from May 1, 1979 through April 30, 1980, a total of 253 business days. Both include a constant term. Each variable for the Hunts comprises all accounts alleged to be part of the manipulation, including those of the so-called Conti group, and is measured in units of 5,000 troy ounces.

With this expanded list of explanatory variables, any hint of the association between the Hunts' trading and the changes in the price of silver disappears. Taking the results literally, on the days the Hunts took delivery of bullion on futures contracts or on EFPs there was a small fall in price when the effect of movements in other metals are accounted for. Individually and collectively, the variables concerning the Hunts are statistically insignificant. The explanatory power of the whole regression would be essentially the same without them, the important variables being gold and platinum.

These more detailed tests accord with those done in Section 4.1 without the effects of metals included. Regardless of whether other precious metals serve as proxies for political news, regardless of whether the Hunts' positions disaggregated, regardless of whether lags are included, and regardless of whether special days are excluded, no connection is apparent between the Hunts' trading day by day and changes in the price of silver day by day. Many other possible regression specifications – such as allowing the effect of the purchase of silver to depend on the amount of silver previously purchased – likewise fail to reveal a connection between the Hunts' trading and day-by-day movements in the price of silver. This conclusion was the defense experts' major argument. Some specification not yet considered might suggest a relationship,[24] but such a finding is surely far from robust. In any event, that missing specification relating day-by-day changes in the price of silver to changes in the Hunts' trading was not located by the plaintiff's experts.

4.6   Limitations on econometric tests of causality

Among economists, skepticism about the results of regression analysis abounds because of the all-too-common practice of "data mining." A researcher computes regressions among all combinations of variables in a large data set until a startling relationship is found. The researcher publishes in a journal article this one regression, piously bowing to the god of the significant t-statistic. The readers rightly suspect that the statistical significance is overstated and rightly fear that with a minor alteration in specification the economist's startling results disappear.

In the Hunt case, data mining was not the problem. The experts for each side computed their many regressions using different sample periods, different proxies for political events, and different constructions of the Hunts' positions, all for a good reason: to demonstrate the robustness of their conclusions. Nonetheless, skepticism about the results from those regressions is

---

24   One possibility would be to account for the declining liquidity in the silver market over the period, so that the same size trade would have a larger price effect in February 1980 than in June 1979.

well founded, for they were robust only within the single style of statistical analysis each expert pursued.

Any explanation of the price of silver in 1979 and 1980 needs to be consistent with the evidence at different degrees of scrutiny, whether prices are measured over long intervals or whether prices are measured transaction by transaction. For instance, the effect of freezes in Florida stand out when orange juice prices are measured annually or when they are measured daily (Roll, 1984). The effect of the breakdown of the International Coffee Agreement in June and July 1988 stands out in a graph of prices measured annually for several years before and after, in a graph of prices measured monthly during 1988, and in a plot measured daily through June and July as reports of the negotiations became public.

No explanation for silver is consistent over all the intervals at which prices can be measured. When the price is measured annually every January, the year 1980 stands out as showing by far the biggest increase, with the timing making it feasible for either the Hunts or political events to have been the cause. Measured at the scale of months, the Hunts' causal connection becomes less tight, because the main price move occurred six months after their principal purchases. On this monthly scale, political events, such as the Soviet invasion of Afghanistan, coincide much better with the price moves. On a daily scale, however, the political events coincide less well, and the Hunts' trades not at all. As the interval of observations becomes finer, so it becomes more difficult to discern the true causal relationships; indeed, the temporal connection of cause preceding effect may no longer apply. Traders might take hours or days to comprehend the full implications of particular news while in other instances, traders might have anticipated news days or weeks ahead.

The defense experts pursued a methodology that imposed perhaps too demanding a causal connection. They claimed that changes in the Hunts' trading day to day should be related to the changes in the price of silver day to day. All actions by the Hunts, they argued – whether futures trading, deliveries taken, or EFPs arranged – should be understood by other traders within a few days, even though most of the obvious political events fail to pass this standard. In their regression methodology, the defense experts made no provision that other traders, for example, might become aware a week or two before the delivery period that the Hunts would likely stand for delivery. Of course, such anticipations are difficult (if not impossible) to measure, but in the regression methodology selected by the defense experts, the possibility of those anticipations was ignored from the start.

As we have seen, the plaintiff's experts pursued relatively complicated econometric methodologies, such as correcting for autocorrelated errors and purging gold for the Hunts' effect. Nothing is wrong *per se* with more complicated methodologies, but mistakes can be made more easily. Because such methodologies revealed the Hunts as having a major influence on the price of silver, as the plaintiff's experts were predisposed to believe, they did not authenticate their techniques. The defense experts did test the techniques, by replacing the Hunts' position with the daily temperature in Buenos Aires – a variable that clearly did not cause the price of silver to rise. According to the technique of the plaintiff's experts, the temperature in Buenos Aires has a strong relationship to the price of silver, a finding that brings into question the entire style of analysis on which the plaintiff's experts depended.

The plaintiff's experts argued that the Hunts' effects might be long delayed, yet no one acknowledged that such an argument transformed the analysis from one of direct to indirect measurement. Presumably, should the price rise directly with the Hunts' actions, or with some action related to the Hunts (such as the arrival of first notice day each delivery month or the meetings of the Hunts with exchange officials), the Hunts' effect on prices could be measured directly. If no such alignment were to be found, the timing of the price rises might be used to infer the timing of the other traders' reactions. In effect, such was the plaintiff's argument. Yet it verges on tautology, for the timing of the price changes are used to infer traders' expectations about the Hunts, which are supposedly the reasons for the prices themselves.

Other experts in the case made indirect measurements of political and economic events and they, too, faced certain irreconcilable problems with their method. The defense experts and one of the CFTC Division of Enforcement's experts used the price of gold as an indirect measure of political and economic events influencing silver. Yet, by doing so, they were prevented from finding that an event peculiar to silver had or had not influenced gold.

Professor Kyle, the expert for the CFTC Division of Enforcement, revealed much with the logic implicit in his attribution to the Hunts' movements in the price of silver not related to movements in the price of gold. He took it as obvious that some events would manifest themselves in both silver and gold prices. He readily accepted that he could not measure all these events, but that a correlation between gold and silver would indicate a common cause. He took it as obvious that, with events affecting both markets at much the same time, causality meant change from one day to the next. These are the assumptions made by the defense experts, except that they tested for the Hunts' effect directly.

Had the experts on each side pursued broader regression methodologies, they might have established the robustness of their results one layer deeper. The CFTC Division of Enforcement's expert discovered something unusual in the silver market by relying on a single proxy for all political and economic events and by measuring the Hunts' effect indirectly. Had he also measured the Hunts' trading directly and applied his proxy to additional commodities such as platinum, any positive conclusion would have been more persuasive.

The plaintiff's experts found a causal connection between the Hunts and the price rise by relating the price level to the Hunts' total position, without considering the temporal connection between the Hunts' trading and the price rise. Had they demonstrated such a connection, their conclusion would have been much stronger. The defense experts examined the timing of the Hunts' purchases and the price rises in silver, finding that the Hunts' day-by-day trading had not caused the day-by-day price rise. Nonetheless, they should also have considered those longer units of time in which the full effects of the Hunts' actions would have become evident. Had they been able to show that no such effects were apparent over a longer time scale, their conclusion would have been more persuasive.

The markedly different approaches of the experts to testing for the cause of the price rise in silver derived from their initial perceptions of the style of argument they would need to make. The CFTC Division of Enforcement's experts intended to provide an upper bound on what silver's price might have been without the Hunts, and so approached the subject of causality indirectly through gold rather than directly through the Hunts' trading. The plaintiff's experts believed that the jury should not be burdened with detailed analysis. Hence they conceived of time in broad intervals, in which it was natural to relate the price level to the size of the Hunts' position. Because the defense experts came from the field of finance, in which the day-by-day price change is overwhelmingly the most common unit for analysis, they believed from the start that daily data would reveal more about the cause of the price rise than less frequent observations.

By leaving unarticulated their decisions about methodology, the experts may have given the impression that they had concocted their approach and conclusions for the benefit of their lawyers. From this perspective, the defense experts probably looked worse, for, intuitively, their conclusion seems less plausible. To insist that the Hunts' huge purchases of silver barely increased its price, appears willfully to ignore nearly self-explanatory evidence. Yet, those who thought they had proven statistically that the Hunts indeed caused that increase, not only failed to do so, but failed to recognize the errors that skewed their results.

4.7   Econometrics and proximate cause

Although causality for legal purposes would seem to be a simple concept, it is in fact complex and subtle, as many commentators, such as Borgo (1979) and Wright (1985, 1988), have observed. The style of this debate over causality is well summarized by the classic conundrum of whether the smoker, the cigarette, the paper in the wastepaper basket, or the oxygen caused the fire (Hart and Honoré, 1985). In the Hunt case, however, the dispute over the cause of silver's price rise was not over which element in a sequence should be considered the proximate cause, but which of two possible explanations was dominant.

The issue of causality in the Hunt case shares many features with litigation over substances alleged to be toxic. Like the connection between the Hunts' purchases on a particular day and the price of silver, the connection between a particular chemical and an individual's disease is more difficult to trace than might at first appear. Toxic tort cases invariably involve expert witnesses and highly technical testimony, including considerable discussion of statistics. Consequently, they have become a highly controversial area of the law (Farber, 1987; Brennan, 1988; and Green, 1992), with many proposals to reduce the emphasis on technical testimony (e.g., Brennan, 1989). Many of the controversies, moreover, are really about the appropriate evidence of causality, rather than judicial suspicion of expert testimony.

In some respects, the issue of causality in the silver market offers even more difficulties than toxic substance torts. Although many people traded in the silver market, there was only one price spike involved. This single event is not like an industrial accident that releases some chemical throughout a neighborhood whose effect might take months to emerge. Instead, it would be as if only one person claimed to be sick because of long-term but variable exposure to some chemical, with her health and exposure to the chemical having been recorded daily. The analysis of causality would be complicated by the possibility of cumulative effects, interaction with other environmental factors, and build-up of tolerance.

Most people who serve on juries do not think about causation in the probabilistic perspective appropriate to toxic substances and commodity markets but in the simpler style of mechanistic causal chains that serves in everyday life (Vinson, 1986, Chapter 3). Knowing jurors' tendencies, both the plaintiff and defense reduced their interpretations of causes and events in the silver market to very simple terms. The resulting simple stories not only diverged sharply, they were also too obviously incomplete.

The plaintiff's lawyers tried to remind the jury at all times that the Hunts bought a great deal of silver whose price rose considerably. However, the individual price moves in silver rarely coincided with the Hunts' trading more than approximately. Why, if the Hunts caused the price of silver to rise, did the effects of their purchases take months to appear? A rejoinder arose during the trial that other traders did not realize the size of the Hunts' positions until the Hunts began taking deliveries and negotiating exchanges for physicals. Under these circumstances, the plaintiff's story is no longer simple. It must not only connect the price rise to those specific actions, but also explain how the Hunts disguised, then signaled their manipulation, and how other traders gained knowledge, then formed expectations about the Hunts' actions.

The defense, in its simple story of causality, repeatedly told the jury that other factors, such as world political unrest, primarily caused the price of silver to rise. But the defense identified few specific causes for the changes in the price day by day, leaving the category "unknown factors" large. Political news most important for silver, such as reports from Afghanistan, did not immediately affect the price. To complicate matters, economic and political developments often transpired on the very days on which the Hunts traded.

Because these stories of causality could not be simple, some statistical analysis was brought to bear. As it played out, the econometric analysis, which was introduced by the defense, did no harm to the plaintiff's case. Supposedly, the plaintiff should provide the convincing statistical evidence of its theory of causality (Jacob, 1985); the defense need only cast doubt on that explanation and suggest alternatives. In practice, it seems that the defense experts' negative result, that no connection existed between daily changes in the Hunts' positions and daily changes in the price of silver, failed to sway the jury from the plaintiff's explanation. The suggestion of political and economic connections evidently needed to be demonstrated with clear examples.

The defense also failed to turn to advantage the incompleteness in the plaintiff's explanation of the price rise. The crudest statistical analysis, the one relating the price of silver to the level of the Hunts' position, accounts for only 51 percent of the daily movement in the Comex close from April 30, 1979. The defense would have been advised to present a week or two of hour-by-hour silver prices, and have the plaintiff's expert identify the price changes due to the Hunts' activities. The burden of proof might have subtly altered, because the connections of those price changes to the Hunts' actions would not have been obvious.

Among lawyers, skepticism abounds about experts testifying to juries about econometrics – and the record of the Hunt case seems only to have increased this skepticism. Nevertheless, the lesson should not be to avoid such testimony. The period May 1979 through April 1980 witnessed many political and economic developments, frequent trading by the Hunts, and continual price changes in silver. Because of the sheer complexity of events and their potential causes, the use of statistical techniques to study them becomes unavoidable. Even so, any issue uncovered through econometric techniques can also be described without econometrics. The lesson should be that it is better to make the statistical analysis explicit and accessible, for the advantage goes to the side making its reasoning clearer to non-specialists.

For example, the controversy over whether to use daily changes or the daily price level in the various regressions concerned fundamentally how long the effects of any of the Hunts' actions would plausibly take to appear fully. The defense should have reiterated at every opportunity the fact that the Hunts bought in June and July 1979, whereas the price rose six months later. How then could this six-month gap indicate proximate cause? Presumably, the jury would have grasped this point had it been presented to them in non-econometric terms.

Determining the appropriate price of a good is the main activity of experts in many fields, for example, those appraising privately held firms for tax purposes, those appraising houses for mortgages, or those appraising fine art for auction reserves. Often such experts testify in court. At the Hunt trial, the economist expert witnesses all expressed opinions about what the price of silver would have been without the Hunts' trading. Because the appropriate – the "competitive" – price of silver directly determined damages, the experts were asked to name a specific dollar value per troy ounce. As typical in trials distinguishing liability from damages, their appraisal was considered a distinct issue, separate from their other opinions about the silver market and the way it functioned.

In naming the "competitive" price for silver, the experts at the Hunt trial disagreed by several hundred percent. At one end of the spectrum, Professor Houthakker pronounced the price without the Hunts' trading to be $8 to $10 per troy ounce, up slightly from the $6 prevailing in January 1979. At the other end of the spectrum, Professor Edwards, the defense expert who testified most directly on this issue, proposed something like $45 per troy ounce, just slightly below the peak price of $50 reached in January 1980. Of the two experts for the CFTC Division of Enforcement, Dr. Burrows favored the range $10 to $12, but conceded silver could have increased as much as gold, which would have placed it around $22; Professor Kyle pursued arguments that would have placed his estimate between $22 and $45.[1]

The difference between the highest and lowest valuation for silver without the Hunts' trading is astonishing, for appraisers of other goods, especially

---

[1]   Recently, Professor Kyle has said that an increase in silver's price close to gold would have been reasonable, which would imply a price around $22. This $22 would be his preferred estimate, although his analysis of spreads and coins would suggest the higher number.

135

ones as homogeneous as silver, rarely disagree by more than 10 to 15 percent. Were an IRS expert and a bank trust department's expert to vary by a factor of five in valuing a bequest of closely held shares, almost certainly the IRS would pursue a tax case. Were real estate appraisers to differ so much, a mortgage company would suspect fraud. Were an auction house's expert to misestimate the reserve to such an extent, the house would attract few consignments. How, then, could reasonable economists propose such a great range for the appropriate price of silver?

Cynics might answer that the lawyers' exigencies dictated the economists' various opinions. The plaintiff pursued two components in its damage claims.[2] First, the short positions it placed in late October and early November at approximately $17 per troy ounce had to be closed out in mid-December for failure to meet variation margin calls at approximately $24, a loss of some $7 per troy ounce apart from gains on inventory it owned.[3] Second, had Minpeco been able to maintain its short positions, it would eventually have been able to close them out at a profit, for it anticipated that market fundamentals otherwise indicated a price fall.[4] Thus, Minpeco's damages would be maximized under the first claim if no other factors contributed to the price rise during early December and maximized under the second claim if the competitive price were lower. Seemingly in direct support, the plaintiff's expert claimed the competitive price would have remained nearly constant and below $10. Meanwhile, the defendants' experts insisted that the Hunts' trading added insignificantly to silver's "competitive" price. The CFTC Divi-

---

2   Both of Minpeco's claims are predicated on an argument, common in calculation of damages in securities litigation (Thorup, 1990), that Minpeco would not have been enticed into the market except for the false signal of the manipulated price of $17.

3   Judge Lasker ruled (686 F.Supp. 420 [S.D.N.Y., 1988]) in favor of the defendants that Minpeco had to take into account its gains on the 2 to 3 million troy ounces in its inventory. (The precise amount was not known because of incomplete records.) In passing, it is worth noting that the gains on the inventory, which was silver located in London or silver in lead concentrate needing additional refining (just as coins need refining into .999 bullion), were measured dollar for dollar with the price of bullion in exchange-approved vaults. This approximation, however sensible given the other imprecisions in the damage calculations, contradicts the tight definition of deliverable silver used elsewhere in the trial.

4   Judge Lasker ruled (676 F.Supp. 486 [S.D.N.Y., 1987]) in favor of the defendants that Minpeco was not entitled to lost profits from having the manipulation dispelled after it had entered into its positions, lost profits of perhaps $8 per troy ounce depending on the "competitive" price to which silver would have returned. Judge Lasker did allow Minpeco to make an abbreviated lost-profits claim, namely, had Minpeco entered into its short positions even at a price undistorted by manipulation, it would only have done so with some hope of profit, $1 or $2 per troy ounce at most, the precise amount for the jury to determine. This lost-profits claim is a difficult legal issue because it requires an approach for determining not only what the price of silver would have been had the Hunts been absent from the market but what Minpeco would have done at that price.

sion of Enforcement's experts could concede a price rise in silver to the extent of gold and still support the Division of Enforcement's desire to find the Hunts liable for having affected price to any measurable extent.

Despite appearances, the range in expert opinion arose not because of pressure from the lawyers but from various simplifications the economists felt necessary to make before proceeding with their analyses. Determining the appropriate price for silver requires consideration of both a vast supply and a world market, a task that is orders of magnitude more difficult than the appraisal of a single firm, a single property, or a single painting. The task is comparable to the evaluations often attempted of large public programs, for instance the Strategic Petroleum Reserve's effect on the price of oil or the Export Enhancement Program's effect on the price of wheat. Such analysis is complex. Proper evaluation of the Strategic Petroleum Reserve requires information on how willing oil users are to switch to other fuels and how quickly the supply of those fuels can increase; evaluation of the U.S. Export Enhancement Program requires knowledge of the wheat market worldwide, including how other exporters might retaliate. Analysis on such a scale would hardly be possible without breaking the task into simpler questions to be answered. Each simplification can lead to an important insight and yet remain inadequate because no one question will address the subject fully.

This chapter examines the four methods used by the experts in the Hunt case to determine silver's appropriate price. The first method arrived at that price by measuring the supply and demand fundamentals for silver, such as new mines, industrial uses, and stockholdings. The second used multiple regression analysis relating the price of silver and the Hunts' trading to estimate the price without the Hunts' trading. The third, which can be called a market-based model, equated the appropriate price of silver with the prices of futures contracts for very distant delivery dates. The fourth measured traders' expectations of silver prices by the current price for silver in the months immediately following the end of the supposed period of manipulation and labeled that the appropriate price.

Although these four methods are widely recognized as plausible paths toward determining price, the opposing experts in the Hunt trial differed sharply as to the applicability of each method to silver in the 1979–1980 period. Both sides emphasized supply and demand fundamentals but were divided irreconcilably on whether investors or industrial consumers were the main source of demand and whether existing stocks or new production constituted the main source of supply. Regarding the use of regression analysis to remove the effect of the Hunts' trading, the plaintiff placed it at the center of numerical computations of silver's competitive price while the defense was unprepared even for questions about the approach. The reverse applied to the use of distant futures prices to approximate the appropriate price of silver; the defense favored this approach while the plaintiff ignored it. As for looking to silver just after April 1980 for its appropriate price, the defense experts argued the point, while the plaintiff's expert maintained that the Hunts' presence contaminated the silver market for two years after that date.

The expert witnesses never spoke of their methods as necessary simplifications that did not preclude the validity of other approaches. For example, while the defense characterized the supply of silver as fixed and the plaintiff described it as flexible, neither side fully reconciled that silver displays aspects of both. The experts were also too willing to end their analysis without sufficiently examining the internal consistency of their findings. For example, those representing the plaintiff and the CFTC Division of Enforcement, after studying trends in mine production and industrial consumption, concluded that the price of silver would have increased only slightly in 1980, and so attributed the further increase to the Hunts' trading. They did not, however, explain why the peak price was $50, and why this $50 prevailed not just for immediate delivery but also for delivery far into the future. Conversely, the defense experts emphasized that, on the day the price peaked at $50, people willingly traded distant futures contracts at even higher prices. But why were the prices for all the delivery dates not around $30 or $70 instead? In explanation, the defense needed some assessment of mine production and industrial consumption before its analysis would be complete.

Some of the problems with internal consistency trace back to the nature of a trial for damages, such as *Minpeco v. Hunt*, in which a complaint and its defense are distilled into two simply stated opposites. The plaintiff reasoned: The price rise was not due to these other factors; thus, it was probably due to the Hunts. The defense reasoned: The price rise was not due to the Hunts; thus, it was probably due to other factors. Nothing in the nature of the trial compelled the expert witnesses to confirm the implicit second step in their arguments or reconcile their two starting points.

The nature of the trial encouraged the expert witnesses to make easily grasped arguments for determining silver's appropriate price, testimony not always consistent with their other statements, especially about the definition and tests for manipulation. The jury, in order to choose among the various simplified, partial arguments made for its benefit, nonetheless needed a deep and comprehensive understanding of the influences on silver prices. Ironically, what was difficult for the economists to achieve was expected as a matter of course from the jury.

5.1   Models of supply and demand for silver

The economist expert witnesses agreed that the fundamentals of supply and demand determine the price of silver but they differed sharply in whether those fundamentals as applied to silver are stock-dominated or flow-dominated. An extended example helps to differentiate the two types. To keep close to the subject of silver, consider ancient Roman silver coins and subscription newsletters reporting current prices for such coins. The newsletters contain ephemeral information, whereas the coins remain the same over time. Although more copies of the newsletters can be printed (or another publication founded) if collecting interest grows, the Roman coins themselves are in fixed supply. The situation of coin-collectors' newsletters versus Roman coins closely approaches the extremes of the spectrum of flows versus stocks. The contrast teaches a number of lessons. Of particular interest is the behavior of prices for the coins and for newsletters as numismatic enthusiasm waxes and wanes.

Most people, including economists, conceive more easily the "supply and demand fundamentals" of the newsletter market. The supply fundamentals reflect the cost of newsprint, the speed with which new newsletters can enter the market, and so on. The demand fundamentals of the newsletter market reflect the number of collectors, the subscription rates for competing journals, and so on. The supply-side and demand-side are distinct.

In the old-coin market, the supply-side and the demand-side are not distinct. Collectors sell while collectors buy. In a sense, those who own coins but do not sell in a particular period participate in the market, because in choosing not to sell, they behave as if they were newcomers buying. Who buys, who sells, who stands apart from the market, all result from differences in enthusiasm for Roman coins and in the opportunity cost of collecting, as when a Texas businessman eagerly takes up the Roman-coin hobby, or when an impecunious classics professor parts with a few coins to fund a trip to Italy. Such fundamentals are much more difficult to measure than those influencing the newsletter market. One thing is easy to measure, however. If the holdings of one group of collectors, say Texans, increase, the holdings of other collectors collectively must decrease, because no more coins can come into existence even if the price rises.

The price for Roman silver coins represents what a buyer must offer to induce others to part with their holdings or what a seller must offer to entice others to add to theirs. A widespread rise in collecting interest may increase the price of coins without increasing the number of transactions in the coin market. In the newsletter market, in contrast, a widespread increase in collecting interest is likely to result in higher subscription rates and more newsletters sold.

The two markets also show different tendencies to huge price changes in response to changes in demand. A widespread increase in collecting interest of Roman silver coins may require a sharp increase in price if few current holders will part with their coins. And if collecting the coins proves to be a fad, the price may fall precipitously. Subscription rates for coin-collectors' newsletters, in contrast, are likely to remain more stable because, for one, the supply of new newsletters can expand and contract relatively easily.

Most important, the two markets differ by the predictability of their price changes. In the midst of an upward trend in collecting interest – say visitation at coin shows has been rising for close to a decade – a forecast of rising subscription rates for coin-collectors' newsletters is likely to be accurate, because the only newsletters that can fill this demand are newly printed ones. Anticipated demand for subscriptions to coin-collectors' newsletters does not induce people to buy and store copies of a soon-to-be-out-of-date newsletter. Any forecast about coin prices is less likely to be accurate. Even though people can attempt to anticipate the trend by buying coins, sellers are no fools. Able to wait, they need not part with their coins unless at a price that includes the known upward trend in demand. Because everything predictable about the future manifests itself quickly in coin prices, there need be no close temporal connection between changes in demand and price.

Silver bullion displays characteristics of both flows and stocks, in that silver is continuously mined and yet much of what has ever been mined remains accessible. Unlike Roman silver coins, the amount of refined silver can be increased. In 1979, some 300 million troy ounces were mined for use in the photographic, electronics, and jewelry industries. Unlike coin-collectors' newsletters, silver retains its value when stored. In 1979, when perhaps 600 million troy ounces existed as bullion, another 500 million to 1,000 million troy ounces were in the form of demonitized coins nearly of bullion quality, and a comparable quantity existed in forms whose jewelry or numismatic value was such that a price rise might induce its reconversion into bullion. At some price, much more of the silver lost in photography or electronics would be recovered.

Although all the expert witnesses in the Hunt case mentioned both stock-related inventory demand and flow-related industrial uses, the emphasis in their approaches were nearly as far apart as that for Roman coins and coin-collectors' newsletters. Those economists who viewed silver as a flow-dominated commodity included the compilers of the original CFTC report in the aftermath of the 1979–1980 turmoil, the CFTC Division of Enforcement's Dr. Burrows, and Minpeco's experts. The three defense experts were at the stock-dominated end of the spectrum along with the Division of Enforcement's Professor Kyle. No expert combined an analysis of flows with stocks, or strove consciously to weigh their importance. Rather, because analysis of commodities in the middle of the spectrum is much more difficult, each expert attempted to simplify the issue by concentrating on one end or other of the spectrum. Which end they decided upon for silver, determined their conclusions about its appropriate price.

How the characterization of silver shaped the analysis can be seen in a crucial diagram (see Figure 5.1) from the CFTC's published report on the silver market during 1979 and 1980 (CFTC, 1981, p. 96). It represents, in Figure 5.1(a), the Hunts as adding to the investment demand for silver, that is,

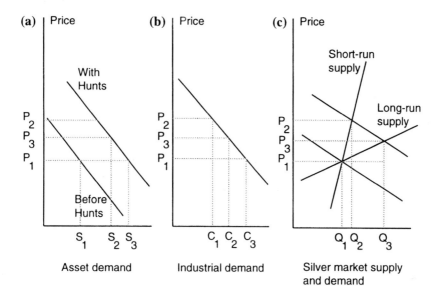

Figure 5.1. Supply and demand representation of silver price movements during 1979 and 1980, according to the CFTC's *A Study of the Silver Market* (1981, p. 96)

causing an outward shift in the whole curve. As represented in Figure 5.1(c), the short-run effect of this shift in demand causes a substantial increase in price, at least relative to the long-run price once additional production is forthcoming, which fits the pattern of the spot price over 1979 and early 1980. As the standard model of microeconomic textbooks, the posited long-run supply response is very large compared to the holdings of stocks. Figure 5.1, although distinguishing the short run from the long run, does not make the number of periods explicit. Nor does it equilibrate the short-run supply (the bullion available) with long-run supply (the exploitation of mines at the optimal rate). Most important, the investment demand is represented as a function of the spot price of silver, not the differential between the short-run and long-run prices, which emerges as a substantial premium for immediate delivery. Other investors' demand remains unaffected by either the Hunts' demand or by political events over the period. The investment demand in Figure 5.1(a) is structurally similar to the industrial demand in Figure 5.1(b).

Dr. Burrows and Professor Houthakker approached their analysis less abstractly, by looking directly at the flows in the silver market. Figure 5.2 is essentially one Dr. Burrows used in his report to the CFTC and one Professor Houthakker presented to the jury. It shows estimates from Handy &

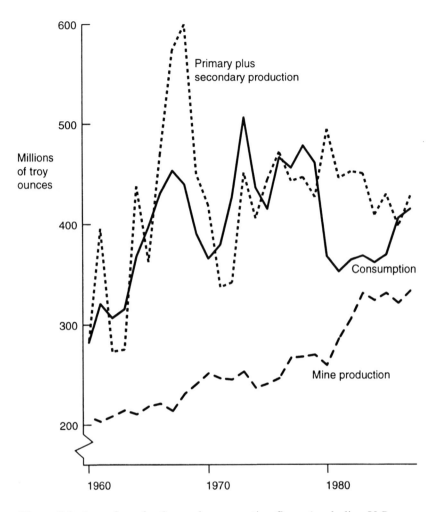

Figure 5.2. Annual production and consumption flows (excluding U.S. coinage), 1960 through 1987

Harman (the major compiler of statistics on silver) of the annual supply of silver, whether from mines or scrap, and the annual demand for industrial uses, including a small amount of coinage outside the U.S. Although silver production and consumption both fluctuate, the fluctuations are small. No break in either series is prominent around 1979. Hence, both experts stated that supply and demand fundamentals did not justify the substantial increase in the price of silver at that time.

In his report to the CFTC, Dr. Burrows used a second model to conduct a range of experiments with higher prices for silver, concluding that the silver market would have been in balance in 1980 at a price under $12 per troy ounce. He described the model only in the most cursory manner, claiming it as proprietary to Charles River Associates. The model is actually an engineering-based analysis in which the production costs and the ore bodies of every mine are documented, along with the specific prices at which individual industrial users would switch to other metals for every application. The model emphasizes flows, and does not include stocks except as a residual.[5] Dr. Burrows' experiments all used a stand-alone spot price for silver, whereas a stock-based model would include the relationship between spot and futures prices. In essence, this second model is a careful application of the official CFTC report's general flow-oriented model of Figure 5.1.[6]

In contrast to the flow-dominated approach toward silver employed by the plaintiff and CFTC, the defense relied upon stock-dominated thinking. Several quotations from Professor Ross's testimony embody this emphasis: "In a typical year the flow into the silver market is small compared to the total stock of silver that is available" (Trial Transcript, p. 13282). "Supply consists of the billions of ounces of silver that there are actually in the world" (Trial Transcript, p. 13285). "Changes in the political and economic environment have dramatic effects upon the demand for this commodity" (Trial Transcript, p. 13280). Investor demand includes "the demand on the part of those people who already own [silver] to retain what they have" (Trial Transcript, p. 13281). Professor Ross presented these propositions as self-evident. He presented no equivalent engineering-based study of the distribution of silver storage costs. Nor did he relate the amount of stocks to the spread between spot and futures prices. Although he did feature a graph of the type of stocks comparable to Figure 5.2, he did so to buttress his testimony on deliverable supplies rather than his discussion of silver prices.

Because silver occupies neither end of the flow–stock spectrum, all the economists distorted silver's properties to some degree and hence misjudged the appropriate price without the Hunts. Those who defined silver as a stock

---

5   In 1992, Charles River Associates conducted a similar extraordinarily detailed worldwide census of all stocks of silver, from antiques to dental X-ray scrap.

6   Charles River Associates' model provides engineering-based estimates of supply and demand functions. Another approach would be to estimate those functions econometrically. Indeed, econometric models of commodity markets are widespread – the World Bank, for example, is a major user and its *Market Outlook* reports are typical applications (World Bank, 1992). These econometric models too, with few exceptions, are flow-dominated. Stocks, if they are explicit at all, are represented as a structural equation as a function of the spot price much like an equation for industrial demand. Such econometric models would suggest an appropriate price for silver in early 1980 much as the other flow-dominated models.

exaggerated its asset-like properties by overlooking the impact of mining supplies and industrial demand. Silver's role as a store of value, sensitive to general political and economic events, rests on its present and future industrial uses. Hence, the statistics on mining and consumption flows were relevant to the determination of silver's appropriate price.

Those who approximated silver as a flow-dominated commodity were led to a rather larger number of faulty judgments about silver's properties and hence its appropriate price. First of all, the decline in silver holdings among people other than the Hunts was said to indicate a lack of general investor interest in silver.[7] However, given the relative paucity of mine production, the increase in the Hunts' holdings had to come from sales by owners of silver, who could reasonably be interpreted as so wanting to hold their stocks that they were enticed to sell only at an extraordinarily high price such as $50 per troy ounce. Those who chose not to sell at $50 were effectively investors valuing their holdings at that price or higher.

Another error in the flow-dominated arguments was in the treatment of the demand for inventories, which was measured as simply the change from one year to the next of silver in private hands rather than the far larger total held privately. The demand for inventories was likewise incorrectly represented as merely a function of the current spot price rather than also a function of spot prices in the future. Thus, expectations about the future could not be directly represented as a "demand fundamental."

Perhaps the most insidious error in the flow-dominated arguments was this prominence given to the spot price of silver while ignoring the relationship between the spot and futures prices. That price relationship is always consistent with the amount of the commodity being held in stock; therefore the model should reflect that consistency. Because spot and futures prices are determined simultaneously, one price in the constellation of delivery dates – the spot price – is not more significant than the others.

The relevance of the simultaneous determination of spot and futures prices can be seen in Dr. Burrows's calculation of the appropriate price of silver for 1980 by using the conditions in mining and industrial usage as of 1979. He concluded, relying on his engineering-based model and his analysis of silver production and consumption, that an increase in the spot price from $6 to $8 per troy ounce of silver was justified from January 1979 to January 1980 based on circumstances known in January 1979. His prediction of an

---

7   The decline in the open interest in silver futures contracts was also interpreted as a fall in investor interest in silver. However, because there is a seller for every buyer of a futures contract, this decline in open interest could just as well be portrayed as indicating a decline in bearish sentiment, at which point the short sellers bought back their contracts. Thus, the magnitude of open interest itself says little about the sentiments of traders.

increase from $6 to $8, namely 33 percent, is inconsistent with a basic arbitrage relationship, which is that a commodity can be purchased, stored at the prevailing interest cost, and delivered on a futures contract. During January 1979, when the price for immediate delivery was $6.00, the January '80 contract was trading on the Comex at a price of $6.60, which, not accidentally, was above the $6 spot price by the rate of interest (10 percent) for the year's time. This price of $6.60 for January 1980 delivery is no more, or no less, relevant than the simultaneously quoted $6.00 for January 1979 delivery. Put bluntly, Dr. Burrows' model cannot duplicate the circumstances of early 1979 in both the spot and futures markets.

5.2   Models of the Hunts' direct price effect

Coefficients from linear regressions measure the contribution of one variable while other variables are held constant. In effect, multiple regression analysis determines what the dependent variable would have been without a particular independent variable. Because of this capability, multiple regression analysis has become a standard tool in price-fixing cases, where it is used to measure the effect of a conspiracy apart from changes in raw material costs and demand patterns (Finkelstein and Levenbach, 1983), and in litigation over employment discrimination, where it is used to measure wage differences due to sex and race apart from education and experience. As regards silver, the regression analysis of whether the Hunts' trading caused the price of silver to rise (the topic of Chapter 4) estimates what the price of silver would have been without the Hunts' trading. Similarly, that regression analysis estimates what the price of silver would have been without the political and economic events represented in the price of gold, much as in insider-trading cases it is used to estimate of how much a particular share price would have moved due to stock-marketwide factors (Mitchell and Netter, 1994).

The plaintiff's experts used regression analysis to determine the appropriate price, although they did not appreciate fully the consistency required of the use of regressions in testing for causality. The defense experts, having found no statistically significant association between the Hunts' trading and the changes in the price of silver, dropped regression analysis from further consideration. I myself had not thought through the full implications of this dual use of regression analysis. Under cross-examination I was confronted with a figure very much like Figure 5.3 which shows the Hunts' contribution to the price in January 1980 according to regression analysis. The amount reaches as much as $7.70 per troy ounce. Figure 5.3 uses the regression (see the upper half of Table 4.7) that suggests the largest effect for the Hunts among the regressions used by the defense and reported in Chapter 4. At the trial, the plaintiff had selected a regression that made this effect appear to be over $20. This $20, or even $7.70, far exceeded the small price effect to

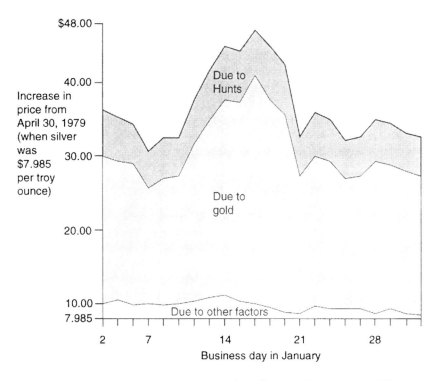

Figure 5.3. An estimate of the Hunts' price effect, during January 1980, using regression analysis

which I had testified. In response, I sputtered about the relatively minor point that the regression the plaintiff had selected included nonsensical coefficients (e.g., a negative sign on the variable London forwards), and so should not be used for such a purpose (Trial Transcript, pp. 13813–15).

I now understand that more important issues are involved in the dual use of regressions than whether a graph like that in Figure 5.3 is constructed from one whose coefficients are sensible. One issue concerns the confidence that can be placed in any estimate based on regression analysis. Ideally, this confidence interval is small. According to the regression reported in Table 4.7 itself, however, the 95 percent confidence interval in Figure 5.3 for the Hunts' largest effect is from –$0.53 to $17.32. This range is so great as to remove from the numbers in Figure 5.3 all precision, especially the precision required for damage calculations.

Another issue involved in the dual use of regressions concerns the measurement of the Hunts' cumulative effect when the effect is estimated for a percentage change. With regard to the price effect measured in dollars rather than percent, it matters very much the sequence in which the various factors are considered. Figure 5.3 was constructed by taking the observed price change for each day and subtracting the estimate of the Hunts' effect (from Table 4.7); the price without the Hunts for a particular day in January 1980 is the cumulation of these calculations for the previous days from May 1, 1979. In turn, gold's effect is subtracted from the daily percentage charge adjusted for the Hunts. (It is $30.78 per troy ounce at silver's peak.) The remaining percentage change can be attributed to "other factors." (It is $1.78 per troy ounce at silver's peak.) Just as reasonable would be to start with the price on May 1, 1979 and add the Hunts' effect day by day. In turn, gold could be added to the contribution by the Hunts. This estimate of the Hunts' (and gold's) effect by January 1980 is just as valid, but is much lower, with "other factors" now much more important.[8]

The discrepancy is no sleight of hand but the result of the compounding of percentage changes from different bases. If the Hunts' purchase of 1,000 futures contracts in June 1979 is thought to have caused, say, a 1 percent increase in the price – equivalent to $0.08 per troy ounce – is it $0.50 that is carried over to January 1980, which is 1 percent of the price at that time, or the $0.08? It might seem that performing the regression analysis directly in terms of dollars per troy ounce rather than in terms of percent would avoid this problem of interpreting the contribution of gold or "other factors." Unfortunately, an approach using dollars and not percent leads to nonsensical "appropriate" prices for another reason, which is yet another issue involved in the dual use of regression analysis and perhaps the most important.

Similar computations can be done based on the plaintiff's regressions relating the Hunts' trading to the price of silver. The regression in Table 4.5 presents one of the larger estimates of the percentage effect of the Hunts' trading. According to its coefficients, the peak price of silver would have been $18.07 were it not for the Hunts.

The "competitive" price of $18.07 implied by the plaintiff's expert's regression analysis contradicts his own testimony, based on analysis of supply and demand fundamentals, that the price would not have risen above $10. This contradiction was not apparent at the trial because he presented regression results showing a maximum under $10; indeed he emphasized how his regression analysis accorded with his other approach. But this number as presented excluded the category "other factors" in the computation of the price without the Hunts. In effect, the plaintiff's expert removed not just the Hunts but also all other new influences on the price of silver. The mistake

---

8   The precise numbers are $1.54 for the Hunts, $29.87 for gold, and $8.84 for "other factors."

was an easy one to make, given the complexities of regression analysis with corrections for autocorrelated error terms.[9] The defense understood that this mistake had been made, but concluded that an attempt to explain it to the jury would itself become bogged down in the technical issues of econometrics.

The defense did not, however, appreciate that another problem would have arisen in the plaintiff's expert's analysis had he computed the peak price correctly at $18.07. The methodology applies to every day in 1979 and 1980, not just the peak day. If the Hunts' effect according to the plaintiff's expert is removed from every day, the price in early August 1979 would have been as low as $5.50 (down from $7.985 on April 30, 1979) and again as low as $4.00 in March 1980, both implausibly low prices. (Under some versions of the plaintiff's regression analysis, the price without the Hunts would have been negative, which is absurd.)[10] According to the plaintiff's expert himself, nothing in the fundamentals of mine production and industrial usage changed so much over the year. The problem then resides in the method for estimating the Hunts' effect, namely the regressions reported in Chapter 4.

The more anyone argued that the peak price in January 1980 is attributable to the Hunts, the less plausible the estimates of the price of silver without the Hunts in months other than January would have appeared.[11] Fundamentally, the dilemma arises because the Hunts had essentially the same positions, in both size and composition, from August through March. If the effect of those

---

[9]   More specifically, the plaintiff's experts used the fitted values in an AR(1) regression without the Hunts. That is, their RESID variable representing the increase in gold ostensibly not due to the Hunts alone was added to the initial price of silver. Additions to the (autocorrelated) error term were implicitly set at 0.0. But removing the effect of both the Hunts and "other factors" amounts to asking what would have been the price of silver if all new influences on its price were absent – not surprisingly, the regression analysis says the price would have remained constant. The proper approach would have been to subtract the estimate of the Hunts' effect from the actual price of silver on a particular day, which includes the influence of "other factors.".

[10]   The appropriate price of silver would have been negative according to the regression specification of Table 4.5, which uses as the dependent variable the percentage increase in the price of silver from April 30, 1979. The estimated coefficient times the increase in the Hunts' position by August works out to 200% of the initial price, or $16. Thus, whenever the price is below $16 after August 1979, the price without the Hunts would seem to be negative.

Actually, the plaintiff's experts used the natural logarithm of the silver price as the dependent variable. For small changes, the difference between two logarithms is equivalent to the percentage change (and percentage changes are easier to understand). The correspondence breaks down when the changes are large, as for silver. I have used here the version with natural logarithms equivalent to Table 4.5. The low price is no longer negative, but it is still implausibly low.

[11]   If the maximum price without the Hunts in January 1980 were to be $12, the regression coefficient in the logarithmic version of Table 4.5 would have to be such that the price of silver in early August 1979 would be $3.50.

positions is taken away from January's price, the prices in the other months must be adjusted to a similar extent.

The regression analysis ought to yield estimates of the Hunts' effect so that its implicit estimate of the price without the Hunts be sensible for every day of the period from 1979 through 1980. This constraint was not recognized (let alone exploited) by the economist expert witnesses. It was a major collective lapse.

The dual use of regression analysis – for determining the strength of the statistical association between the Hunts' trading and the price use and for determining the price of silver without the Hunts – has one more implication little understood at the time of the trial. What is the interpretation of the "error term" in the regression? In Figure 5.3, this component has been labeled "other factors," as if it were some other influence such as platinum. It could, however, be classic "measurement error," as when the price quotations are not synchronous; or it could be a "specification error," as when the relationships are not linear or alter over time. If a specification error, the effect labeled "other factors" could be due to the Hunts or conversely, some of the effect assigned to the Hunts could be due to other factors. This problem in interpretation is the origin of the confidence intervals mentioned earlier, but here the regression analysis, by its nature, provides an incomplete representation of what silver prices would have been without the Hunts.[12]

Also, regression analysis provides less understanding of the relationships between silver and gold, even though changes in the price of gold "explain" a substantial fraction of the changes in the price of silver. In testing whether the Hunts caused the price rise, gold could reasonably be put forth as a proxy for political and economic news. When determining the appropriate price of silver, that approach looks like a much blunter instrument. In the terminology of econometric models, gold represents an "unrestricted reduced-form," in which little knowledge of the interaction of political events, macroeconomic forces, and metals markets is exploited. That is, in the regression, gold at best measures the average effect of political and economic events. To understand silver prices, we need to identify the differential effect of an event in various settings, such as when news about the Soviet invasion of Afghanistan arrives just after bad news about inflation or just after good news about inflation.

In sum, the application of regression analysis involving both the Hunts' trading and gold over the period 1979–1980 serves mainly to cast more doubt upon some of the tests for the causes of silver's price rise. Further conceptual

[12] In litigation over wage discrimination, this problem is known as "under-adjustment bias," and has lead to controversy whenever regression analysis provides the main evidence.

problems emerge with the defense's use of gold as a proxy for political and economic news. The plaintiff's regression techniques, which lead to the conclusion that the Hunts had a large effect at the time of the price peak, lead to implausibly low prices without the Hunts at other times. Precisely because the appropriate price of silver was treated as a subject distinct from tests of the Hunts' statistical association, these inconsistencies were not made clear; indeed they were not even recognized.

5.3   Models of distant futures prices

At the trial, the defense argued that the appropriate price for silver during the period of the Hunts' trading could be found in the prices for distant futures contracts in silver that were then being traded. In late 1979 and early 1980, silver futures extended as far as two and one-half years ahead on the CBOT, and two years ahead on Comex. These very distant contracts were traded in low volume, but the important fact is that they were traded, and not by the Hunts. When people are freely trading, the resulting price supersedes any alternative calculation from an engineering-based model or an econometric study of what the price would be.

Of course, in late 1979 and early 1980, other people besides the Hunts traded silver for immediate delivery. Although market-determined, the resulting price cannot be said to represent a price without the Hunts' trading. Likewise, prices for intermediate delivery dates might not be free of an influence from the Hunts even if the Hunts had no position in those futures contracts. Prices for delivery dates sufficiently far ahead that the demand the Hunts placed on the bullion market could be satisfied out of new mining and secondary refining would represent the price of silver without the Hunts.

The plaintiff ignored this technique for observing the "competitive" price of silver, whereas the defense made it a central argument.[13] Professor Edwards presented two large graphs illustrating the course of silver prices from June 1979 through March 1980, one graph showing the price for immediate delivery and the other graph showing the price of a futures contract for delivery always one year ahead. These two graphs when overlaid clearly indicated that price for the distant delivery date closely tracked the price for immediate delivery, also rising above $50 per troy ounce.

As simple as Professor Edwards's point is, it can perhaps be made even clearer with the aid of all the prices on a single day. Figure 5.4 shows silver prices on January 16, 1980, which was chosen because it was near the price peak observed later that week and had relatively stable prices throughout the

---

[13]   A comparable argument could have been made about the price of coins reached in January 1980, but the defense did not present that evidence.

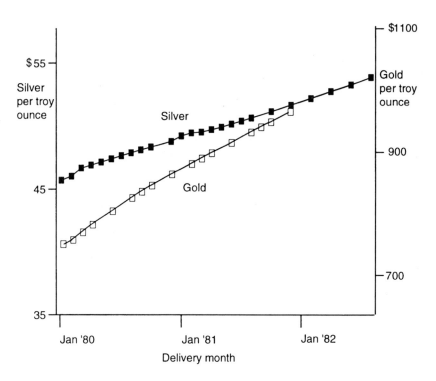

Figure 5.4. Gold and silver prices for deferred delivery, close of trading, January 16, 1980

day.[14] Designated by the black squares are the prices for all twenty-six delivery months available on either the CBOT or Comex.

Figure 5.4 also includes the available delivery dates and prices for gold futures (on either Comex or the Chicago Mercantile Exchange depending on the delivery month). Because of the abundance of gold bullion, gold prices for different delivery dates essentially expressed full carrying charges.[15] Had even more distant delivery dates been traded for gold, they would have been

[14] Because price-move limits applied to the distant contracts, I have reconstructed the prices from the straddle market, using procedures comparable to Figure 6.2. Nothing is artificial about these prices; they would have been perceived by traders at the time.

[15] The nearest delivery dates, most unusually, were slightly above full carrying charges as measured by the Eurodollar interest rate, because of tight credit conditions for precious metals dealers. This differential – 20 percent per annum instead of 15 percent per annum – widened later in January.

extrapolations of available prices with interest rates taken into account.[16]

The profile of gold prices can be superimposed on the profile of silver prices, as in Figure 5.4. This comparison amounts to saying that the gold/silver ratio between distant futures prices (a ratio of 19:1 on January 16, 1980) reflects the competitive price of silver.[17] Because gold prices display full carrying charges, the spot price of silver (if silver displayed full carrying charges among nearby delivery months) can be read off on the scale for silver, namely $39.80 per troy ounce. This $39.80 is a minimum estimate of the "competitive" spot price on January 16, because the profile of silver prices could not be steeper than full carrying charges. That minimum estimate also ascribes all the difference between $45.70 and $39.80 to the Hunts.

The difference between $45.70 and $39.80, namely $5.90, is none other than Professor Kyle's premium for the immediate delivery of silver, also known as the extent that silver spreads were below full carrying charges, which he studied for indications of manipulation.[18] The analysis of intertemporal spreads for indications of a manipulation contains within it a model of the "competitive" price of silver, namely that the prices for distant delivery dates are free from manipulation. Perhaps it is fairer to say that this market-determined approach to the appropriate price of silver contains within it a theory about manipulation. As Mr. Gorman's cross-examination made clear, Professor Edwards viewed the Hunts' alleged manipulation as synonymous with a corner, one in which the spot price would go to a substantial premium to distant delivery dates (Trial Transcript, pp. 14050–4).

Professor Edwards considered a manipulation of the silver market as analogous to one of the wheat market, in which the last old-crop futures contract could be squeezed but in which the abundant supplies available with the new crop would leave the new-crop contracts undistorted and their prices a minimum estimate of the appropriate old-crop price. He determined that two and one-half years would be more than sufficient for new mine production and bullion from scrap to overwhelm the demands of any manipulator of silver. He believed that traders, recognizing the magnitudes of those flows, would only transact at an untainted price, and in particular, distant spreads would be at their normal condition of full carrying charges. (The extent that

[16]   The bend to the profile of gold prices reflected the descending term structure of interest rates: 15 percent per annum for two months and 12 percent per annum for two years.

[17]   Figure 5.4 is similar to Figure 3.9, except that Figure 5.4 is in terms of the price of gold rather than the gold/silver ratio.

[18]   Figure 5.4 has been constructed to make this difference as large as possible, by supposing gold spreads beyond the contracts traded would have been slightly higher (in percent) than the silver spreads. If distant silver spreads were at full carrying charges, the premium for January '80 bullion would have been about $1.25 less. The remaining $4.65 is close to the charge Professor Kyle observed in the refining services market. Price relationships were consistent.

the silver spreads were below full carrying charges did indeed attenuate with time ahead; that is, the price profile in Figure 5.4 became more nearly parallel with that of gold.)[19] His same logic applies to gold, in which case the whole profile of gold prices is "competitive" since people were freely transacting at those prices.[20]

Of course, not many people traded these distant futures contracts. On January 16, 1980, volume in silver futures contracts more than fifteen months distant was merely 1,327; over the whole week, volume in those contracts on both exchanges totaled 5,710.[21] Yet the fact remains that people freely bought distant futures contracts at those high prices. Moreover, anyone, such as a mine operator, who would have silver by August 1982 could have sold it in January 1980 for future delivery. By not selling, those with silver by August 1982 were accepting the prevailing prices as "competitive." The analogy with Roman coins applies, namely that the volume of trading does not necessarily correspond to sentiments about the price. Indeed, because futures markets, unlike the Roman coin market, permit selling by those who do not possess the physical commodity, everyone who paid attention to the silver market and did not sell distant silver futures contracts accepted those prices.

Those purchasing distant futures contracts in January 1980 at $50 for silver or $850 for gold seem foolish in retrospect, but so do those who, in January 1978, sold silver at $5.75 for delivery in January 1980 or gold at $205. One party to every trade in silver or gold futures will *ex post* regret the trade to some extent. This does not mean that the price was not reasonable *ex ante*. Had some different situation developed, the loser in a trade might have been the winner. More generally, the very variability of commodity prices, especially those for storable commodities like silver, implies that any "best estimate" of an appropriate price is surrounded by a considerable range of uncertainty. None of the experts paid much attention to such "confidence intervals" implicit in the history of spot and futures prices themselves.

5.4   Models of expectations feedback

The narratives of the silver market over 1979 and 1980 all end with the dramatic events of late March when the Hunts were sold out of many of their remaining futures positions. On March 27, 1980, the price touched a low of $10.40 per troy ounce. This price seems to confirm Dr. Burrows's and Professor Houthakker's opinion that the appropriate price for silver had been $8

---

[19]   The most distant silver spreads are at full carrying charges.

[20]   The implications of this reasoning for the issue of whether the Hunts caused the price rise in gold were not brought out at the trial.

[21]   The corresponding volumes for distant gold delivery months were 1,807 and 6,231.

to $12 all along. Yet, in the summer of 1980, the price rose above $15 and remained there, and on September 22, 1980, it reached $24.20.[22]

The defense argued that the state of the silver futures market in the months just after the end of the Hunts' presence offered a reasonable guide to what prices might have been earlier. More important, the defense used this approach to argue against the approach determining the appropriate price based on the flows of supply and demand. A price of $24 following $10 by just a few months is fundamentally inconsistent with the plaintiff's and the CFTC's analyses, because nothing concerning silver production and industrial consumption had altered so profoundly over those months.

The plaintiff's expert dismissed the evidence of a price rise in the summer of 1980, saying that it was contaminated by the lingering effects of the Hunts' previous trading (Trial Transcript, pp. 8731–6). Indeed, the markets themselves showed the lingering effects of the events through March 1980. The CBOT silver market was fatally injured despite the rapid recovery of prices, and the volume on Comex did not return to the levels of 1979 until several years later, as Figure 5.5 shows. The open interest, namely the number of contracts outstanding, has never recovered, principally because the open interest had been inflated through tax-motivated straddles.[23]

The low volume of futures trading after March 1980, the wide bid–ask spreads in the bullion market, and the jumpy prices all accord with the silver market's remaining disturbed by the events climaxing in March 1980. Yet for determining the price effect of the Hunts' trading, it is the level of prices after March 1980 that matters. The plaintiff's expert did not substantiate his proposition that the Hunts had a sustained effect on price by relating that price rise after March 1980 to the Hunts' positions during the summer, as he had done for the price rise of the fall and winter of 1979–1980. Rather, he shifted his style of analysis to a theoretical discussion of how other traders would have reacted to the disruptions of early 1980 and how they might have anticipated another attempt at manipulation by the Hunts because they retained substantial amounts of bullion.

What one supposes to be the effect of the Hunts' trading on the price in 1980 or much later depends in large part on what one believes the Hunts did in 1979–1980. If the Hunts attempted to corner the silver market, the dismal outcome of their scheme would not encourage anyone to try again and the effect on prices of any attempted corner could only have been transitory. The event itself was too brief for any new mines to open and, although coins and scrap became more concentrated in dealers' hands, such miscellaneous

---

[22]   The price of gold also revived over this period, though not as much as silver. The gold/silver ratio corresponded to early June 1979.

[23]   In the early years in Figure 5.5, the turn-of-year contribution of tax-motivated straddles can be discerned.

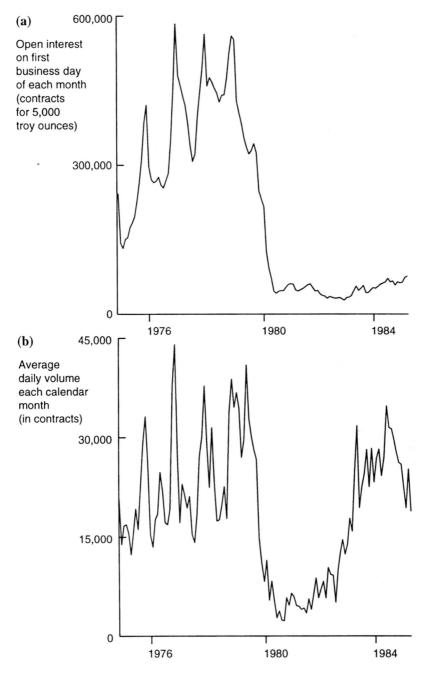

Figure 5.5. Activity in silver futures, all delivery months (Comex and CBOT)

sources of silver remained abundant throughout. If the Hunts attempted to fool others into overestimating investor interest, the events of March 1980 would make it unlikely that anyone would be misled again. And again, no effect would linger in prices.

If the Hunts were legitimate long-term investors, the lingering effect of their trading is even more problematic. The large stocks of silver the Hunts bought, they would eventually resell. If the Hunts had bought for a reason unique to themselves, those buying from them in turn would lack that unique motivation, and so would bid nothing extra. At most, the Hunts would increase the price for as long as their holding period. For a storable commodity, this effect would be seen as spreads being below full carrying charges over that interval. Yet the evidence is clear that by April 1980, silver prices for delivery dates as far ahead as two years displayed full carrying charges (and remained at full carrying charges even at the price peak in September). Thus, if other traders anticipated later Hunt actions, whether an increase or decrease of the Hunts' holdings, the spot price reflected those expectations as much as the more distant futures prices, and as much as the hypothetical futures prices for delivery dates beyond those traded.

The plaintiff's expert, given his observation that prices were at full carrying charges in early April and his claim that, by early April, prices had returned to normal, contradicts his own argument that price levels were later distorted due to lingering effects. For storable commodities, anticipated lingering effects are compounded into current prices; price changes such as the increase in the price of silver to September 1980 must reflect something new.

The effect of future conditions on prices of storable commodities can perhaps be understood by continuing the example of collectors of Roman silver coins and imagining contracts for future delivery of such coins far into the future. Should an elderly wealthy gentleman suddenly become an avid collector, he might well have to drive the spot price of Roman coins up considerably to entice them from other collectors. But if only one such collector's taste has changed, the prices for delivery at dates after his probable death are unaltered, because the coins will be returned to the pool. The elderly collector at most affects the carrying charge, namely, a premium for current delivery. If the carrying charges are observed to remain full even as a new collector is buying aggressively, one of two things may have happened. Possibly, the new collector may be part of a general increase in collecting interest; his coins will be bought on his death by other new collectors and the price rise sustained. Or possibly, current holders of Roman silver coins are persuaded to part with them at a negligible premium knowing they can buy them back soon. In either case, the anticipation of the new collector's future sale are reflected in the currently quoted prices for the different delivery dates. If those prices are judged at some moment to be normal, they cannot later be abnormal because of the supposed lingering effects of the new collector.

For an even more telling example of the effect in the present of future conditions, consider the gold market in recent years. Controversy surrounds the price effects of a number of mines selling their future output forward and of some sales of bullion by a few small central banks. It is difficult to understand the first controversy, however. Unless the forward sales induce the mines to expand output, the gold market would have had to absorb a spot sale at the time of production. Any current buyer of gold would anticipate that production. Hence, whether ownership changes hands in the present or in the future should not matter to price, which would have changed when the ore body was first discovered. Sales by central banks might be a different matter, though. Private investors might reasonably have concluded that central banks would lock their gold away in vaults forever, so that sales by any one bank might persuade private investors that many other central banks will soon sell. Hence, the price fall might be out of all proportion to the size of a sale.

These arguments recognize that when stocks are held, the present spot price reflects expectations about the future. Similarly, when spreads are at full carrying charges the prices for future delivery reflect current conditions. These points, first made long ago by Working (1948), cannot be overemphasized for understanding the price behavior of commodities, especially that of one so easily stored as silver. As profound as this simple insight is, however, it does not explain everything about commodity prices. The spot price may reflect expectations of future investment demand, but why does the reasonable expression of future investment demand result in a price of $50 rather than $30 or $70?

The expression in current prices of current events, future events, and the possibilities for future events, makes all too clear that the issues of causality, type of manipulation, and the Hunts' intent are not distinct from the determination of the price of silver had the Hunts not been present in the market. Yet the style of courtroom delivery encouraged each of these issues to be treated as distinct subjects and, as a result, an inconsistency in an expert's testimony was often concealed, sometimes even from the expert himself. The defense experts emphasized how political events could influence the investment demand for silver, which is fundamentally a stock-dominated interpretation of silver prices. Yet the defense experts also defined manipulations to be about corners more than expectations, which supposes the targeted commodity to be closer to the flow-dominated end of the spectrum. The defense experts never reconciled these two views of the determination of silver prices. Just as the plaintiff's expert argued that prices after March 1980 reflected the possibility of another attempt at manipulation, his theory of manipulation more generally emphasized expectations. In that instance, he was making a plausible argument based on stock-dominated model. Yet, his method of determining the appropriate price of silver was based on a flow-dominated model, in which expectations about the future bear no connection to the present.

5.5   Models as necessary simplifications

In sum, the great and puzzling range of the experts' proposed prices for silver without the Hunts' trading reflected primarily the range of models they utilized to determine that "appropriate" price. It was not that one expert's model was wrong and another's correct. Rather, each model was a simplification whose ability to isolate an important feature of a real-world situation led to just one of the possible insights. Current silver prices do reflect expectations about economic and political conditions in the future, because the stocks of it are huge and therefore the same silver will continue to exist over time. Yet the price of silver does depend on the current and future industrial uses of the metal, for if it had no such uses, no one would want to hold silver stocks. Moreover, the price of silver does move with other metals. And the price of silver does represent only what people are willing to buy and sell it for. No expert's model came close to determining the relative importance of all these insights and hence to explaining silver prices fully.

In any case, a comprehensive model would be difficult to achieve. It would respect the minutiae of engineering costs in the present and the future, would allow for the quantity, form, and distribution of stockholding, would deal with the formation of traders' expectations, would make the connection to political events explicit, would encompass the exchanges' responses, would determine spot and futures prices simultaneously, and would account for the volume of trading. A comprehensive model would itself determine the weight given to each of its components. Such a comprehensive model, however, would far exceed a jury's ability to appreciate it. Moreover, if economists were to develop such a prescient model of the silver market, they would not be expert witnesses – they would be rich.

How is the trial process itself able to deal with a variety of modeling approaches to determine silver's appropriate price, each offering a valid insight but each incomplete? Poorly, I would say, for at least four reasons.

First, the accepted style of testimony and cross-examination prevents the limitations of a modeling approach from being suitably acknowledged. In the Hunt case, one example can be found in the defense experts' emphasis on the influence of political and economic events. Presumably that relationship is systematic, so that political events twice as important, for example, would have twice the price effect. Quite reasonably, the plaintiff would want to confirm this. But the trial setting discouraged each defense expert from providing details of his model, for these would only have assisted an opposing expert to conduct that test or have invited a vigorous cross-examination. Because any explanation of commodity prices, however detailed, is always incomplete in some way, some inconsistency can be found, and the expert's valid insight dismissed. Consequently, in the Hunt case, the experts kept any discussion of their analysis as vague as possible. As a result, the jury, during direct examination, was never told enough about the methodologies to evaluate them; neither, as one would expect, did cross-examination produce a balanced picture of the strengths and weaknesses of the various experts' approaches.

Second, a trial presents the expert witnesses as proffering competing explanations. If one expert's insight is convincing, the other's must be wrong. Yet the explanations may not be contradictory as much as incomplete, as the experts may even admit privately. Nevertheless, the lawyers at the Hunt trial would have had apoplexy had their experts conceded that an opposing expert's argument offered an important insight, and worse, one that his own analysis did not contain. Lawyers likewise have misgivings when an expert proposes several approaches or contents himself with arguments of the form "the effect could have been no larger than ...," rightly fearing that such intellectual flexibility will be misinterpreted as equivocation. Dr. Burrows, for example, when he conceded that the price of silver could have risen as much as gold, was arguing that the Hunts must have had an effect, because the actual price rise in silver was so much greater than the price rise in gold. Such reasoning persuades economists, who, knowing the limitations of models, reflexively avoid a precise answer, but fails to impress others, who expect experts to be more decisive.[24]

Third, a trial encourages expert witnesses to defer to the jury's lack of special training by being more simplistic in their explanations than otherwise. Indeed, in the instance of the "competitive" price of silver, the experts compressed their analysis to a single number for the entire 1979–1980 period. The experts at the Hunt trial recognized that concepts like forecasts with regressions, relationships between spot and futures prices, and the aggregation from one mine to worldwide supply are exceptionally opaque to the nonspecialist. Unfortunately, in trying to keep the applications of these concepts simple for the jury, the experts not only made their analyses less multidimensional but conducted them less rigorously than they would have for an audience of other economists. Worse, the simplifications did not help the jury. The Hunt jury, seeing nothing but the great range of the economists' estimates of silver's appropriate price, was probably just puzzled and may well have concluded that there was little analytical reasoning behind any of the estimates.

Fourth, a jury is left to do what the experts cannot, namely construct a comprehensive approach. To weigh the various insights offered by the experts, that is, to conclude whose "competitive" price seemed most reasonable, the Hunt jury had to contemplate the nature of traders' expectations, the

---

[24]   As Mayer (1993) would put the issue, in economic analysis, there is a trade-off between precision and understanding.

relative importance of stocks versus flows, the significance of the distant futures prices. They were, however, hardly able to glean from the experts' testimony any of the methodological subtleties behind these points. Nor were they helped by testimony that treated manipulative intent, causality, and the appropriate price of silver as separate subjects and so left the internal consistency of each expert's arguments unexplored.

The Hunts' involvement with the silver market in 1979 and early 1980 was incessant. They hardly spent a day without taking delivery on some futures contract, without adjusting the composition of their positions through roll-overs into other delivery months, without negotiating some exchange for physicals, without communicating with CBOT and Comex officials. At the time and in the subsequent legal proceedings, the Hunts were credited with an overarching rationale for their actions. From that quite natural supposition arose an inductive logic: some of the Hunts' actions could betray the purpose of all their actions, whether the purpose be investment, as the Hunts maintained, or manipulation, as the plaintiff charged. The intention behind the Hunts' actions was paramount because under the relevant statutes as they have come to be interpreted, no wrongdoing ensues without the specific intent to manipulate.[1]

The CFTC Division of Enforcement characterized a number of the Hunts' particular transactions as "manipulative acts." In like manner, Minpeco compiled a list of "uneconomic acts" committed by the Hunts, which supposedly were unprofitable by themselves but furthered a manipulative scheme as a whole. According to the defense, many of these actions had innocent interpretations or were economically rational. It instead pointed to other actions consistent with the objectives of long-term investment as indi-

---

[1]   The CFTC has stated most straightforwardly the intent element within a manipulation charge: "It must be proven that the accused acted (or failed to act) with the purpose or conscious object of causing or effecting a price or price trend in the market that did not reflect the legitimate forces of supply and demand ..." (*In re. Indiana Farm Bureau Coop Assn*, CCH Commodity Futures Law Reporter ¶21,796 [1982–84 Transfer Binder] (CFTC, 1982), p. 27,283). However "artificial" the price, a trader is not guilty of manipulation if he influenced the price out of negligence or even out of the knowledge of his influence, provided that he did have the purpose of influencing the price. For more on the nature of "specific intent," see Commissioner Stone's concurring opinion in *Indiana Farm Bureau*, p. 27,303, or Harrington (1984).

cating the Hunts' motives. Despite disagreement over the purposes of particular acts, all the lawyers and economists concerned accepted that detailed analysis of specific transactions could reveal intent.[2] As the CFTC itself emphasized in the widely noted proceedings *In re. Indiana Farm Bureau,* "since proof of intent will most often be circumstantial in nature, manipulative intent must normally be shown inferentially from the conduct of the accused."[3]

Determining intent inevitably involves the weighing of probabilities, simply because no one can know completely another's thinking. In some instances, the inference appears straightforward, as in a trial for burglary where the accused has been found in the upstairs study of a mansion, the bookshelf moved, the wall safe opened, and the jewels in his pocket. Indeed, in such circumstances the formal logical sequence required for inferring intent seems superfluous. Inference of the Hunts' intentions was not as straightforward because the collapse in silver prices in March 1980 halted events in mid course. Their situation is similar to that of a stranger who parked his car in the driveway of a mansion, took a circuitous route through the rosebeds, ignored the gardener's hail, and was arrested at the front door, with a box of chocolates under his arm and a Swiss Army knife in his pocket, the burglary (or social call) stopped before it could be completed. In the subsequent trial, the prosecution would stress the indicia – to use lawyers' jargon – of the Swiss Army knife in the accused's pocket, his unresponsiveness to the gardener, and his failure to take a direct path to the front door. Perhaps an expert would testify that one part of the knife can be used as a picklock and that – to use economists' jargon – a circuitous route significantly rejects the hypothesis of a social call. The defense would counter that the accused likes flowers and that ignoring a gardener's hail is no crime. Its experts would discourse on the knife's usefulness for opening the box of chocolates. Despite the opposing theories about the accused's intent, all involved in the case would agree that the accused's purpose can be deduced from his actions. Moreover, the actions speak for themselves; they are sufficiently simple that experts are not really needed.

Of course, the actions only speak for themselves to the point where the jury must interpret them. In weighing the evidence about the person arrested at the door of the mansion, the jurors bring to bear their own experience about whether people normally carry pocket knives or leave a main path to smell flowers. Ideally, the actions are sufficiently within the realm of the jurors' experience to speak directly to them.

---

2   This focus on the Hunts' acts is the style of analysis recommended by Perdue (1987) as her solution to the ambiguity in approaching manipulation from the perspective of an artificial price.

3   *In re. Indiana Farm Bureau Coop Assn*, CCH Commodity Futures Law Reporter ¶21,796 [1982–84 Transfer Binder] (CFTC, 1982), p. 27,283.

The exercise of inferring intent changes, however, when the jury depends on expert witnesses for a characterization of the path taken as circuitous, for the idea that a professed flower lover would go out of the way to smell roses, and for an understanding of the workings of the object in the accused's pocket. The jury remains unaware of the relevant expert's assumption that the normal path to this house is the front walk, that flower lovers walk out of their way to smell roses, and that Swiss Army knives are used as picklocks. The jury does not know that no study was made of the paths to the front door taken by other visitors, or of the rose-smelling habits of flower lovers, or of the picklocks used by burglars. Although some of the experts' assumptions may have been borne out had formal studies been conducted, the "facts" presented to the jury may be no more than chains of logic following from the experts' private assumptions.

The jury in *Minpeco v. Hunt* seemingly could interpret without the intercession of experts some of the Hunts' actions, such as their meetings at racetracks and horse auctions with members of the so-called Conti group. (One particularly damaging witness testified that he had overheard, in January 1980, Bunker Hunt soliciting a London-based bullion trader to join his group.) Perhaps for that reason testimony about the supposed conspiracy predominated.

Yet even in such simple matters as the Hunts' relations with other silver traders, inferences may have depended on chains of logic from unstated assumptions. Bunker Hunt seemed to have trouble remembering the details of large transactions; it could be inferred that he had something to hide. However, these transactions were perhaps not so large to someone as rich as him. Following that logic, it could be argued, the very rich deploy sophisticated tax and financial planning. The fact that Bunker Hunt could not produce detailed tax calculations and the fact that he could not articulate a sophisticated investment strategy led naturally to an inference that he was not making long-term investments. Yet that inference rests on an assumption that Bunker Hunt is normal, or at least, the normal rich. Incredible as it seems, Bunker Hunt was more likely to remember the food at a business lunch than the multimillion dollar check that changed hands, was in the habit of haphazard tax planning, and, not accustomed to justifying his actions to others, was not particularly articulate. These idiosyncrasies do not mean that an inference about Bunker Hunt's actions in the silver market cannot be made, only that the starting assumption, say that he should have acted in silver investments as he did in oil investments, should have been made explicit.[4]

---

[4] A telling example of the assumptions made implicitly about the Hunts comes from early in the silver litigation. Placid Oil seemed to take inordinately long to produce documents as requested by the CFTC Division of Enforcement's attorneys, which

Unquestionably, the Hunts' specific actions within the silver futures market were neither simple nor could they speak for themselves. No one within the jury could begin to interpret deliveries on futures contracts, EFPs, or tax-motivated straddles. At the minimum, the members of the jury needed experts to elucidate those terms; more likely, they needed experts to classify particular acts as "uneconomic" or as "for investment purposes." The very classification of particular acts depended, however, on the experts' presumptions about normal patterns in futures markets. Their presumptions were rarely stated, let alone tested.

The Hunt jury attended to lengthy expert testimony devoted to specific actions by the defendants. Although this testimony paled in significance compared to the impressions the jury gained from the Hunts themselves (just as the experts' discussion of picklocks would be of little importance to a jury if it became known that the stranger had been seen prowling around other houses in the neighborhood or had a friend who had suggested the visit), the economists' testimony provides the sharpest examples of the difficulties in inferring intent. This chapter will consider five of the defendants' actions and attendant expert testimony: the Hunts' deliveries taken, their EFPs, Lamar Hunt's "switch trading," their trading patterns in the summer of 1979, and their relationship with regulatory officials. These five examples, besides representing most of the broad categories of the Hunts' actions (recall Table 2.4), all demonstrate the danger of experts presenting their hidden assumptions as facts from which intent is to be inferred. (Several also reveal the problems resulting from a lack of any clear definition of manipulation, the subject of Chapter 3.)

Another theme unites the five examples. Frequently, an apparently innocent action by the Hunts was offered as corroboration of manipulative intent, because a rational person would attempt to disguise his manipulation. For example, the trading by the Hunts and the Conti group in different delivery months was interpreted by the plaintiff as a clever disguise for relationships to be expected of conspirators. It would be as if the prosecutor of the accused burglar proposed the box of chocolates as proof of the accused's shrewdness in anticipating the nature of a trial for burglary. Such reasoning undercuts the premise that only one intent can be inferred from a particular act. Depending on the accused's skill at anticipating the reaction of others to his own actions – a level of skill that cannot be demonstrated but must be assumed – any of his actions can plausibly be reconciled with a particular intent. The jury, after hearing the experts' conflicting interpretations of what a rational burglar would do in anticipation of others' percep-

lead them to conclude that the Hunts were hiding something and to press the case harder. They presumed that Placid Oil would have a legal department commensurate with its size – actually, there were merely two in-house lawyers, who were swamped with the request for documents.

tions of his actions, convicts him for the one crime in which intent was beside the point: rudeness to the gardener.

6.1   Deliveries taken on futures contracts

From September 1979 through March 1980, Bunker Hunt, Herbert Hunt, and IMIC among them took delivery on 7,667 futures contracts corresponding to 38,335,000 troy ounces of bullion.[5] The Hunts needed no active decision to take delivery. Someone holding a long position in any futures market who does not close it out or roll it over into a later delivery month eventually receives (and must pay cash for) a warehouse receipt tendered by a short and passed through the clearinghouse.

Many investigators characterized the Hunts' taking of deliveries on futures contracts as a manipulative act. The "massive deliveries," to use the words of the CFTC Division of Enforcement's original complaint, figured as a central allegation in its case. The Division of Enforcement's expert, Professor Kyle, implied over and over again that a rational long-term investor would rarely take delivery of bullion on futures contracts, especially if intertemporal spreads were below full carrying charges (Kyle CFTC Report, pp. 22, 25, 59). At the trial, the plaintiff's expert, Professor Houthakker, classified as "uneconomic" the taking of deliveries when spreads were below full carrying charges (Trial Transcript, pp. 8581–5). Reflecting back on the Hunt case recently, he considered deliveries in any quantity to be the strongest evidence of the Hunts' manipulative intent.

Nevertheless, the Hunts' taking of delivery on many futures contracts offers a prime example of the difficulty of inferring intent from actions. No one disputes that the Hunts took deliveries in large amounts, nor that deliveries can be a symptom of a corner. Rather the dispute arises in deducing whether such actions are necessarily manipulative.[6] Professors Kyle and Houthakker began their analysis of the Hunts' deliveries by assuming deliveries to be rare on futures markets. Indeed, the CFTC Division of Enforcement considered it practically axiomatic that deliveries on futures contracts were unnatural. The defense experts began their analysis with the assumption that tax considerations matter. Neither group of experts inspected its assumptions.[7]

---

5   Other Hunt-related corporations took some deliveries too. Naji Nahas and BPS, members of the Conti group, took deliveries on 1,720 and 4,450 contracts respectively over this period.

6   As mentioned in Chapter 3, it might have been argued that the Hunts took so many deliveries as to be far beyond the optimal number for extracting a premium from anyone who wanted bullion, with the implication that they were not manipulators.

7   Imwinkelried (1988) would recognize this discussion of deliveries as another instance in which in the syllogistic structure of scientific testimony, the "major premise" goes unexamined.

To presume deliveries to be rare on futures markets would have seemed reasonable to economists familiar with futures trading. The view in Hieronymus (1977a, p. 340), a standard text, is typical: "In [futures] markets that work, delivery is rarely made or taken; futures contracts are entered into for reasons other than exchange of title."[8] To many unfamiliar with these markets, a most perplexing aspect of "contracts for future delivery" is the infrequency with which they culminate in delivery. Hence economists have gone to great lengths to explain how futures contracts are used as temporary substitutes for more specific merchandising contracts to be arranged later. But in explaining how futures contracts need not culminate in delivery, economists may well have left the impression that delivery should never occur.

As it happens, deliveries are far more common on futures contracts than anyone has supposed, whether in terms of their absolute number or in proportion to the size of the market. In perhaps the only contribution to general knowledge about futures markets to have come out of the Hunt silver case, I investigated the level of deliveries for a range of commodity futures markets. Table 6.1 provides summary statistics for silver, gold, copper, and platinum, evidence I presented at the trial; and for hard wheat, evidence I compiled since then (Peck and Williams, 1991). Sometimes as much as 50 percent of exchange-certified stocks changes hands during a month through deliveries. The Kansas City Board of Trade wheat market and the Comex copper market show considerable variation in the number and timing of deliveries within the delivery month, mostly in conjunction with the seasonal variation in carrying charges. Although gold and platinum deliveries are less obviously connected to carrying charges, they vary considerably. For any particular month in any particular commodity, it is very difficult to say when a particular level of deliveries is unnaturally high.

In silver itself, deliveries are often substantial, as Figure 6.1 shows clearly for the five principal contracts on Comex each year. Even if only first-day deliveries are considered – some warehouse receipts are retendered until they arrive in a pair of "strong hands" where they are held for some time – more often than not, 25 million troy ounces change hands each delivery month.[9] Whether in terms of value, in terms of the peak open

---

8   Another long-established text, Baer and Saxon (1949, pp. 127–8), provides another example: "The fundamental purpose of traders in the *physical* markets is *to make or take actual delivery* of specific grades of the physical commodity when the contracts mature to delivery date ... On the other hand, the fundamental purpose of the traders in *exchange* [i.e., futures] contracts is primarily *not to make or take delivery*, but to cancel out every purchase by an offsetting sale (and vice versa), thereby avoiding all deliveries and settling all differences by cash payments" (emphasis in original).

9   Because the records of the Kansas City Board of Trade distinguish original from retendered deliveries, Table 6.1 for hard wheat includes both ways of measuring the importance of deliveries.

Table 6.1. *Average deliveries on futures contracts for various commodities (standard deviations in parentheses)*

	Deliveries in 1,000 contracts	Deliveries as percent of contract's peak open interest	Deliveries as percent of certified stocks
Comex silver, 1977–1987[a]			
Entire month	8.842	31.56	44.23
	(4.023)	(15.42)	(12.45)
First day	4.086	13.92	19.89
	(2.422)	7.41	(7.91)
Comex gold, 1978–1987[b]			
Entire month	13.716	35.57	53.88
	(5.426)	(11.59)	(21.15)
First day	5.436	14.41	21.18
	(2.811)	(6.75)	(10.45)
Comex copper, 1977–1987[a]			
Entire month	6.330	19.99	43.98
	(3.420)	(11.39)	(19.78)
First day	3.357	10.26	21.20
	(2.315)	(5.95)	(10.58)
NYMEX platinum, 1975–1987[c]			
Entire month	1.572	25.12	39.84
	(1.102)	(15.22)	(21.50)
Kansas City wheat, 1973–1987[a]			
Entire month	1.018	8.85	26.20
	(0.952)	(8.77)	(20.10)
First day	0.360	3.36	7.81
	(0.561)	(6.04)	(10.86)
Original deliveries	0.722	6.51	18.55
	(0.710)	(7.20)	(14.08)

[a] Five delivery months annually: March, May, July, September, December.
[b] Six delivery months annually: February, April, June, August, October, December.
[c] Four delivery months annually: January, April, July, October.
Stocks are measured at the end of the preceding month.

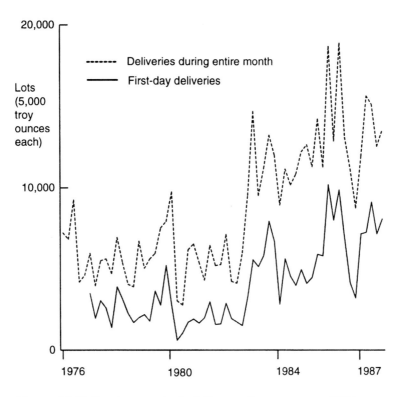

Figure 6.1. Deliveries on principal Comex silver contracts, 1976 through 1987

interest, or in terms of exchange-certified stocks, silver deliveries are substantial. Equally relevant, silver deliveries vary considerably from month to month and year to year.

If the substantial average level and variability in deliveries for commodities in general and silver in particular had been more widely appreciated, perhaps the experts characterizing deliveries as manipulative acts would have been more circumspect. More to the point, their characterization rested on an assumption that deliveries on futures contracts are rare, which was never later confirmed. For that matter, my assertion that it is difficult to identify the Hunts' deliveries as out of line in the silver market also rests on an assumption, namely that long-term investors are prominent among those taking delivery in precious metals. My need to make an assumption is perhaps the more defensible, given that I would have needed access to the records of many individual traders to test it, whereas a test of the assumption that deliveries are rare could have been conducted by glancing at Comex yearbooks. Embarrassingly for all experts on futures markets (I too had written an incantation about the rarity of deliveries [Williams, 1986, p. 4]), the dogma of negligible deliveries has long gone unchallenged. Had a fraction of the effort spent on the trial instead been spent on studying delivery practices in the silver market, an inference about manipulative intent from the Hunts' deliveries would have been much more soundly based.

Professors Kyle and Houthakker found particularly suspect the Hunts' taking of deliveries when spreads fell below full carrying charges. Here, too, their analysis began with an assumption, namely that no rational investor would take delivery if spreads were less than full carrying charges as conventionally measured. More precisely, the assumption hides within the conventional definition of carrying charges. "Full carrying charges" are defined to be warehouse fees and interest expenses; subtleties like taxes are ignored. Oh, the complications from taxes! Put briefly, the tax laws prevailing in 1979 and 1980 gave an incentive for someone whose long position had appreciated to take delivery. Taking delivery was not a "taxable event," whereas closing out the position or rolling it over into a more distant delivery month was. If the capital gain was short-term, a tax rate of 70 percent conceivably applied. Furthermore, taxes would be due on the bullion taken in delivery only when it was sold, whereas interest and vault fees paid to carry the commodity would be deductible when incurred.[10]

I tried to illustrate the complications due to taxes briefly at the trial and at greater length in my report to the CFTC, through the tax computations of a hypothetical speculator. Here Table 6.2 presents a large speculator who enjoys a substantial short-term paper gain by late November 1979 and is considering four strategies for liquidating this position in December '79 futures, which are priced at a slight premium to later delivery dates.[11] As Table 6.2 tries to show, the speculator, depending on her tax situation, would perfectly rationally take delivery despite the spread below full carrying charges. For her, in some situations, the spread is not below full carrying charges. Among the four tax situations, only if the speculator had a large short-term capital loss in tax year 1979 (in which case the effective tax rate on a short-term gain is zero), would it be rational not to take delivery. In the more likely situation of substantial ordinary income in all tax years, the speculator's optimal strategy would be to take delivery while

---

10   Selig and Scmittberger (1977), Schapiro (1981), and Rudnick et al. (1983) explain some of the arcane tax rules applicable at the time, many of which were unsettled, due to the IRS often changing its interpretations.

11   Table 6.2 supposes that any tax-loss carried forward will be used eventually. It also supposes that no new opportunities might arise in future tax years that would cause the speculator to regret having used the capital losses earlier. Finally, it does not distinguish between the before-tax interest rate and the after-tax discount rate. Any of these complications is likely to add to the reasons for taking delivery.

Table 6.2. *A hypothetical speculator's delivery decision in various tax situations*

===

Hypothetical situation

In mid-August 1979, a speculator bought 100 December '79 silver futures contracts at $9.00 per troy ounce. By late November 1979, the contracts' price has increased to $19.00. Whereas the interest rate is 1% per month, the prices for more distant delivery dates increase from the December '79 price at 0.5% per month: Silver spreads are slightly below full carrying charges conventionally measured. Believing that prices will increase no further, the speculator wishes to end this exposure while preserving as much of the $5 million gain as possible from taxes.

Possible strategies

Strategy *a*: Offset December '79 contracts through a direct sale.
Strategy *b*: Sell January '80 contracts, take delivery on December '79
   contracts, make delivery eventually on January '80 contracts.
Strategy *c*: Sell August '80 contracts, take delivery on December '79
   contracts, make delivery eventually on August '80 contracts.
Strategy *d*: Sell January '81 contracts, take delivery on December '79
   contracts, make delivery eventually on January '81 contracts.
(Any deliveries taken are financed with borrowed funds.)

Tax rules to consider

i.   Gains from futures held less than six months are short-term.
ii. Gains on the commodity taken in delivery are long-term if
       commodity held one year from inception of futures position.
iii. Interest expenses are deductible against ordinary income.
iv. Capital losses can be deducted only against capital gains of like
       kind but can be transferred forward to subsequent tax years.
(Short-term gains and ordinary income taxed at 70%, long-term, 20%.)

	Effective current tax per troy ounce	Extent the spread would have to be below full carry for delivery not to be taken
Speculator has $6 million short-term capital loss in tax year 1979		
Strategy *a*	$0.00	—
Strategy *b*	0.88	> 0.0 % per month
Strategy *c*	> 1.45	> 0.0
Strategy *d*	> 2.17	> 0.0
Speculator anticipates $6 million short-term capital loss in tax year 1980		
Strategy *a*	7.00	—
Strategy *b*	0.88	32.7
Strategy *c*	1.45	4.6
Strategy *d*	> 1.68	2.7
Speculator anticipates $6 million long-term capital loss in tax year 1980		
Strategy *a*	> 8.58	—
Strategy *b*	> 7.88	4.2
Strategy *c*	0.89	6.3
Strategy *d*	2.18	3.1
Speculator anticipates substantial ordinary income in all tax years		
Strategy *a*	7.00	—
Strategy *b*	6.30	4.1
Strategy *c*	2.44	3.9
Strategy *d*	2.26	2.4

recommitting for redelivery in the most distant tax year possible. Spreads would have to be far more below full carrying charges, specifically 2.4 percent per month, equivalent to a substantial backwardation in silver prices, for delivery not to be the speculator's "economic" choice.

Generally speaking, investigators ought not conclude that someone's financial dealings are irrational or manipulative without knowing the underlying tax situation. (And each individual's tax situation would depend in part on his own forecast of the type, size, and timing of future capital gains and losses, a forecast that may be difficult to reconstruct after the fact.) In the Hunt case, none of the expert witnesses understood the effect of taxes on the Hunts' actions. The plaintiff's and the CFTC Division of Enforcement's experts characterized the Hunts' deliveries as irrational in the face of spreads below full carrying charges and thereby assumed that the Hunts were free of tax considerations. Although the defense experts (including a tax expert) explained how tax considerations could have mattered, they failed to say whether such considerations had actually played a part in the Hunts' decisions, because they did not have access to the relevant tax records.[12] The Hunts in their own testimony only alluded to their approach to taxes. No memos detailing calculations of the potential tax consequences were forthcoming, nor was the tax treatment of their previous silver deliveries offered as evidence of the interactions of delivery strategies and taxes.[13] In the end, the jury was left to rely on experts who themselves had left many issues unexplored about "economic" deliveries.[14]

6.2   Exchanges for physicals

While Bunker Hunt, Herbert Hunt, and IMIC were taking delivery on many

[12] Minpeco's attorney, in the closing argument, took me to task for this (Trial Transcript, p. 16576).

[13] From other testimony at the trial, it seems that Herbert Hunt, for one, paid taxes in 1979 at the "alternative minimum tax" rate of 25 percent. Given that this rate applied regardless, the effective tax on a rollover in late 1979 might have been zero. Then again, a transaction involving an appreciable number of futures contracts might have induced a large enough gain to supersede this tax rate. Furthermore, in 1979, Herbert Hunt did not take delivery when spreads were below full carrying charges conventionally measured. Only a complete picture of Herbert Hunt's tax planning in both 1979 and 1980 would reveal whether his deliveries could be explained through the complications from taxes.

[14] Market professionals would not necessarily have provided better analysis. Joe Ritchie, who conducted the highly specialized arbitrage between Chicago and New York silver futures, discussed the Hunts in an interview reported in Schwager (1992, pp. 342–62). He emphasized the Hunts as taking deliveries uneconomically in the face of spreads below full carrying charges, yet misrepresented the premium for immediate delivery as $15, not $3 to $4, and mentioned taxes not at all, although he surely considered taxes in his own arbitrage operations. In short, this topic of deliveries may be too complicated for any one person to understand fully.

futures contracts, they consummated exchanges of futures for physicals (negotiated with the principal commercial dealers) for an even greater amount of silver. In its complaint, the CFTC Division of Enforcement classified these EFPs as manipulative acts because they absorbed silver that otherwise would have been available to the market. Their expert's supporting analysis consisted of brief, sweeping statements such as the Hunts "did not use the EFP transactions as opportunities to roll forward deliveries later into 1980, but instead negotiated delivery schedules which matched closely the deliveries that would have occurred on their futures positions" (Kyle CFTC Report, p. 61). Echoing the CFTC Division of Enforcement's interpretation, the plaintiff's expert testified that "the net effect of these EFPs was to reinforce the defendants' control of the market" (Trial Transcript, p. 8652). Yet he elaborated not at all, offering no analysis of particular EFPs. In response, I testified about the EFPs slightly more extensively. Yet my testimony aimed merely at broad conclusions (even though I had studied each and every EFP in its excruciating detail). None of the Hunts' counterparties testified. Thus, the jury, although expected to deduce the Hunts' purpose for the EFPs, learned little about the particulars of the transactions.

That the jury was not asked to endure detailed analysis of the EFPs is not surprising. Even the most straightforward of them were exceedingly complex, as the one arranged on January 16, 1980 between Philipp Brothers and Bunker Hunt demonstrates. In the EFP reproduced in Table 6.3, the essentials of the agreement, namely the exchange of Bunker Hunt's 1,400 March '80 contracts for the equivalent seven million troy ounces of bullion at the previous day's settlement price of $37.50, do not jump out. Because the bullion was to be delivered other than on the first business day in March, the prices were adjusted with less than obvious premiums and discounts. The discount for the segment for January 30 delivery to $36.985 corresponds to 15 percent interest over the thirty-three business days to March 3 – not that the agreement itself explained this. The premiums over $37.50 for the segments for March 31 delivery and for July 1 delivery correspond to interest computed from March 3 at 6 percent per annum, not 15 percent.[15] Again these computations are not manifest in the agreement itself.

These premiums and discounts for delivery dates other than March 3 correspond to the spreads prevailing in the futures market on January 16, which is to say, Phibro (or Bunker Hunt) could have made much the same rescheduling through the futures market directly. Phibro, however, received three advantages not available through the futures market, and not mentioned in the agreement itself. First, its bullion, although not in Comex-approved vaults, was treated in exactly the same way as deliverable bullion. Second, Phibro did not post any security, such as a letter of credit, while

---

[15]   Put differently, Phibro paid $0.25 per troy ounce per month to delay delivery.

Table 6.3. *Text of EFP between Phibro and Bunker Hunt, January 16, 1980*

This confirms the exchange agreement whereby we [Philipp Brothers] agreed to sell and deliver to you [Bunker Hunt] and you agree to purchase and accept from us 7,000,000 troy ounces .999 Bar Silver at times and places and for the amounts set forth in the annexed Schedule A against payment in immediately available funds wire transferred to Philipp Brothers' account, Chase Manhattan Bank, in the amount calculated as provided in the annexed schedule and you have sold and delivered to us and we have purchased and accepted from you January 16, 1980 1,400 Comex contracts for the purchase of March 1980 Silver in the amount of 7,000,000 troy ounces. We will give you telex advice two business days prior to each delivery.

This transaction is an exchange for physical (EFP) as provided by the rules of the Commodity Exchange, Inc., New York, New York and as to the 1,400 contracts is priced at U.S. Dollars $37.50 per troy ounce, and as to the physical metal is priced as set forth on the annexed Schedule A.

... [paragraph on force majeure] ...

You have converted to us your right, title, and interest in and to certain silver described below as collateral security for the performance of your obligations set forth herein. The silver consists of:

(A) 2,730,000 troy ounces of Silver which we have sold to you pursuant to our exchange for physical (EFP) sale to you of January 14, 1980, and

(B) 1,200,000 troy ounces of Silver which you represent that you have purchased from Sharps–Pixley, deliverable ex Engelhard Industries Refinery, Newark, New Jersey, on March 3, 1980.

... [paragraph on arbitration of claims] ...

... [signatures] ...

Schedule A

Quantity	Place of delivery	Date of delivery	Price
2,000,000 troy ounces	Engelhard Industries Refinery, NJ	January 30, 1980	$36.985 per troy ounce
2,000,000 troy ounces	Engelhard Industries Refinery, NJ	March 31, 1980	$37.677 per troy ounce
3,000,000 troy ounces	London Silver Market at Derby & Co. Ltd.	July 1, 1980	$38.2585 per troy ounce

Bunker Hunt did (by pledging physical silver). Third and most important, Phibro received what amounted to a substantial interest-free loan for the term of the EFP. This feature results from the price-move limits in effect on the March '80 contract, which was trading through the straddle market at the equivalent of $47.70 at the close on January 15.[16] Phibro faced prospective variation margin of some $9.70 per troy ounce payable nearly immediately. (Recall the discussion of the problems of commercial shorts in Section 2.4.) By avoiding the interest on $67.9 million of variation margin until delivery of the physical silver, Phibro gained about what it lost in spreads at 6 percent instead of 15 percent.

Did the EFP on January 16 between Phibro and Bunker Hunt relieve the immediate demand for Comex-certificated stocks? Did Bunker Hunt extract an advantage from Phibro? These were the questions the jurors needed to answer. But they could not possibly have interpreted the EFP in Table 6.3 themselves, because it and the other EFPs were so complex. The intermediation of experts was required. Indeed, because the jury never actually read the EFPs, either when deliberating in the jury room amid all the evidence formally submitted or when hearing the EFPs discussed during testimony, the jury's impression of the mechanism and purpose of EFPs came solely from the experts. Accordingly, the assumptions from which the experts reasoned, even if not obvious, determined the information the jury received.

The reasoning of the CFTC Division of Enforcement's experts and the plaintiff's experts went like this: It is unnatural to use futures contracts to obtain physical silver; the EFPs resulted in the delivery of physical silver, hence the EFPs must be unnatural and manipulative. This characterization of EFPs rests on the same assumption as that behind their view of deliveries as a manipulative act. At the very least, therefore, the EFPs were not separate indicia of manipulation.

The defense experts' analysis of the Hunts' EFPs had the same starting point as their analysis of the Hunts' deliveries – namely, someone such as the Hunts with a long position had the contractual right to receive certificated bullion in a specific month. The chain of logic continued like this: While permitting shorts some flexibility, a cornerer would extract an advantage; because the Hunts offered generous terms to their counterparties in the EFPs, they could not have been manipulators. Thus, the defense implicitly assumed that any generous act disproved manipulative intent. Because the CFTC Division of Enforcement implicitly assumed that all acts

[16]   It may seem that from a price of $36.985 for January delivery while the spot price was $46.30 Phibro was selling its bullion at below market value, in order to leave the silver market at any cost. On the contrary, the price-move limits in effect on the March '80 contract are the reason for the strange price. Bunker Hunt surrendered his futures contracts at a corresponding amount below their market value. Fay (1982, p. 156) and the SEC (1982, p. 37, note 16) make this mistake in interpreting the EFPs.

ought to be generous, two such opposite characterizations of the EFPs as contributing to or relieving congestion were inevitable.

Strangely, no expert offered any evidence about the use and terms of EFPs by any traders other than the Hunts. The Hunts' EFPs were simply assumed to be unusual. Yet EFPs, like deliveries, may be more common than generally thought.[17] From data Comex has made available about the silver market (unfortunately not including the years before 1980), it would seem EFPs of the size of the Hunts' occur on 10 percent of days; the daily average of EFPs involves some 1,000 futures contracts, predominately in the months nearest to the delivery period. Without such standards of comparison, experts, let alone a jury, would have difficulty deducing the purpose of a particular EFP.

Still more troubling was that Minpeco's lawyers suggested the Hunts' EFPs were part of a super-rational plot. My testimony that the Hunts extracted little advantage from their EFPs with the principal commercial shorts was met with the idea that the Hunts were generous to those shorts to persuade them to acquiesce in the squeeze of the remaining shorts. Quite apart from whether the interpretation is plausible, it undermines the notion that the Hunts' intent can be inferred from particular actions.

6.3   Lamar Hunt's switch trades

Lamar Hunt purchased distant silver futures contracts on eight days in late December 1979 and mid-January 1980, when trading in all but the January '80 contract was restricted by price-move limits. On those days, trades in the more distant delivery months, say September '80, required two steps: a purchase of the unrestricted January '80 contract at the open market price and a "straddle" (with the short leg in the January '80 contract and the long leg in the September '80 contract) at the straddle's open market price. These "switch" trades, as they came to be called at the trial, received attention out of all proportion to the number of contracts involved. Before the trial, they were the subject of lengthy affidavits. At the trial, the plaintiff's expert singled them out, inviting lengthy, indeed the most acrimonious, cross-examination. Similarly, they constituted a significant portion of my own testimony.

The switch trades were battled over primarily because they connected Lamar Hunt and his financial resources to Minpeco's case. (The CFTC Division of Enforcement had not included Lamar Hunt in its complaint.) In a videotaped deposition replayed at the trial, Lamar Hunt fielded questions

---

[17]   In the grain markets, seemingly, EFPs are frequently used just before a futures contract approaches the delivery period. In NYMEX's crude oil market, cumulative EFPs often outnumber the peak open interest in a delivery month.

about his handwritten trading records, especially the recorded losses computed from the January '80 contracts involved with the switches. Although he only dimly remembered his broker's explanation of the style of trading on days affected by price-move limits, he made the unguarded statement that the losses on the January '80 contracts – as much as $7 per troy ounce – were a sacrifice he had to make to get more contracts.

The plaintiff's expert, quoting this testimony, characterized Lamar Hunt's switches as "repeatedly forcing his way into the market on limit days in an uneconomical manner through the use of straddles" (Houthakker affidavit, 4 September 1987). He computed Lamar Hunt's losses on the January '80 component of the switches to be some $20 million. He asserted that such switches were a highly unusual form of trading, from which Lamar Hunt's intent could be inferred as manipulative (Trial Transcript, pp. 8591–4).

Switches are actually a standard form of trading, although they are hardly straightforward transactions, easily grasped by a jury.[18] Switches, or more properly, the style of trading on Comex on days with price-move limits in effect, requires much knowledge of institutional details of that exchange. Lamar Hunt did not understand them. Neither did the plaintiff's expert.[19]

The nature of switches can be understood with the aid of Figure 6.2, which shows the course of silver prices during Monday, December 31, 1979. (See also Figures 4.4 and 4.7 for other analyses of price movements on this date.) Throughout that Monday,[20] the price of the January '80 contract stood considerably above the previous Friday's closing price of $29.35. Figure 6.2(b), based on Comex's Time and Sales Report, shows the timing of each change in price.[21] From the opening to the close, the March '80 contract was "locked up the limit" at $29.05, $1.00 above its previous settlement price. No seller would offer the March '80 contract at $29.05. Nevertheless, that Monday's volume in the March '80 contract was 1,153 contracts, of which Lamar Hunt's were merely 23. Lamar Hunt and others traded the March '80 contract by way of the January '80 contract and a "straddle" January '80–March '80. This straddle market is a real market,

---

[18]   Minpeco itself used switches during the last days of December while closing out some positions on Comex.

[19]   Professor Kyle, who for his study of spreads (reported in Section 3.4) used the straddle market on days with price-move limits, took Comex's institutional details as self-evident. Over 1979 and 1980 while working for a CBOT member firm, he had observed the silver market's operations during days with price-move limits.

[20]   The market closed one hour early for the New Year's holiday.

[21]   Lamar Hunt's outright trading in the January '80 contract occurred in three approximately ten-minute segments, for they can be identified from his records of prices paid. The timing of his trades in the straddle market is more difficult to reconstruct (except for eight straddles at the close, because their price of $0.915 was unique that day).

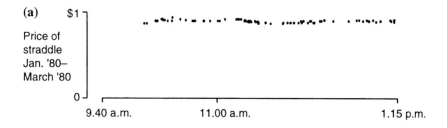

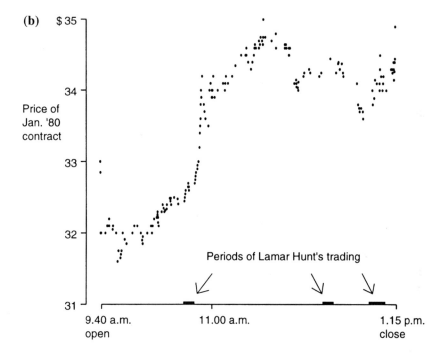

Figure 6.2. Comex straddle and spot month markets, December 31, 1979

with a market price, as shown in Figure 6.2(a), where each trade that day is plotted. Rarely did as many as five minutes pass without some transaction in this straddle market, all within the range $0.870 to $0.920.

The nature of transactions in the straddle market were manifest only to those familiar with Comex. Although participants in the straddle market bargained over this price of some $0.90 per troy ounce, the clearinghouse recorded it differently. The March "leg" was entered at $29.05, officially the maximum permissible price, and the January "leg" at $29.05 minus $0.90, namely $28.15. The $5 loss on buying a January '80 contract at $34.00 and selling it within minutes at $28.15 was purely an artifice of the clearinghouse's accounting. The March '80 contract was booked by the clearinghouse at the same $5.00 below its market value. This gain would have been realized as soon as the limits on settlement prices caught up with the market.[22] Put differently, if the March '80 contract had traded directly, its price would have been some $0.90 above the January '80 contract's price at any moment during December 31. This technique of circumventing the price limits (with the full acquiescence of the exchange) worked so smoothly that many outside investors would not even have been aware of it.

If this exposition of Lamar Hunt's switches on limit-move days continues to leave them unintelligible, the main idea of this section has been accomplished. No jury could possibly understand such trading techniques intuitively. And the testimony necessary to instruct the jury would amount to overkill. First, a preliminary and simple definition of a price-move limit would be required. Second, the arbitrage between the straddle market and the market for individual delivery months would have to be demonstrated, including testimony about how Comex records straddles on its Time and Sales reports. Third, the similarities among the straddle market on days without price-move limits, on days with price-move limits for some hours, and days with price-move limits throughout would need to be established. (Recall Figure 2.2.) Fourth, the importance of the free market in the spot month would have to be emphasized. Fifth, some testimony about floor brokerage practice would be needed, to make sense of why orders are broken into smaller lots and why the spot month is sometimes executed before the straddle and sometimes after. No doubt, to place this testimony in the category of "facts" rather than expert opinion, actual Comex floor traders would be required to testify, with their inevitable jargon – "opened up the limit," "tick," "back leg" – of no help to the jury's comprehension. And should the jury have been led by means of all this testimony to understand Comex floor practices on days with price-move limits in effect, they would still have faced the task of inferring Lamar Hunt's intention.

Far from simple actions, like the switch trades, depend for interpretation on an expert witness, whose opinion in turn depends on assumptions. An expert witness resists reflecting on the chain of reasoning behind his opinion while being cross-examined. Under cross-examination, I, for example, admitted only grudgingly that my interpretation of the Comex's Time and

---

22 Because the purely book-keeping loss on the January '80 leg was recorded in one tax year and the purely book-keeping gain not recorded until the next tax year, Lamar Hunt (and others) may have received a tax benefit too, under the tax laws at that time. Nevertheless, the motive for such trades was not tax deferral.

Sales reports was based on the assumption that the spot month trade was connected to a straddle inasmuch as the reports did not name the individual trader (Trial Transcript, pp. 13742–5). Even after thirty minutes of cross-examination about Lamar Hunt's single switch trade of January 15, the plaintiff's expert had not conceded that he had assumed the long leg of that switch to have made no profit on paper (Trial Transcript, pp. 8966–86). What cross-examination could possibly have revealed his crucial assumption that price-move limits on Comex operated identically to those on grain markets where they originated?[23] The plaintiff's expert, who, unlike most economists, had a general knowledge of price-move limits, reasonably would consider his assumption plausible, even though it was wrong.[24] Comfortable with his assumption, he would have fended off almost any question on cross-examination.

Under cross-examination, the plaintiff's expert ultimately agreed that he described Lamar Hunt's switch transactions as uneconomic because he believed Lamar Hunt had bought his long positions at excessively high prices (Trial Transcript, p. 8986). In other words, Lamar Hunt's purchases were at issue regardless of the method of effecting them. Indeed, the relevant issue was why some of these positions were in the congested March '80 contract. From these trades broadly considered, perhaps the jury could have inferred intent without the "filter" of an expert. The experts' discussion of the switches was extraneous.

6.4   Changed patterns in trading

Although Bunker and Herbert Hunt had traded silver futures contracts for a number of years, they altered their style of trading about mid-June 1979. As described in Chapter 2, they had previously established new positions and had rolled expiring contracts into the nearest delivery months, yet from mid-June 1979 onwards, they employed delivery months much more dis-

---

[23]   As of 1980, all the grain contracts, including the spot month, were subject to price-move limits and so when prices moved up the limit, trading in all delivery months would cease. On CBOT grain markets now, no price limits apply to the spot month during the month-long expiry. Thus, during five of every twelve months, the CBOT grain markets need not be closed by price-move limits, in exactly the fashion for Comex metals markets in 1979 and 1980. Since 1986, as it happens, Comex has rescinded its price-move limits; all delivery months trade freely. Meanwhile, some of the financial futures markets that previously had no price-move limits have instituted a system of a mandatory thirty-minute pause in trading after a large price move (so-called circuit breakers). In sum, these institutional details vary exchange by exchange and period by period.

[24]   Professor Houthakker is not alone in misunderstanding the Comex straddle market on days with price-move limits. Bailey and Ng (1991) construct an elaborate test of intertemporal spreads in Comex silver during 1979 and 1980 without recognizing that they need not guess the spreads on days with price-move limits.

tant, at least six months ahead. Whereas formerly they had outright long positions, in mid-June 1979 they added substantial straddles, with both legs in 1980, the long legs the nearer of the two delivery months. Prior to this, they had traded on their own account, but after mid-June, they and two others formed IMIC as a separate corporation with the avowed purpose of acquiring physical silver.

The CFTC Division of Enforcement and Minpeco pointed to the changed trading style that began in the summer of 1979 as the start of a manipulative scheme.[25] The shift to longer maturities, they said, was a plan to target the February '80 and March '80 contracts. The straddles, they said, "were a low-cost way [for a manipulator] to establish quickly a large long position in a particular contract month in the next year without attracting notice" (Kyle CFTC Report, p. 58).

Mid-June 1979 coincided with the arrival of a new financial advisor to the Hunts, who attempted to reduce the expenses of their in-and-out trading. Attempts were made to consolidate the Hunts' positions into fewer accounts. Also, as of mid-June, tax-loss carry forwards from some investments in earlier years looked to be exhausted. The straddles placed in June were at least consistent with the well-known tax deferral scheme described in Section 2.1.

The straddles placed in June 1979 undoubtedly are significant, for no other reason than they expanded considerably the gross long position. Were it not for Herbert Hunt's long leg in the February '80 contract and Bunker Hunt's long leg in the March '80 contract, the Hunts' positions would have much less of an appearance of targeting particular delivery months, as can be seen in Table 6.4. Surely, if silver prices had moved into marked backwardation, with the February '80 and March '80 contracts much higher in price than contracts for later delivery, these straddles would have been the centerpiece of the allegations of a manipulation. As it was, the Hunts lost money on these straddles, even at the price peak in January 1980. Even though the March '80–July '80 spread, for example, was below full carrying charges, the distant leg had appreciated more than the nearby leg, approaching $1.00 per troy ounce. Had the Hunts' positions been even more strongly in straddles, they would have experienced net losses at the peak price, and it would have seemed ludicrous that such straddles were the main component of a manipulative scheme.

The plaintiff, however, drew attention in closing arguments to the straddles because of the very losses incurred (Trial Transcript, pp. 16580–2). The losses, according to the plaintiff, proved the straddles to be "uneconomic," and because no rational investor would undertake uneco-

---

[25] No one seems to have dwelt on one constant aspect of the Hunts' trading: their habit of taking deliveries.

Table 6.4. *Futures positions of Bunker Hunt (NBH) and Herbert Hunt (WHH) on February 15 and August 15, 1979 (contracts short in parentheses)*

February 15			August 15 without straddles			August 15 with straddles		
Delivery month	NBH	WHH	Delivery month	NBH	WHH	Delivery month	NBH	WHH
Mar '79	926	316	Sept '79	0	15	Sept '79	0	15
April	920	1,092	Oct	0	31	Oct	0	31
May	2,219	2,199	Nov	0	0	Nov	0	0
June	900	55	Dec	0	299	Dec	0	299
July		0	Jan '80	0	200	Jan '80	0	200
Aug		50	Feb	3,030	846	Feb	3,030	2,266
Sept		0	Mar	6,048	330	Mar	11,838	330
Oct		31	April	0	0	April	500	(1,420)
			May	6,048	330	May	0	2,670
			June	0		June	0	0
			July	150		July	(2,500)	(4,500)
						Aug	0	
						Sept	(740)	
						Oct	0	
						Nov	0	
						Jan '81	0	
						Feb	0	
						Mar	(2,550)	
						April	(500)	

nomic investments, the straddles therefore exposed the Hunts' manipulative scheme. This argument surreptitiously twists the standards of inference, for the *ex ante* purpose of the straddles was to be inferred from the *ex post* outcome.[26] More important, this type of argument produces a no-win situation for the defendants: If *ex post* the straddles made money, the jury should infer manipulative intent; if *ex post* they lost money, again the jury should infer manipulative intent. Needless to say, Minpeco and its expert did not make the assumptions behind this reasoning clear to the jury.

The analysis of IMIC also shows that an inference about intent requires

[26] By this *ex post* standard, the Hunts' positions in their entirety should be judged an investment because they made substantial gains through January 1980, or September 1980, for that matter.

some preliminary assumptions about the nature of manipulation. If "manipulation" means the creating and taking advantage of congestion, a steady delivery schedule, which would put no pressure on any particular month, would presumably minimize congestion. According to Table 6.5, which shows the distribution of IMIC's futures and forwards the day they reached their peak, IMIC's positions look close to the non-manipulative ideal.[27] Although IMIC's delivery schedule was consistent with its avowed business purpose of acquiring bullion and becoming a dealer, the plaintiff's expert claimed that to use futures contract to do so was contrary to sensible practice. This claim, again, rests on assumptions about the purpose of futures markets. Moreover, the plaintiff's expert also argued that, because normal business practice for dealers is to be "hedged" (i.e., to have a short futures position in distant delivery months against their bullion holdings), IMIC's lack of short hedging revealed another purpose, namely manipulation. Yet, had IMIC established these short positions together with its bullion, the effect would have been the same as straddles. Bunker and Herbert Hunts' straddles, which would have allowed them to "bury the corpse," supposedly indicated manipulative intent. Thus, the presence and absence of essentially the same action were both construed as revealing manipulative intent.

The plaintiff also pointed to the Conti group's positions *vis-à-vis* the Hunts' in the summer of 1979 as evidence of manipulative intent. The Conti group's positions were primarily in the December '79 (Comex) contracts, whereas Bunker and Herbert Hunts' holdings were primarily in the February '80 and March '80 contracts. According to the plaintiff, this trading in different delivery months, far from suggesting a lack of coordination between the Conti group and the Hunts, indicated a meticulously laid and subtle plan to disguise their collaboration from regulators. Such a plan is at least conceivable. However, had the Hunts' positions been predominately in the December '79 contract, surely that overlap with the Conti group's positions would have been presented as evidence of coordination. Thus, almost any combination of the Conti group's positions and the Hunts' positions could be presented as indicating manipulative intent.

All actions taken by the Hunts prior to the market turmoil of December 1979 through March 1980 are inherently ambiguous about intent because of the considerable passage of time. For example, perhaps the straddles were put on quite innocently in June 1979, but some time later, because of intervening events, the Hunts might have realized conditions were ripe for a corner. It is also possible to imagine a scenario in which the straddles were placed with evil intent but later, due to changed circumstances, the scheme

---

[27]   This impression is all the stronger upon remembering that no November contract is traded and the January contract is lightly traded.

Table 6.5. *IMIC's positions on August 31, 1979 (including London forward contracts in 5,000 troy ounce units)*

Delivery month	Number of contracts
September '79	709
October	580
November	0
December	1,863
January '80	75
February	925
March	1,035
April	1,000
May	955
June	990
July	1,000
August	226
September	135

was quietly abandoned. The greater the number of intervening events, the less the act of purchasing the straddles can reveal intent.

In their own testimony, the Hunts only made their actions of the summer of 1979 seem more ambiguous. For example, Herbert Hunt testified that he had placed the straddles as long-the-nearby and short-the-distant because he was "bullish" on silver. In most commodity markets, this type of straddle is indeed called a "bull straddle," for the simple reason that when the price of such a commodity rises, the nearby contracts typically appreciate relative to the more distant delivery months.[28] This relative appreciation in price is just a tendency, however, and one not usually seen in precious metals, where, consequently, the straddle short-the-nearby and long-the-distant carries the name "bull straddle." Not least because he mischaracterized his straddles as "bullish," Herbert Hunt was made through particularly effective cross-examination to look evasive. Furthermore, he offered no explanation of why, even if he wanted to be long-the-nearby, the long leg was not in a much more distant contract than February '80.

In sum, the jury's attention was drawn to the patterns of the Hunts' trading in the summer of 1979, with the general proposition before them that they could sensibly draw inferences about intent from these actions. The jury, however, was given an essentially impossible task, for the general

---

[28] That is, high prices and backwardations tend to coincide, as in the base metals shown in Figure 3.5.

proposition was wrong. Whatever the *ex post* outcome of a trade and whatever the connection of these actions to the Hunts' other transactions, an equally plausible argument could be made for manipulation or for an investment strategy. Whatever the intent at the time of the action, it could have changed in the course of events.

6.5   Relations with regulators

On October 22, 1979, Herbert Hunt assured the Business Conduct Committee of the CBOT that he would not take delivery on his February '80 contracts should spreads remain below full carrying charges. The jury heard testimony from a representative of the Business Conduct Committee that Herbert Hunt had said "you can call me a liar if I do," then took delivery despite spreads below full carrying charges. On his list of the Hunts' actions from which could be inferred manipulative intent, the plaintiff's expert included a category, "misrepresentations to regulators," by which he meant this specific incident.[29]

On January 7, 1980, Comex imposed position limits effective on February 18. As mentioned in Section 2.4, the following day, Bunker Hunt rolled back 468 of his March '80 contracts, into the January '80 contract, and to that extent evaded the position limits. Professor Kyle in his report for the CFTC Division of Enforcement represented Bunker Hunt's action as having been made to thwart the desires of Comex officials.

Although both these actions seem simple enough to speak for themselves, the discussion of them at the trial demonstrated otherwise. Most revealing was an exchange, not before the jury, concerning whether the plaintiff's expert should be allowed to state his own conclusions about Herbert Hunt's statement before the CBOT Business Conduct Committee. Mr. Robinson, an attorney for the defense, argued that the jury, having heard the relevant testimony themselves, did not need the plaintiff's expert's aid in the exercise of inferring intent. Judge Lasker understood that the plaintiff's expert "is assuming that false statement was made" and would say that, in his opinion, if Herbert Hunt lied, the lie would indicate manipulative intent (Trial Transcript, p. 8600).[30] There the discussion ended – yet the plaintiff's

---

[29]   Several other regulators and exchange officials testified and many more were deposed. Some of their statements were unfavorable to the Hunts and others favorable (such as that by the President of the CBOT, who said in a deposition taken by the CFTC Division of Enforcement that "the Hunts lived up to everything they told me to within the confines of normal, rational, reasonable behavior.") The issue here is not the conflicts among these various statements, which was the jury's concern, but the use of these statements in inferences about the Hunts' intent.

[30]   This careful wording was necessary in part to make Professor Houthakker not rely for his opinion on the credibility of another witness. For a discussion of the problems that arise from an expert's opinion about a witness's credibility, see Berger (1989).

expert's reasoning requires the proposition that only those who intend to manipulate are less than forthcoming with the Business Conduct Committee.[31] His reasoning also requires that a manipulator would plan to antagonize regulators. An expert could just as well deduce that Herbert Hunt's "lying to regulators" demonstrated his innocence of a larger manipulative scheme. (The jury might have, and probably did, draw from this incident as recounted by the Business Conduct Committee's representative some inference about Herbert Hunt's general commitment to tell the truth. The issue here, however, is whether the incident should be used by experts to infer the existence of a manipulative scheme.)

In addition, these two actions involving regulators cannot speak for themselves because they cannot be disengaged from events in the silver market at large. From October 1979, when Herbert Hunt promised not to take delivery on his contracts, to February 1980, when he did so, the CBOT and Comex had formulated rules on position limits and trading for liquidation only, whose combined effect fell strongly and disproportionately on the Hunts. Herbert Hunt could reasonably have concluded that the CBOT itself had so changed its policies as to release him from his announced plans. In the meantime, the liquidity of the straddle market on the CBOT had declined, which made it more difficult than in October for Herbert Hunt to roll over the February '80 contracts into later months. Finally, by mid-February, Herbert Hunt rolled 2,939 May '80 Comex contracts into September '80. Because the May '80 contract was in the group of "congested" delivery months along with the February '80 contract, these rollovers accomplished for the silver market as a whole most of the benefits of any rollover of February '80 contracts.

Likewise, Bunker Hunt's rollback of 468 March '80 contracts to January '80 needs to be placed in the context of the many March '80 contracts he did roll into more distant months. From January 15 through February 15, his rollovers of March '80 contracts into later months totaled 5,789, more than ten times the number of the action in dispute. Most prominently, on January 18, 1980, the day on which silver prices peaked, he rolled 2,500 March '80 contracts to September '80.[32] Thus, if these two actions involving regulators are placed in the context of the silver market over those months, it becomes less clear that the Hunts acted to thwart the regulators.

In the broader context of a decade of the Hunts' trading in many com-

---

[31] What ended was the discussion of Professor Houthakker's inference from the account of Herbert Hunt's appearance before the Business Conduct Committee. The defense attorneys later argued on appeal that Minpeco had failed to disclose that the Business Conduct Committee's representative had agreed to testify as part of an agreement in which Minpeco cropped its suit against the CBOT.

[32] Also, the spread between the January '80 and the March '80 contracts was at full carrying charges; delivery taken in January instead did not add to congestion.

modities, however, the ambiguity inherent in interpreting the purpose of the Hunts' two actions increases. To put the matter with some understatement, the Hunts and the regulators had had dealings before. Besides the dispute centered on the old-crop soybean futures during the spring of 1977, the Hunts also tangled with regulators over the size of their positions in soybeans in 1974. Their long history of being embroiled in controversy in commodities markets cuts both ways when considering the Hunts' intent in the silver market. From one perspective, the Hunts should have known that their every action would be scrutinized (as did happen), and hence they should have known not to make unguarded statements about their plans if they were engaged in a manipulation. From the other perspective, the Hunts could have concluded from the small penalties previously imposed that they could essentially ignore regulators' admonitions.

The Hunts' behavior toward regulators allows but one conclusion to be drawn unambiguously. Although during the silver crisis the Hunts broke no reporting requirement, exceeded no position limit, and ignored no written regulatory request, they did not cooperate fully with officials responsible for monitoring the markets.[33] For instance, they did not offer assistance to the CBOT Business Conduct Committee when the price of silver peaked in January 1980, nor did they propose to lease silver through CFTC auspices to anyone needing it. Although the Hunts may not have transgressed, they were never fastidious about public displays of deference to authority.

6.6   Intent in commodity markets

Because the jury had to decide whether the Hunts intended to manipulate the silver market, the lawyers directed attention to a number of the Hunts' specific actions. But inference of intent from such actions fails, for at least three reasons. First, a jury is provided with little idea of the range of actions in normal periods, which they need since they themselves have no experience with commodity markets. Second, the actions are rarely so simple that they can speak for themselves; an expert must interpret them. More than likely, the expert organizes that interpretation by assuming, perhaps without realizing it, one of the theories of intent, which the actions are supposed to reveal. Third, the logical chain from purpose to action is far from clear. If someone contemplating a manipulation can foresee the possibility of a trial, for example, his actions might be different. All three problems, moreover, are exaggerated by the very nature of a trial. A trial itself suggests that the actions under scrutiny are abnormal; it discourages an expert from acknowledging the chain of reasoning behind the interpretation of a par-

---

[33]   Imwinkelried (1984) would classify much of this evidence about the Hunts' relations with regulators as pertinent to the "uncharged misconduct" of not cooperating fully.

ticular action; and it encourages multiple explanations for a single action.

All trials shine a spotlight on particular actions of defendants. Often the actions themselves are in dispute. By the start of the Hunt trial, there was consensus at least about the number of deliveries they had taken, the days and amounts of the EFPs, and so forth. Yet there was no consensus about the actions of parties other than the defendants, such as the frequency of EFPs in futures markets under normal circumstances. It may be that EFPs in metals markets are rare, in which case the Hunts' EFPs look suspicious; or they may be common, in which case the Hunts' actions look normal. The jury was barely told such background information, mainly because no one knew it. After all, the legal proceedings were not arranged to fund sober academic study of the use of EFPs in futures markets.

The trial could have achieved a standard of comparison for the Hunts' actions, had the actions of the shorts, including Minpeco, been subject to the same scrutiny as that given to the Hunts. If any of the shorts were shown to have had manipulative intent, the style of analysis would have been exposed as flawed. Perhaps an even better comparison would have been with the U.S. government. It had a huge stock of silver, some 180 million troy ounces, which it held steadfastly through 1979 and 1980. If insistence on physical bullion, if refusal to "lend to the market" in times of less than full carrying charges, and if reluctance to exchange bullion for coins are all manipulative acts, could not the U.S. government have been accused of manipulative intent? Such a comparison verifies the considerable range of non-manipulative behavior.

The jury's only source of information on normal practices in commodity markets were the expert witnesses. Professor Kolb, an early witness for the plaintiff, instructed the jury on the peculiar terminology and practices of commodity markets. The defense attorneys found Professor Kolb's explanations dismayingly opaque and worried about the degree of understanding the jury had obtained. The jury received little further sense of normal practices from the experts who appeared later in the trial. Their testimonies were arranged not as disquisitions about commodity markets but as expressions of opinion. Ironically, the less those experts justified their own sense of normal practices and their chains of reasoning from particular premises, the more convincing their conclusions sounded. The plaintiff's Professor Houthakker was especially effective when cross-examined about his list of "manipulative acts," because he took every occasion to assert his conclusions rather than justify his path to them.

Furthermore, the piecemeal consideration of the Hunts' actions hid from the jury's inspection the degree of internal consistency among each expert's analysis of particular acts. As noted in Chapter 3, at no time in the trial was the plaintiff required to state explicitly and succinctly its theory of the Hunts' strategy of manipulation. The plaintiff's expert could propose that the conspirators, by trading in different delivery months, pursued an extremely far-sighted strategy for deceiving regulators and, on another occasion, propose that one of them, Herbert Hunt, pursued an extremely short-sighted strategy for deceiving regulators. Similarly, at no time in the trial was the defense required to state explicitly and succinctly its theory of the Hunts' plan for long-term investment. Examining each action separately, the defense experts could variously present the investment strategy to have been dominated by tax considerations, by concern about the integrity of futures markets, or by bullish sentiment for silver. It is difficult to imagine how any cross-examination, however skillfully conducted, could have exposed to the jury's inspection such subtle alterations in the experts' premises. Nor would testimony by opposing experts about the need for synthesis have succeeded, for the testimony would risk sounding pedantic, or worse, risk reinforcing the first experts' conclusions through repetition.

Even had the plaintiff and defendants been compelled to put forth comprehensive theories, they could have found plausible ones. Here then impends the fundamental futility in trying to infer intent from the actions in the silver market. Whether intending manipulation or investment, the Hunts were in a "game" against sentient, forward-looking opponents, traders as well as regulators. Any action by the Hunts can be associated with some particular purpose, depending on their presumed skill in forecasting their opponents' reactions to their own actions.

One example may suffice to demonstrate the problem. It can be argued that the Hunts were rational enough to realize that the silver market was too large to manipulate. Yet others argue – witness Stephen Fay's book *Beyond Greed* – that the Hunts selected silver because no regulator or commercial dealer would suspect anyone of planning to corner such a market. According to this line of reasoning, the very audacity of the scheme proves its existence. On the contrary, this line of argument demonstrates merely how problematic in such settings is the inferring of intent from actions.

How might the difficulties of inferring intent from actions in commodity markets alter the requirement in civil legal proceedings that the preponderance of the evidence be against a defendant for the defendant to be found liable? Consistent with the presumption of innocence, it might be argued that it is insufficient to establish that some of the Hunts' actions were consistent with manipulation. If some subsection of the Hunts' many trades are reasonably long-term investments, those trades should be presumed not to be part of the manipulation. If enough trades are removed from the tally of those thought to be part of the manipulation, the whole supposed edifice may crumble.

Because a plausible, innocent explanation can be found for almost any act, by this extension of the presumption of innocence, the jury's conclusion about the Hunts' intent should have been other than perfunctory. I suspect the very complexity of so many of the Hunts' actions invited the speedy inference of manipulative intent. That is, the jury may have accepted, perhaps unconsciously, that something they did not understand had something suspicious about it. Hence, the analysis, conducted to help the jury to infer intent, itself shifted the presumption from not liable to liable.

In parallel with the effects of complexity, the scale and frequency of the Hunts' actions may have shifted the presumption from not liable to liable. Although the Hunts may have viewed it as only normal practice for substantial traders to extract advantages out of a regulation or a negotiation, the jury might well have applied a higher standard to large traders and expected them to forgo the pettiness of extracting every dime's worth of advantage. If the Hunts, as the largest private holders of silver, were expected to be exemplars of fair practice, magnanimity, and moral rectitude, as is expected of other public figures, the ambiguity inherent in their actions may have further predisposed the jury towards inferring manipulative intent.

The predicament of economic analysis in the courtroom

As the jury deliberated, Judge Lasker encouraged one last attempt at settlement. Minpeco offered to accept $30 million, close to its offer at the start of the trial six months before and far below the $450 million it might be awarded. Nonetheless, the Hunts, true to their inclinations, hazarded the jury's verdict.

The jury found the defendants liable on virtually every charge against them. It found Bunker Hunt, Herbert Hunt, Lamar Hunt, IMIC, and Mahmoud Fustok liable for manipulation, monopolization, fraud on the market, and conspiracy; it found all but Lamar Hunt liable for racketeering.[1] It awarded Minpeco $65.7 million in damages,[2] an amount trebled under the antitrust and racketeering statutes. Given the $64.7 million received by Minpeco in previous settlements, the defendants therefore became liable for just over $132 million.

Just after the jury's verdict was officially recorded in late August 1988, the Internal Revenue Service obtained a lien on Bunker Hunt's and Herbert Hunt's assets to the full $600 million of taxes that it claimed were due from

---

[1] Evidently, the jurors were upset and puzzled that Minpeco's brokers were not defendants at the trial. It seems, from the post-trial interviews conducted by Minpeco, that the jurors would have found the brokers liable on just the evidence presented incidentally in the case against the Hunts.

[2] Of the $101 million compensation Minpeco claimed for losses on futures and forwards, the jury awarded $63 million. The jury concluded that Minpeco would have made $1 per troy ounce profit on its short positions under normal conditions, out of the $2 to $4 Minpeco requested, for another $12.1 million. The jury awarded 50 percent of the $48.9 million in interest on loans supporting futures losses (as damages rather than prejudgment interest; see Freund et al. [1985] for an explanation of prejudgment interest in commodities litigation), while denying entirely the plaintiff's claim for losses on loans of physical silver from the Peruvian Central Bank. Offsetting these various awards, the jury applied the maximum estimate of the gains Minpeco made on its own inventory.

the early 1980s, principally on silver transactions. Unable to conduct their financial affairs with their assets frozen, on September 21, 1988, Bunker Hunt, Herbert Hunt, their wives, and trusts in their names filed for bankruptcy. The two brothers were forced to divest themselves of most of their personal assets, for instance, Bunker Hunt his prized antique coin collection and racing stables. The Hunt family's major oil holdings, Placid Oil and Penrod Drilling, also filed for bankruptcy.

As in a Greek tragedy, a venture flawed by obsession and arrogance ended in seemingly fateful demise. Yet the bankruptcies of Bunker Hunt and Herbert Hunt were less ordained by fate than by the brothers' persistence in staking such a disproportionate share of their wealth on commodity investments. Had the price of oil boomed in the late 1980s instead of collapsing as it did in 1986, the Hunts would have gained handsomely and almost surely would have settled out of court with both Minpeco and the CFTC Division of Enforcement. Ultimately, they lost the bet they had placed repeatedly since the 1960s: invest in physical, not financial assets. Their last spin of the roulette wheel turned up black, not red, and the game of double or nothing ended.

The bankruptcy filings meant that the ranking of creditors took precedence over any decisions in the lawsuits involving the Hunts' silver trading. Minpeco, along with the CFTC Division of Enforcement and other silver plaintiffs, ranked at the bottom as unsecured creditors. When terms were worked out, the banks received many of the assets of Placid Oil and Penrod Drilling, the IRS most of the remaining funds, Minpeco and other silver plaintiffs little.[3] Ultimately, Minpeco received less than 30 percent of the $132 million it was awarded. While Minpeco settled with Mahmoud Fustok for about $8 million, it collected nothing from Naji Nahas, who remained in Brazil throughout the trial.[4] Minpeco's major prospect for recovery remained with

[3]   The Hunt-related bankruptcies were particularly contentious. Several banks holding mortgage rights to Placid Oil's assets became incensed that Placid proceeded with a highly risky campaign of drilling in deep waters off the Gulf of Mexico – a major find would restore the Hunts' fortune while a bust would dissipate the banks' collateral. (Little oil was found.) Bunker and Herbert Hunt, in anticipation of bankruptcy, allegedly moved assets into other family members' trusts (*Wall Street Journal*, 5 February 1991). Only in 1994, when the two brothers' families turned over much of the disputed property to the brothers' creditors, did the contentions over the bankruptcies subside. Also in 1994, the various Hunt family trusts sold for $250 million what remained of Placid Oil, ironically to Occidental Petroleum, which had made money from the silver price spike (*New York Times*, 30 November 1994).

[4]   Others would now like to collect from Mr. Nahas. In June 1989, he abandoned obligations to purchase shares worth $31 million on the Sao Paulo stock exchange, where he had been responsible for upwards of 50 percent of trading volume. His default forced trading to be suspended for one day, and when it resumed, prices fell 54 percent. This affair forced the resignation of the president of the central bank and left eight brokerage houses insolvent. It uncannily parallels his involvement in the silver market:

Lamar Hunt, who had not filed for bankruptcy but threatened to do so if held responsible for the entire judgment. Lamar Hunt settled with Minpeco for some $17 million, out of proportion to his position in silver futures among the defendants.

The bankruptcy also circumscribed the post-trial appeals. The defense attorneys believed several legal arguments worth pursuing. The defense attorneys proposed to re-argue the single entity theory, which Judge Lasker had denied before the trial commenced in part because of the defense's poorly constructed record of whether Peru treated Minpeco's marketing operations as an enterprise consolidated with government-owned mines. They proposed to emphasize that the market necessary for the antitrust charge, namely the restriction to bullion already in exchange-approved vaults, relied on the plaintiff's expert's understanding that a re-assaying process of several weeks was obligatory for silver to be deliverable on futures contracts; Judge Lasker, in his decision denying the defense's motion for judgment notwithstanding the verdict, accepted the limitations of the testimony but concluded that the defense's alerting the jury sufficed. The defense attorneys proposed to contrast the plaintiff's expert's use of terms such as "manipulation" with the defense experts' use of less conclusionary phrases such as "consistent with manipulation."[5] Whether these or other possible arguments would have succeeded cannot be known; any success on such legal grounds would have required a new trial.

As for *Minpeco v. Hunt* as conducted, it nearly had a different outcome since the jury almost hung over the question of damages. Twice during the jurors' five days of deliberation Judge Lasker had to encourage them to come to some decision. Although some of the six jurors wished to grant Minpeco the full $450 million it had sought, at least one wanted to award it much less than the final judgment. The jury's award was a compromise (exactly 50 percent of the interest expenses and exactly $1 per troy ounce in forgone profits), made more to appease personalities than to reflect any careful calculation of the Hunts' effect on Minpeco. Had the jury awarded less than the previous settlements, the Hunts would have been liable for nothing (something the jury did not know) and the adverse verdict on the manipulation charge would

establishment, with the mistaken trust of others, of an unnaturally large position and abandonment of the whole position when the market turned against him. Evidently, when his arrest was imminent in July 1989, Mr. Nahas fled Brazil (*Financial Times*, 13, 14, and 22 June and 26 July 1989).

5   Even as Minpeco's expert was testifying, the Appeals Court with jurisdiction over the Southern District of New York decided that a witness's repeated use of "manipulation" amounted to a legal conclusion outside the permissible scope of expert testimony, because "manipulation" is not self-defining. *United States v. Scop*, 846 F.2d 135 (2nd Cir., 1988), a case involving an "investor-interest" type of stock manipulation.

have had no legal significance for the other litigation pending against the Hunts over silver.[6]

Prior to the trial, attorneys on both sides made use of mock juries, a now-common procedure for learning the predispositions of prospective jurors. Over several hours, the attorneys presented both their own side's main arguments and their version of the other side's approach. Ironically, the mock jury hired by Minpeco's attorneys found the Hunts not liable while the three hired by the Hunts' attorneys all quickly determined that the Hunts had manipulated the price of silver. These three mock juries predicted the outcome of the actual trial, for all disagreed on the amount of the damages, with some of the New Yorkers having strong objections to obligating Americans, even Texans, to pay money to foreigners.

Whether one considers justice to have been served by the jury's verdict in *Minpeco v. Hunt* depends on the degree of punishment one considers appropriate to the offense. Some would say that the silver market itself sufficiently punished the Hunts. As the price of silver fell from its peak, the Hunts were overwhelmed by the costs of financing their holdings, losing hundreds of millions of dollars in the process, more than the maximum damages the jury could have assessed.[7]

Whether one considers justice to have been served by the jury's verdict in *Minpeco v. Hunt* also depends on one's idea of what the offense was. As noted in Chapter 3, neither the judge, nor the lawyers, nor the economic expert witnesses defined the meaning of "manipulation" in a futures market nor identified the type of manipulation the Hunts had allegedly committed. That the Hunts had held large positions when the price had not risen and that relationships within the web of silver prices did not particularly indicate a corner proved less pertinent than the threat posed by their holdings of silver. Their huge positions and their supercilious attitude towards traders and exchange officials persuaded the jury that they were both placed and inclined to violate the law.

That finding by the jury is most interesting, for the holding of large positions was not among the accusations against the Hunts. Indeed, at the time no exchange or CFTC rules limited positions in silver futures. Had that accusation been made explicit, the trial would have proceeded much more quickly, because the positions in Bunker Hunt's and Herbert Hunt's personal

---

6   By the principle of *res judicata*, once an issue, such as whether the Hunts were manipulators, has been determined in court, it is not reconsidered in another trial. Conversely, if no monetary judgment had been entered against the Hunts, other parties to silver litigation, such as the Gordon class action, would have had to re-argue whether the Hunts had manipulated the silver market.

7   Fischel and Ross (1991) would offer the financial outcome for the Hunts in support of their argument that manipulations are self-deterring and are not in need of statutory prohibitions.

accounts were large by any standard and the brothers had made no effort to conceal them. Much of the expert testimony would have been irrelevant and unnecessary. Experts would still have been needed to discuss such subjects as the size of warehouse stocks or the market's liquidity in absorbing a huge order, but their discussions could have been brief.

This chapter investigates the problematic role played by the economic arguments in the Hunt trial and the broader lessons to be learned about economic analysis in the courtroom. Section 7.1 reports on the jury's process of deliberation and considers how it weighed the economic arguments before it. Section 7.2 considers how the verdict reflected the evidence relevant to the accusations of manipulation and monopolization. Section 7.3 considers how the economist expert witnesses were utilized in the litigation process and trial. Section 7.4 considers the lessons about the role of economic analysis in other disputes over manipulation. In the Hunt case, the various means by which the economic analysis was presented in the courtroom ultimately nullified the instructive benefit such analysis was meant to provide.

7.1   Economic evidence and the Hunt jury

Several months after the trial, Minpeco's attorneys interviewed five of the six jurors. Those five remembered the deliberations as unpleasant, with the disputes often too personal, although the trial itself had been an exciting experience. All could still recall minute aspects of the testimony, which even the attorneys had by then forgotten.

According to that interview, the jurors easily agreed that the defendants were liable for manipulation, monopolization, and so forth, deciding all the charges in the first hours. They found agreeing on the damages much more difficult. (One stumbling block was the poor state of Minpeco's records about the inventory whose gain in value offset losses on futures.) During five days of acrimony, they made little attempt to explain their reasoning behind the level of damages proposed. Some jurors became unwilling to talk to one another. The jurors reached unanimity only with prodding from Judge Lasker, who reminded them that the entire trial would have to be repeated were they not to come to some agreement.

According to the post-trial interview, the jury found the Hunts to be unconvincing witnesses, often unresponsive, inconsistent, and less than frank in explaining their actions. Much of this impression arose during the presentation of the plaintiff's case. To avoid being called as plaintiff's witnesses, the Hunts did not even attend the trial until the defense introduced its case – a tactic often deployed so that a jury first encounters a defendant while a positive narrative is being presented, leaving the plaintiff to read from dull depositions. But the Hunts had been deposed several times on videotape. When edited into sequences according to subject, these videotapes not only enabled the plaintiff to tell its story twice, they presented a devastating image of Bunker and Herbert Hunt as evasive and contradictory. Particularly damaging was Bunker Hunt's changing his testimony about his role in the silver-backed bonds as Minpeco uncovered more documents. By the time the Hunts took the stand in person, they faced a jury very skeptical of their commitment to the entire truth.[8]

The Hunts' behavior during the videotaped depositions may have reflected their inarticulateness from little practice at explaining themselves or a true inability to remember a lunch with Naji Nahas, a mundane experience for them but something the jurors might have considered a memorable, once-in-a-lifetime experience. Nevertheless, their behavior during the videotaped depositions exemplified their habitual strategy of evasion, obstruction, and delay. That strategy, perhaps advisable when the prospect of a trial seemed remote, became extremely damaging in the context of the trial. By contesting every request for documents during the process of discovery and deposition, the Hunts' attorneys at Shank, Irwin so exasperated the magistrate-in-charge that she began to be skeptical about their requests. Because of the trouble Professor Houthakker was put through while reconstructing the Hunts' trading records, he developed, he has said, an almost personal animosity towards the Hunts.[9] At the trial, the Hunts' long record of denying any knowledge of their specific trades or of their fellow longs precluded them from asserting that their actions and associations were conducted openly and aboveboard, perhaps their most powerful defense. In general, the Hunts were fearful – some would say paranoid – that the legal system was stacked against them, but they misjudged the effect of their own attitude and failed to understand that they invited much of the ill will against them.

According to the post-trial interview, the jurors found particularly significant the sheer size of the Hunts' silver positions and magnitude of the price rise, which they perceived as a single event. The plaintiff's attorneys cleverly reinforced the simplification of silver's price rise by keeping on display a chart of twenty years of silver prices (here Figure 1.1), which inevitably compressed the period 1979–1980 to one sharp spike. The broader lesson would seem to be that, as evidence becomes more complicated and a trial longer, the power of a simple, memorable argument increases.

---

8   As he stated recently, Judge Lasker believes the decision to postpone the Hunts' arrival at the trial to have been a major tactical error. He would not be surprised if the jury had come to resent the time wasted. (Had the case been a bench trial before him alone, he would have stopped the redundant presentation.) The Hunts attorneys, however, continue to believe that as unimpressive as the Hunts appeared through the videotapes, they would have made an even worse impression as live witnesses during the plaintiff's part of the case.

9   Actually, the Hunts' records were in such disarray that even their own experts became frustrated when reconstructing their silver positions.

In debriefing the jurors, Minpeco's attorneys inquired about the impressions made by the expert witnesses. A commonly held view is that opposing expert witnesses simply cancel each other out; when one contradicts the other, a jury concludes that neither is reliable. The Hunt jury, in contrast, found the plaintiff's expert Professor Houthakker's interpretation of the price spike of 1979–1980 convincing and was swayed by few, if any, of the defense experts' arguments. The jury was troubled by Professor Ross's use of a graph (basically Figure 4.5) in which the price moves of many commodities were reduced to the same scale. Even though he had changed the scale to highlight the similarity in timing of the price moves, the jury interpreted this choice as an attempt to obscure the magnitude of silver's price rise.[10] A contentious exchange between Professor Edwards and Mr. Gorman over a comparison of the silver price spikes of 1973–1974 and 1979–1980, in which Professor Edwards insisted on checking Mr. Gorman's computations, persuaded the jury that Professor Edwards would battle any point made against the defense. Mr. Gorman's cross-examination of my testimony (as in Figure 5.3) convinced the jury that my regression results (as in Table 4.7) showed the Hunts causing part of the price rise, which I had denied. (During recess, one member of the jury was overheard muttering, "They should shoot that professor.")

During closing arguments, Mr. Robinson, one of the Hunts' attorneys, belittled Professor Houthakker for making a number of self-evident mistakes in his statistical analysis. Mr. Gorman countered with a synopsis of Professor Houthakker's credentials, arguing that a well-respected scholar and advisor to Presidents such as he would surely conduct statistical analysis sensibly. With the choice presented in this way, the jury credited Professor Houthakker's background, and found offensive Mr. Robinson's attacks on him.

A jury's impression of a particular expert witness both reinforces and derives from other aspects of the case. It may be that, if the other evidence appears strong for one side, the jury will be predisposed towards that side's expert and will validate its inclinations by seizing on any flaw in the other expert's presentation; if the other evidence appears balanced to that point, the jury may look more carefully for inconsistencies in that side's expert's testimony and may not ignore the other side's expert's entire testimony upon the first sign of a problem. The Hunts' experts labored under the considerable disadvantage of the impression the Hunts themselves had left while Minpeco's expert's stately yet humorous presence was particularly suitable before a friendly jury.

---

[10]   Mr. Gorman has expressed puzzlement that the defense attorneys did not detect the jury's reaction to that graph, which the defense attorneys used again in their closing argument.

In the post-trial interview, the jurors acknowledged the importance of the experts' analysis, perhaps because the attorneys in their closing arguments had emphasized the economists' testimony and had made some insightful paraphrases of some of the economists' points. Yet before reaching their verdict on liability, they did not review the economic evidence in detail. During the days of acrimonious deliberations over damages, the jurors did not consider systematically what they believed to be the Hunts' effect on silver prices.

One might conclude that the jurors avoided the details of the economic analysis because they found the main points obvious.[11] On the other hand, one might conclude that the jurors had been unable to absorb the details of the economic analysis. Indeed, only two of them had college degrees, and so following the intricate discussions of butterfly straddles or econometric techniques must have been daunting. Their problem was far from unique; in protracted cases, those who cannot avoid jury duty usually lack high levels of relevant expertise and analytical training.[12]

Many commentators (e.g., Adler, 1994) have questioned whether typical jurors can make sense of extensive technical testimony. Despite the seventh amendment to the U.S. Constitution, which explicitly preserves the right of trial by jury in civil suits, some of these commentators argue for a trial before a judge (as practiced in Great Britain in nearly all civil trials) for especially complex cases. Others (e.g., Lunebury and Nordenberg, 1981) propose a "special jury" selected by education and ability for such cases.

Other commentators (e.g., Guinther, 1988, and Friedland, 1990) come to the defense of a jury's role in a complex trial by citing judges' equally uncertain abilities to understand complex cases. Some of these advocates (e.g., Lempert, 1981, and Strawn and Munsterman, 1982) propose to simplify the jury's task by providing it with a logic tree of a case's main points or by breaking a case into a sequence of issues, with a verdict to be rendered after each segment. Such approaches would not have helped in the Hunt case, where the issues were so thoroughly intertwined. (Judge Lasker's experiment to let the attorneys offer mini-summations at the end of blocks of testimony did seem to help.) Still others suggest a neutral master, either a lawyer or an expert, to explain the facts to the jury in simpler terms. Such an approach would probably not have helped in the Hunt case, because the

---

[11] Another possibility is that the jury found the economic analysis irrelevant. As an economist, I am reluctant to advance that interpretation.

[12] In a much-referenced study of a complex antitrust case, Ell (1978) examined the selection path of prospective jurors. In the initial representative panel, the jurors had on average some college education; after a lottery through which a panel was chosen, after exemptions because of economic hardship, and after *voir dire* challenges, the final jurors averaged only a tenth-grade education.

master's imposition of order on the evidence would itself have endorsed a particular conception of normal workings of commodity markets.

No commentator on juries has recognized the problem that plagued the Hunt case – namely that the jury was assigned impossible tasks. Foremost among them was that the jury was expected to understand more than a year's worth of details about the silver market, and not just the Hunts' actions but also the Conti group's, the exchanges' and the commercial shorts', not to mention broader political and economic events. The jurors, only one of whom took any notes, heard the equivalent of the paragraphs in Chapter 2 read out of order and over the course of six months, and then were asked to reconstruct the narrative.

Needed from the opening statements onward was a time line for the jurors' ready reference. Some of the information in it may well have been objected to as prejudicial, for the same reasons that have caused the courts to hesitate to sanction jurors' notes (for items recorded in notes might dominate other pieces of evidence).[13] Yet even more prejudicial was the haphazard piecing together of evidence, which placed an incredible burden on the jury's memory and organizational skills, making omissions, simplifications, and internal contradictions inevitable.

The style of expert testimony hindered the jury's ability to follow the reasoning behind conclusions. The experts' explanations of the complexities of futures transactions arose from assumptions they neither articulated nor tested. For example, one expert stated simply that taking of deliveries on futures contracts indicated manipulative intent and another expert that it did not, making it impossible for the jury to weigh the strength of the opposing declarations.

With regard to econometric analysis, expert witnesses on both sides repeatedly provided conclusions without justifying the methods used to reach them. The plaintiff's expert simply announced that his associates' many regressions confirmed the Hunts as the major cause of silver's price rise. He explained regression analysis concisely but entirely verbally; his testimony on direct examination took under ten minutes. He did not justify how he had specified the speed of adjustment of silver prices to the Hunt's trading and how he had specified other metals' prices as measuring political and economic events. Weeks later, I merely stated that the plaintiff's expert had performed his analysis incorrectly, then asserted my own regressions as showing no association between the Hunts and changes in the price of silver. Although I attempted to explain regression analysis with two scatter diagrams, the testimony, again, was brief.[14] Similarly, although I, like the other

---

13   Discussion of the advantages and disadvantages of jurors' note-taking can be found in McLaughlin (1983), Friedland (1990), Frankel (1990), and Heuer and Penrod (1990).

14   Similarly, the CFTC Division of Enforcement's experts had presented their statistical

defense experts, had discovered a problem with the plaintiff's RESID adjustment to gold, we testified about it in a style relying on our authority as experts, rather than on our skills as teachers, making no effort to illustrate the problem or to provide any intuition about it.

To determine the extent of damages, the Hunt jury was expected to develop a comprehensive model of a worldwide commodity, something no one has yet accomplished. The economists, having recognized the difficulty of assigning a specific number to the price of silver without the Hunts, offered only bounding arguments of the form, "The effect of the Hunts could have been no larger than ..." or "at least as large as ..." The court procedures presumed that calculation of damages would be a straightforward exercise. Yet in making such calculations, one must allow for the effects of other markets, of other traders' expectations, and so forth. The jury was told nothing of such difficulties.

The Hunt jury was asked to conduct its deliberations without anyone at the trial having defined manipulation other than in circular or vacuous ways. Individually, members of the jury readily concluded that the Hunts had done something suspicious and hence had no reservations about finding them liable for manipulation. Yet, collectively, the jury reached no conclusion about the degree of harm the Hunts caused. Perhaps, had the jurors been given a clear definition of manipulation and had they been guided to discuss the type perpetrated by the Hunts, their acrimony in calculating damages would have been avoided. The unstated message, however, was that no such definition or discussion was needed.

To help the jury organize its deliberations, Judge Lasker presented it with a series of questions, written with the suggestions of lawyers from both sides. Under the heading "manipulation," the first question asked, "Has the plaintiff proved ... [the defendants] had the specific intent to cause the price of silver to become artificially high?" Two more questions asked whether the price was in fact artificial and whether the artificial price harmed the plaintiff. The questions about damages were in terms of the dollars to be awarded, that is, the result of the calculations, not their likely and necessary steps. The phrasing and emphasis of these three questions must have discouraged the jury from thinking systematically and consistently about manipulation and price artificiality, especially in the progression of time.[15]

The jury should have been asked questions such as "Did the defendants through an unreasonable demand for physical silver cause the prices of the December '79, February '80, and March '80 contracts to be artificially high compared to the prices for delivery in late 1980 and early 1981? Did they cause the price of bullion to be artificially high compared to coins? Were the

work briefly, emphasizing the results instead of the intuition about the procedures.
[15] No doubt, the phrasing was meant to keep the questions simple, complicated questions and instructions being likely to confuse a jury (Steele and Thornburg, 1988).

defendants responsible for the price rise of September 1979? ... for the price surge of early December when Minpeco suffered its losses? ... for the price fall of January 21–22, 1980?" Questions thus phrased could have helped the jury agree on the type and timing of the manipulation and the extent of the damages to Minpeco.

In sum, even as it confronted numerous assignments that required analytical thinking, the Hunt jury was provided with no analytical aids. Anyone sitting in judgment at the Hunt trial, no matter how technically adept, would have labored under the same considerable handicaps and impossible tasks. Something may be deeply wrong with complex civil trials, but not necessarily because of the jury system itself.

7.2   Economic evidence and the Hunt verdict

The jury implicitly found the Hunts liable because they held large positions during a period in which the spot price of silver rose sharply. That juxtaposition of facts provided a sufficiently self-explanatory proof that the Hunts were liable not only on the charge of manipulation but on the charges of monopolization and fraud as well. Yet the evidence on these other charges is much less obvious than the evidence on the size of the Hunts positions. For example, Chase Manhattan Bank's vault manager testified that bullion can be ready for delivery within a few days, a fact that mitigates the ability of the Hunts to have created a monopoly in month-long delivery periods. That the price of most distant silver futures contracts rose as much as the spot price, even though no defendants traded those contracts, creates some doubt that prices changed solely because of the defendants' fraud on the market.

Of course, the jury, whose task was to render a yes/no conclusion on the various accusations, may have recognized these inconsistencies, which involve relatively minor issues in any case. The point is rather that the charges were connected, even though the separate categories of manipulation, monopolization, fraud, and racketeering suggested that these were distinct offenses to which different pieces of evidence were relevant. The Hunts and their co-conspirators, according to Minpeco's contention, conducted a single scheme whose elements were inextricably linked. The sheer size of the Hunts' positions and the unprecedented magnitude of the price spike dominated the other evidence and carried all the charges.

To most commodity specialists, a manipulation by a long with a large position in nearby delivery months should show symptoms of a squeeze of the shorts; that is, a scramble for deliverable supplies, a premium paid for those supplies, and a long who takes advantage of the resulting price relationships. To some, manipulation means simply the causing of a large price effect, that is, a movement in the price of the commodity relative to others regardless of changes in the relationships within the web of the commodity's

own prices. This price effect might result from a long who, by suddenly purchasing large quantities of the commodity, deceives other traders into behaving as if a broad-based interest in the commodity has developed. To others,
manipulation indicates anything done on a large scale in the market, either
large deliveries taken relative to open interest, large exchanges for physicals
arranged relative to regular commercial dealings, or large positions accumulated relative to visible stocks, regardless of their manner of execution or their
effect on prices. These different conceptions of manipulation and the inherent
problems with large traders determined the expert witnesses' views about the
Hunts.

If the Hunts' large positions were suspect in and of themselves, the
economist experts should have been more direct about whether large positions themselves are pernicious. For more than six years, the Hunts held
large positions both in futures, on which they would sometimes take substantial deliveries, and in physical silver, which they held through thick and
thin. Why were these earlier positions not considered excessive? If the CFTC
and the exchanges had felt large speculative positions in silver to be inherently dangerous, they could have invoked position limits long before 1979.

With the plaintiff's expert's identification of the Hunt's manipulation as a
price-effect manipulation, the evidence on the statistical connection between
the Hunts' trading and the movements in the price of silver should have been
crucial. The timing of the Hunts' silver purchases in 1979–1980 does not
always match the timing of changes in the price of silver. Their purchases
and deliveries, although they may well have contributed to the price surge of
early September 1979, could not have directly caused the far larger price
surge of mid-December 1979 through mid-January 1980, which closely
matches the timing of the Soviet invasion of Afghanistan.

Because the extraordinary price rise induced everyone to look for its
causes, likely candidates were anything that likewise appeared extraordinary
– such as the Hunts' large positions. (Statisticians would say that causality
was tested on a biased sample, because the sample period had been chosen
based on observation of the dependent variable.) When one looks to periods
other than 1979–1980 for evidence of a connection between the Hunts' trading and the movements in the price of silver, however, one finds a weaker
connection than during 1979 and 1980 alone. The Hunts maintained relatively large positions in silver from 1973 to 1979 without the price rising
proportionately. Following their tribulations in March 1980, the Hunts did
not trade from April 1980 through the end of the year, yet the price of silver
rose from $12 to $24 in that period.

The evidence from other metals markets offers little support that the Hunts'
trading affected silver prices. Over 1979–1980, the prices of gold and platinum mirrored the price moves in silver nearly to the day and hour, even
though the Hunts purchased neither gold nor platinum. The Hunts' example

may have inspired others to buy other precious metals, yet only if the Hunts were perceived as legitimate long-term holders of silver, for no one claims that gold and platinum were manipulated. The evidence of price increases in other metals also undermines the style of analysis based on the flows of metals from mines or the flows to uses in jewelry or electronics, according to which the price rise must have been due to the Hunts because the fundamentals of supply and demand changed little. This style of analysis, which claims that the price of silver should have remained below $10 throughout the fall of 1979 and winter of 1980, also predicts that other precious metals' prices would have remained stable, which they did not.

As regards a corner, in which the defendants would have connived to extract a large premium from their short-term monopoly on bullion needed by industry and from shorts unable to deliver on their futures contracts, this area of evidence fails to implicate the Hunts. At the turn of 1980 they responded to the price rise not by taking profits but by accommodating commercial shorts with exchanges for physicals. Had they pursued small gains by bargaining aggressively with the commercial shorts over the EFPs, by offering to take coins at a steep discount to bullion, or by lending bullion at steep fees, such actions would surely have been presented at the trial as those of a classic cornerer. Their deliveries taken on futures contracts despite intertemporal spreads below full carrying charges, seemingly a strong indication of squeezing behavior, needed no other explanation than the tax laws, which favored deliveries after a sharp increase in price.

In mid-January 1980, futures contracts for delivery two years ahead (by which time far more bullion would have been refined or mined than the Hunts could possibly acquire) traded at prices above $50 per troy ounce. Evidently, at least some traders felt that silver's long-run value had fundamentally changed. A corner, which makes short-run supplies extremely tight, perforce would carry over more silver to the future and would depress those long-dated futures prices.

Some of the accusations against the Hunts rely on troubling inconsistencies. One important example concerns the straddles placed by the Hunts in June 1979, which both the CFTC Division of Enforcement and Minpeco cited as surreptitious means to obtain dominant positions and, ultimately, profits. By January 1980, the Hunts had lost money on the straddles, the distant contracts in which they were short having appreciated more than the nearby contracts in which they were long. Minpeco's attorney enticed Herbert Hunt to say that he had placed the straddles because he was "bullish" on silver, then offered as evidence of manipulative intent the losses on the straddles, for why else would an investor desire losses? Apart from the fact that many investors' plans do not in the end provide the profits they wish, Minpeco's argument contradicted its previous characterization of the straddles. Nor did Herbert Hunt's disingenuousness necessarily indicate manipulation. Very likely the straddles were placed for tax-minimization purposes, which, if admitted, would have left the Internal Revenue Service well situated to win the tax disputes.

Of course, several ambiguities appear in the evidence I have emphasized here about price effects and corners. First, if the straddles were primarily tax-motivated, the Hunts, instead of rolling the nearby leg into more distant contracts, could simply have closed them down in January 1980 (a new tax year) at a small loss. Second, in January 1980, they did not take the opportunity to buy coins at the prevailing discount, nor did they offer to lease bullion to others, which would have helped relieve the immediate pressure on bullion, and which would have made clearer that they were taking delivery on futures contracts for tax-related reasons. Third, the behavior of gold prices does not clearly show the dominance of political and economic events. On several occasions, notably the exchanges' restrictions of silver trading to liquidation only in January 1980 and the Hunts' financial troubles in late March, the gold price indisputably moved in accord with events originating in the silver market. The movements of either gold or silver prices, although broadly consistent with events such as the Soviet invasion of Afghanistan, do not accord with the arrival of news hour by hour or even day by day.

Because some ambiguity is inevitable in the evidence assessed at a trial, the legal system provides for charges to be decided according to certain standards of ambiguity: preponderance of evidence, clear and convincing evidence, evidence beyond a reasonable doubt. The inevitability of some ambiguity does not, however, excuse that which arose from the failure to define the central charge of manipulation and to identify the type of the Hunts' manipulation. For example, only if "manipulation" means to corner the market are the straddles relevant; in a calculation of a price effect or the size of net positions, they cancel out. Only if "manipulation" means to fool others into buying the commodity is the number of futures contracts outstanding a relevant indicator of investor interest. Had "manipulation" been defined, whole areas of ambiguous evidence would have been superfluous and the ambiguity in the remainder much less pronounced.

If the Hunts were liable to Minpeco for having excessively large positions in the silver futures market, it should have been necessary to consider the size of positions held by others in silver, in other commodities, and in other periods. The principal commercial shorts (not to mention Minpeco itself) had large futures positions in the fall of 1979, of the same order of magnitude as the principal longs. It may be that these shorts' positions were likewise exceptionally large compared to other periods or markets. The trial provided little sense of the mean and standard deviation of the size of such positions and yet it demanded a judgment about how unusual was the Hunts' position. Of course, the plaintiff was not placed to demand from all other traders the sizes of their futures positions, the frequency of their deliveries, and the style of their exchanges for physicals in 1979–1980, and in other periods, to provide the range of behavior against which to measure the Hunts. The CFTC Division of Enforcement was situated to make such demands, which makes its accusation of the Hunts before answering these questions particularly troubling.

Despite the Congressional Hearings, official reports, depositions, and trial testimony, much remains unknown about the Hunts' actions in the silver market during 1979 and 1980. For everyone to be more confident in the verdict, it would have been helpful to know who selected the particular months for the straddles, whether the brokers acted on vague directions from the Hunts, in which case the straddles look much less like part of a manipulative scheme, or on specific directions about the delivery months, in which case the more sinister interpretation gains strength. It would also have helped to know more about the EFPs in January 1980. If the commercial shorts approached the Hunts with the terms, the picture painted of these EFPs as part of the Hunts' plan to remove bullion from free stocks looks less plausible. If the Hunts approached the shorts or refused to be flexible with terms, the more sinister interpretation gains strength. Further information about those who made and took delivery through the futures market would have helped to classify the Hunts' activities. Finally, knowing the activities of the principal dealers in physicals as well as futures would have helped to assign the causes of the price relationships that developed in 1979 and 1980.

No doubt, even a clarification of these issues would have left much unknown and unresolved about the causes of the silver price spike. By the standard of "preponderance of the evidence," to which the charges of conspiracy, manipulation, and monopoly applied, the jury's verdict against the Hunts is not patently unreasonable. The charge "fraud against the market," however, required the evidence to be "clear and convincing." By that higher standard, the case against the Hunts as having cornered the silver market or as having caused the price rise is hardly proven. Nevertheless, the jury did find the Hunts liable for fraud against the market. On what evidence? Unambiguous by any standard was the Hunts' demeanor and the size of their positions, which may have been given disproportionate weight because the other evidence seemed so unclear.

Unfortunately, the verdict presented little insight into the specific effect of the Hunts' trading in silver. Although the jury did not award all the damages Minpeco sought, the verdict indicated neither the degree to which the Hunts contributed to the price spike nor, by extension, the share of the price rise resulting from other factors.[16] It did not indicate how their trading caused the

---

[16]   With the price having risen $7 per troy ounce while Minpeco's short positions were open and with the jury awarding about $4 per troy ounce, it might seem that the jury assigned to the Hunts 4/7ths of the price rise from mid-November to mid-December

individual surges within the spike.[17] Because the verdict focused on the Hunts, it did not indicate why the price rise was not principally due to political and economic events. These unresolved issues remain, however, as principal concerns for any economist studying commodity markets and for any attorney seeking precedents in the Hunt silver case.

7.3   Economic analysis and opposing expert witnesses

The economists involved in the silver litigation examined the same evidence. Yet they came to decidedly different opinions about whether the Hunts manipulated and monopolized the silver market. How could such experts so fundamentally disagree?

Other economists would reflexively explain the differences of opinion by observing that members of their profession are notorious for not agreeing. Legal professionals would reflexively explain that the expert witnesses had to disagree. "Lawyers typically retain experts for one reason only: in order to help win the case" (Lubet, 1993, p. 440). In its most cynical form, this view supposes economists who involve themselves in trials to be "professional" expert witnesses, testifying repeatedly about such subjects, even soliciting such business.

Legal specialists may have come to expect disagreement between opposing expert witness without appreciating how the trial system itself is responsible for it.[18] The first few minutes of the first cross-examination teaches experts never to volunteer information, never to express the nuances of an opinion, never to show their ability to examine many sides of an issue, any of which could be used later to discredit them. "The process of selecting expert witnesses overemphasizes disputes; the process of preparing evidence helps perpetuate them; and, if there are any surviving issues on which the opposing experts might agree, the process of presenting expert testimony reduces the chances that these areas of agreement will be detected [by the jury]" (Gross, 1991, p. 1184). Indeed, the format of the Hunt trial made the economists circumspect in their testimony, exaggerated the apparent conflict among them, made them disinclined to achieve consensus, and ignored what consensus they did achieve.

When interviewing the various economist experts several years after the trial, I was struck by the fact that all had been isolated from one another's

1979. Yet this calculation surely reads too much into the jury's award. The jury's awards on the various components of the damages were not internally consistent.

[17] McDermott (1979, p. 224) argued, before any suits such as Minpeco's proved the opposite, that private actions seeking damages were preferable to regulatory agencies' administrative actions "because of their ability to pinpoint when the 'squeeze' began and ended."

[18] For an example of the expectation of disagreement, see the panel discussion on experts in antitrust cases (Reasoner, 1992).

work.[19] The CFTC Division of Enforcement's two experts worked entirely alone and did not read the other's report. Only one of them read the defense experts' responses. The experts for the defense, although sharing some data, did not read each other's reports to the CFTC until after they were submitted, nor hear one another testify. The plaintiff's expert, who went to great lengths to construct essentially the same data sets as everyone else, read the two Division of Enforcement's experts' reports only when most of his own analysis had been completed. He did not hear the defense experts testify, his part in the trial having ended.[20] Quite apart from whether the counters to his arguments would have convinced him, to this day he does not know what they were.

The enforced isolation of experts exaggerated their tendency to believe that their analysis revealed the "truth." The defense experts had determined their main conclusions at an early stage, just after the silver cases were filed in 1981. In 1987 when the defense experts were approached again, no time remained to reconsider that earlier analysis or to study the silver market in other ways. The plaintiff's expert had analyzed and formed an opinion on the Hunts' trading by 1985, before much of the particulars of the Hunts' EFPs and so forth were available to him. The discovery process and depositions froze further any analysis, for a change in light of other experts' work would have been interpreted as hiding a flaw rather than making an improvement. In effect, all the economists conducted what in the normal academic cycle would be only the preliminary analysis.

To improve the interplay between opposing experts while preserving the adversarial relationship, Gross (1991) recommends arranging the opposing experts' testimony for the same point in the trial (to hear and react to each other's testimony), constructing large databases together, and meeting informally, perhaps under the court's supervision, before the start of the trial. Such simple interchanges in the Hunt case might well have improved the analysis the economists offered.

In an important recent case, the U.S. Supreme Court addressed the procedures for admitting expert testimony.[21] Accepting that experts would express

---

19 Experts are kept isolated for what may be good reasons, not least the lawyers' real concern of an expert being asked questions about another expert's testimony. If an expert witness applauds part of an opposing expert's testimony, he enhances the credibility of the whole. If he expresses any reservations about a team member's work, he may discredit the entire testimony. It is much safer for him to reply that he never heard nor read the other experts' analysis.

20 Professors Kolb and Spiller did hear the other experts testify, as part of their preparation as rebuttal witnesses.

21 *Daubert v. Merrill Dow*, 125 L.Ed.2d 469 (1993). The testimony of several experts had been disallowed despite their appropriate credentials, because their analysis of the connection between birth defects and a drug taken by pregnant women had not been published in peer-reviewed journals.

contrary opinions, the Court presumed that regular courtroom procedures could differentiate sound from unsound opinions. "Vigorous cross-examination, presentation of contrary evidence, and careful instruction on the burden of proof are the traditional and appropriate means of attacking shaky but admissible evidence." The Hunt case confirms, unfortunately, rather the opposite of what the Supreme Court would like to believe.

In proposing that competing experts expose weak analysis, the Supreme Court presupposed that it is an easy matter to explain what is wrong with a particular analytical framework. It usually is not. For example, the journalistic accounts of the events of 1979–1980 all suggest that the price of silver moved in response to the Hunts' will. Every economist, I am sure, feels uncomfortable with such personifications of a market. Economists might accept that the other traders' expectations about the Hunts influenced their own transactions but they would not accept that the silver market responds with higher prices simply because that was the Hunts' plan. Nevertheless, economists cannot easily explain why such personification is misguided.

The legal system does not contemplate that a style of analysis, pursued with good intentions, may be wrong due to some technical detail that few analysts are aware of. To take one minor but telling example from the Hunt case: The plaintiff's expert claimed that Lamar Hunt accepted substantial losses to trade in distant delivery months on days with price-move limits. Actually, Comex, which did not limit the price of the spot contract, made it possible to trade in distant months by using a combination of regular trades, so that Lamar Hunt paid nothing more than a slightly higher commission. Professor Houthakker did not intentionally misrepresent the procedures on Comex; he simply thought them similar to those in the CBOT grain markets where trading would have been unnatural in any delivery month during a day of price-move limits. Faced with his earnestness, his competence in other areas of economics, and his lack of stake in the trial's outcome, the jury accepted his interpretation, for he clearly was not lying.

The trial format is also ill-suited to uncovering the hidden assumptions behind experts' opinions. For example, the defense experts assumed that prices would reflect the Hunts' trading or general economic events in the matter of a day or two, an assumption buried deep in the discussion of causality. The plaintiff's expert emphasized that the Hunts went against normal practice by taking delivery on futures contracts, which rested on an assumption that deliveries were uncommon. Although some assumptions may be more sensible than others, assumptions are inevitable; all should have been stated clearly, but by the nature of the trial they were not.

Contrary to the Supreme Court's claim, the trial format is ill-suited to uncovering internal inconsistencies in an expert's testimony. (As the previous chapters have emphasized, there were many in the Hunt case.) However open-minded when first examining the data from the silver market, the experts reached an opinion at some point, then marshaled their powers to convince others of that opinion. Indeed, economists are accustomed to the need for making an argument, for economics, more like the trial advocacy system itself and less like an experimental science, emphasizes the style of convincing others (McCloskey, 1985). Economists who have learned to persuade other economists are unlikely to have vigorous cross-examination expose any internal inconsistencies or any incompleteness in their analysis.

Not one of the economists involved with the Hunt silver case could have been challenged as unqualified for expert testimony. Yet surely some were better analysts than the others on the specific topics involved. Moreover, one expert's analysis may be much more competent than an opposing expert's in one area of the testimony but not another. The legal procedures encourage a jury to accept or reject the entirety of an expert witness's testimony, as they do for a normal witness.

The Supreme Court seems to envision circumstances in which the body of knowledge represented by the expert witnesses is so clearly defined and so thoroughly studied that sensible expert analysis would resolve indisputably the issue in question. Under such conditions, skilled cross-examination can indeed reveal which of the opposing experts more closely followed accepted experimental or diagnostic practices or which expert was more familiar with published studies in closely related areas. When the vagaries of a small sample are the most likely cause of scientific uncertainty, for example, either of the litigants can reduce the uncertainty by funding a new experiment.

Nothing like these imagined conditions applied in the Hunt case. Given the available information about traders in precious metals markets, further study would not have determined the cause of the silver price spike. Sensible economic analysis neither confirmed nor dismissed either the theory emphasizing the Hunts or the theory emphasizing political and economic events. Neither theory offered a convincing explanation of price changes at intervals of hours and days. Neither theory explained why the price reached $50 per troy ounce and not $30 or $70. That price, up 500 percent in less than a year – a price at which people freely traded – cannot be reconciled as a corner, or as the effect of a large purchase, or even as a sensible reaction to political and economic news.

Scholarly inquiry into futures markets has long been characterized by a disjunction between the understanding of practice and theory. Practitioners (floor traders, for instance) tend to be too close to their day-to-day activities to generalize about them. Academic economists, on the other hand, generally lack the detailed knowledge of normal trading in each and every market and where some traders can be relatively large; indeed few specialize in commodity markets at all. This state of affairs, very different from that, say, in structural engineering, has resulted in the absence of a body of knowledge that serves as the basis for all study in futures markets. As a consequence, broad and sometimes irreconcilable disagreements among scholars in the field are not unusual, especially over matters like the silver price spike that are themselves extraordinary. Yet the areas of insufficient knowledge often include issues that end up in a courtroom.

Also to the detriment of resolving issues about which there is expert testimony, the trial system overlooks the relevance of areas of agreement among opposing expert witnesses. Indeed, to evaluate which expert's conclusions are the most sensible, it is helpful to know the extent of agreement between them. Outside a trial setting, a patient having to contemplate the disagreement between two physicians – one advising surgery and the other advising bed rest and monitoring of the condition – needs to know what the two physicians agree upon. If the physicians agree that the condition is life threatening but occasionally reverses itself, the patient's decision would be very different than if the physicians do not agree that the condition is serious.

Economists do agree on an important subject, namely how to clarify why they reach different conclusions. They have agreed to use "models," in which the assumptions are clearly stated and which can be checked for internal consistency. In essence, economists have agreed to let others inspect their reasoning as well as their conclusions. As a result, economists at academic seminars tend to discuss conclusions less than the style of analysis, which explains why many of the economists involved with the Hunt case tried to instruct the jury in a particular style of reasoning. The court procedures, however, emphasized the economists' conclusions at the expense of their reasoning.

In the Hunt silver case, the opposing economists agreed, most obviously, on the importance of economic analysis for determining the existence of manipulation, which, after all, is an economic crime. They further agreed on the importance of price relationships, the importance of the timing of price changes, and the importance of the fundamentals of silver demand and supply for determining whether an "artificial price" existed.

If it seems obvious that economists should agree on these issues, consider how the legal professionals ignored that consensus. The lawyers and judge, with all attention to proper legal forms and precedents in Jury Charges in other manipulation cases but without consultation of the economists, crafted the central question posed to the jury:[22] "Did the defendants cause the price of silver to be artificial?" As phrased, this question is incredible to me and, I believe, to anyone familiar with commodity markets. If this book has made anything clear about commodity markets, it is that there is no single price for silver; the phrase "the price of silver" merely approximates for the web of sil-

---

[22] The defense attorneys did, however, recommend more specific questions about the types of silver, to emphasize a corner as the relevant type of manipulation and deliverable supply the key analytical concept.

ver prices, in which are contained the indications of manipulation. If this book has made anything clear about determining the causes of those price relationships, it is that causality is manifest in the details of the timing of price changes. By compressing the silver web to a single price and by compressing the many price changes during 1979–1980 to a single event, the legal system's carefully crafted question about price artificiality offered no place for all the testimony by the economists about the premium for immediate delivery of bullion, the coin/bullion differential, the responses of the commercial shorts, the timing of the Hunts' actions or political events relative to price changes. In short, the legal system's phrasing of the central question dispensed with much of the economic analysis.

Of course, the central issue ought to be presented succinctly – problems come, however, when succinctness becomes oversimplification. As phrased, the central question to the jury amounted to asking whether silver had reached an extraordinary high during 1979–1980. The answer to that question is obvious with a mere glance at a twenty-year plot of silver prices. Unasked, and hence unanswered, were the difficult but fundamental questions of why silver prices rose at the times they did, why they rose to the extent they did, why they rose in the proportions they did.

7.4   Economic analysis and manipulation cases

By almost any measure, the situation in the silver market during 1979 and 1980 was exceptional. Silver prices rose and then fell to a degree not seen in commodity markets before or since. Bunker and Herbert Hunt amassed unusually large positions in physical silver and futures contracts for single investors, and they supposedly conducted a manipulation not for the few hours or days of most alleged manipulations but for at least nine months. The resulting legal cases against them were likewise exceptional. *Minpeco v. Hunt* lasted six months, involved dozens of lawyers and expert witnesses, and culminated in a damage award of nearly $200 million. It seems most improbable that such events will ever be repeated.

Even so, since the end of the Hunt case, many allegations of manipulation have surfaced, not only in commodity markets but in financial and securities markets as well. Three such allegations have been widely reported: Ferruzzi Finanziaria's fractious dispute with the CBOT over the right to hold a large anticipatory hedge position (similar to Minpeco's) in the July '89 soybean contract, Salomon Brothers' scandal over its bids at the two-year U.S. Treasury note auction in May 1991,[23] and Sumitomo Metal Mining's flap

---

[23]   Other firms were said to have squeezed the two-year notes issued in April 1991 (*Wall Street Journal*, 29 November 1993). See Jegadeesh (1993) for an analysis of the price relationships among T-notes during this period.

with the LME over copper in the summer of 1993. Other controversies have prompted headlines such as "Cadmium 'Hit by Manipulation'" (supposedly by dealers trying to influence the price of long-term contracts),[24] "Brokerage House in Japan Corners Silk Futures Market,"[25] "Inquiry Rules Out Stock Market Manipulation" (supposedly by traders wanting to influence the expiry price of the February '91 FT–SE 100 index option contract),[26] and "Traders Find the Squeeze Is Back in Treasury Note Market" (supposedly due to one bank's sizable holdings in the five-year note due in June 1997).[27]

In all these instances, the accused traders, like the Hunts, held large positions at a time of unusual price relationships. All the accused traders were active participants in the market, trading day by day or hour by hour, with an eye to the incessantly moving prices. All viewed themselves as trading against an impersonal market, not against individual traders known to them.

Because of these characteristics of alleged manipulations, the normal trial system provides a clumsy means for determining whether a manipulation indeed took place. Most lawyers, judges, and jurors have little experience with markets characterized by opportunistic, frequent, and anonymous transactions. The trial system has evolved to consider a few distinct events by a few obvious actors with pointed testimony by eyewitnesses, whereas allegations of manipulation concern numerous, often simultaneous, events by numerous, often anonymous, actors and circumstantial, often difficult-to-interpret, evidence.

Once manipulation is alleged, the culture of trials takes precedence. Personal agents become the cause for injuries and a defendant's actions are considered without regard to the actions of all other market participants. When some other market participants are found behaving in a manner similar to the defendant, the culture of trials makes it natural to suppose a conspiracy. The culture of trials also places great weight on intention, for in many crimes the intention naturally translates into the action.

Economic analysis, in contrast, frequently deals with impersonal agents and the ambiguity of simultaneous events. (Traders transact for many different reasons and by influencing the price may affect others with whom they do not deal directly.) Economic analysis frequently concludes that no one agent can be blamed, rather the injury derives from the collective behavior of many independent agents. (Many people, without consulting one another, may decide to buy at the same time, unintentionally harming anyone with a commitment to buy.) Economic analysis often concludes that inten-

24   *Financial Times*, 23 August 1989.
25   *Wall Street Journal*, 23 February 1990.
26   *Financial Times*, 7 March 1991.
27   *Wall Street Journal*, 20 August 1992.

tions cannot be translated into actions. (All traders initiate their position with the hope that prices will move favorably, but prices may not so move.)

Lawyers, predisposed to finding an agent who is responsible for every event, must be perplexed when economists say that no agents are individually responsible or that some agents ought to be lumped into a random error term in an econometric study and ignored. Economic analysis at least makes recognition of ignorance explicit. The nature of the Hunt case, the nature of anything connected with commodity prices, is such that finding a specific agent for each event is impossible.

For manipulation cases, the style of the legal proceeding, the vagueness in the definition of the offense, the emphasis on circumstantial evidence, and the reliance on experts combine to alter a trial to something far from the ideal of the "rule of law," however carefully legal forms are otherwise followed. An expert, without ever publicly defining manipulation or without specifying how the evidence would relate to that definition before inspecting the evidence, pronounces particular actions in the context of particular price relationships to be (or not to be) the offense of manipulation. That expert may be nearly consistent with other experts in the case or with what legislators intended (or with herself in previous testimony), but the trial process does not ensure that consistency. Individual jurors, instructed to determine whether the price artificially reflected other than basic forces of supply and demand, may arrive at some intuitive notion of manipulation. (More likely, the jury concentrates on the personalities, which takes manipulation cases even farther away from the impersonal qualities meant by "the rule of law.") Nothing ensures that a single juror's definition of manipulation is consistent with those of other jurors, or those of any of the experts, or indeed with jurors' implicit definitions in other manipulation cases, let alone with the definition the defendant might reasonably have presumed before the controversy began. Thus comes the main lesson from the Hunt silver case: Law involving such complex subjects is, in effect, created retroactively.

The Hunt silver case has established not that manipulation of futures markets can be unambiguously detected but rather that a large position acquired or held at the time of a substantial price move is suspect. The lesson to others could be to avoid large positions, especially large speculative positions, and to appear cooperative to regulators. Unfortunately, those who apply that lesson may still not avoid trouble, because "large," "cooperative," and "at the same time" are imprecise terms, so apt to be defined with hindsight. Thus, *Minpeco v. Hunt*, especially its principal legacy in its Charge to the Jury, fails Jeffries's test (1985) that an individual case as a precedent should reduce the uncertainty about proper behavior among those who intend to abide by the law.

For others to know *ex ante* where illegal behavior begins, at the minimum, "manipulation" should be defined within the statutes.[28] This definition should not be yet another of the circular and vacuous definitions shifting the burden to other terms. To be sure, a precise definition may encourage the usual human ingenuity in finding profitable activities on just the right side of the definition.[29] However, to say that large positions are permitted provided no one later interprets them as a manipulation opens the door to arbitrary prosecution. Throughout 1979 and 1980, the exchanges and the CFTC monitored the Hunts' trading and the price of silver and, although troubled by the course of events, did not label them a manipulation; indeed, they went on record that the silver market was not manipulated. Yet those same events were later to be labeled a manipulation by the CFTC Division of Enforcement. In the spring of 1994, when the price of silver rose some 25 percent in a few months, rumors abounded of several investment funds (whether in collusion or in imitation of one another) enticing small investors into the silver market, by buying some 200 million troy ounces and "uneconomically" removing some of this bullion from Comex vaults to give the appearance of a shortage.[30] No regulator or aggrieved short has yet accused the investment funds of manipulation, presumably because the positions (comparable to the Hunts') and the price effect (comparable to that during the period of Minpeco's losses) were not "large."

Even more important than defining manipulation within the statutes, regulators should proscribe specific actions that are thought to make manipulation excessively likely. The CFTC's main lesson from the events of 1979 and 1980 proved to be the need for position limits in silver trading.[31] Similarly, some exchanges have moved to limit the number of deliveries that any one speculator can make or take in any one month. These and other proscriptions of specific actions may not eliminate manipulation but they will surely reduce the chance of an extreme instance of it. If something deemed detrimental happens when all traders avoid the proscribed actions, the list of those proscribed actions should simply be expanded.

The best way to discourage manipulation is to ensure that futures contracts be designed with safety valves for particular situations, which would decrease the prospects for and allegations of manipulation.[32] An exchange,

---

[28]   As Levi (1948) documents, the interpretation of the wording in statutes can change.

[29]   In the emerging futures markets in China, there have been allegations that some traders exploit the troubles others have in making payment through the cumbersome banking system.

[30]   *Financial Times*, 11, 25, 28, and 29 March, 15 April, and 2 December 1994.

[31]   Recently, the CFTC itself has proposed relaxing position limits to accommodate "commodity mutual funds," such as those trading in the silver market in early 1994.

[32]   Lower (1991) also recommends this approach, instead of giving the CFTC more powers to intervene in markets. Such policies "would have the CFTC become the greatest and most powerful manipulator of all time" (p. 391).

faced with a long-run decline in deliverable supply of a commodity, could, for example, redesign its contract to allow delivery (perhaps at a discount) at another location or of another grade at the short's option. Contracts could be written (as in the coffee market in France around 1900 and in the new futures markets in China) to allow for delayed delivery at a stated penalty. Such safety valves need not be formally included in the futures contract. For instance, the LME, when it determines that some large trader is unnaturally standing for delivery, permits the shorts to postpone delivery at a penalty per day, which it sets case by case.[33] Had the silver futures contracts of 1979–1980 been written to permit the delivery of coins or had the Comex Board allowed such a substitution by emergency order, the commercial shorts would not have been hampered by a scarcity of bullion, and the Hunts – if indeed they had intended to manipulate – would have been overwhelmed much earlier by the costs of financing the additional physical silver, if not dissuaded from the scheme beforehand.

In addition, the U.S. government, the main regulator of futures markets, should use its own large positions to deflect manipulative private trading and deter squeezes. The U.S. Treasury has now taken a step in that direction by instituting procedures to "re-open" a specific government bond should one party gain control of a substantial proportion of one issue (Department of the Treasury et al., 1992). Similarly, the U.S. government could take action during unusual and temporary price relationships involving the commodities in which it holds strategic reserves. The U.S. government holds in large quantity not only silver but tin, copper, and oil. Since 1979, each of these commodities has experienced a price spike with a substantial premium for immediate delivery that would have been greatly lessened had the U.S. government lent some of its stocks to the market. In each case the government would have earned money and, were the price relationships due to a manipulation, the release of the stocks would have thwarted the manipulation.[34]

Minpeco v. Hunt would appear to demonstrate the effective use of legal institutions – an exception to Markham's fear that manipulation is an unprosecutable crime (Markham, 1991). A jury convened by a Federal District Court, with due process of law, pronounced the Hunts liable, seemingly punishing them for an offense and providing recovery to an aggrieved party. Meanwhile, the CFTC Division of Enforcement had commenced hearings that would have barred the Hunts from trading commodities ever again. One is tempted to conclude that the Hunt case has confirmed the legislature's premise of governmental oversight of organized markets: "The transactions

---

[33]   These interventions are not without controversy, as in the copper market in 1993 (*Financial Times*, 30 July; 3 and 4 August; 2, 4, 9, and 22 September; and 6, 13, and 20 October 1993).

[34]   The U.S. government's intervention broke the gold market on the infamous "Black Friday" in 1869 (Ackerman, 1988).

and prices of commodities ... are susceptible to excessive speculation and can be manipulated, controlled, cornered, or squeezed, ... rendering regulation imperative ..."[35] One is tempted to prescribe, as does Markham, energetic staff at the CFTC Division of Enforcement, vigilant surveillance departments at exchanges, and courts open to those who have lost while trading, in order for more manipulation cases to be brought and for manipulation to be deterred more effectively.

Minpeco v. Hunt also tempts one to conclude, as does Pirrong (1994), that litigation is the socially most efficient method for controlling manipulation of commodity markets. Detailed and numerous rules circumscribe a trader's flexibility regardless of his manipulative intent and regardless of other traders' ability to accommodate. If it were possible to determine quickly and unambiguously that some trader had harmed some other trader, a single rule of "do no harm or face lawsuits for damages" would allow all traders the maximum flexibility. Yet no quick and unambiguous determination of harmful intent is possible, as the Hunt silver case demonstrates. Litigation is the socially least efficient method for controlling manipulation.

Moreover, the very presence of manipulation cases in the courts runs counter to a major achievement of commodity exchanges. Such markets have evolved to minimize the intervention of legal institutions. By standardizing the terms of contracts, the exchanges reduce the importance of the performance history of the parties to the contract, the intent in the minds of the parties, even the identities of the parties; in short, the exchanges' standardization of contracts renders irrelevant the courts' concern over the specifics of contracts. By the system of daily variation margin and "marking to market," commodity exchanges place traders where they would rather perform their obligations than sacrifice their good-faith deposit; in short, the exchanges minimize the need for court procedures to enforce performance. By the precise, public nature of their prices, organized exchanges encourage a commodity's suppliers and users to react to small differences in space, grade, and time; in short, the exchanges reduce the harm that is the courts' focus and the cause of lawsuits.

---

[35] U.S. Code, Title 7, Chapter 1, §5.

Glossary of commodity market terms

Anticipatory hedge: An anticipatory hedge is one of the many ways in which firms dealing in the physical commodity use futures contracts (q.v.). In a standard hedge (q.v.), a commercial firm's futures position can be associated with specific merchandising commitments, as when a miller has a long (q.v.) position in wheat futures contracts and commercial contracts to deliver some months into the future a corresponding amount of flour at firm prices. In an anticipatory hedge, that association is not so close, as when a miller takes the long position in wheat futures believing that at currently quoted prices many bakers will place orders for flour. Anticipatory hedges are one instance where position limits (q.v.) apply to hedgers.

Arbitrage: In its simplest form, arbitrage is the purchase in one market at a low price while simultaneously selling at a higher price in another market, that price more than covering the relevant transportation expenses, storage fees, interest costs, and so forth. The positions in an arbitrage operation need not involve the immediate delivery and redelivery of the commodity; the positions could be held for some time. Nor need the arbitrage operation be absolutely riskless. These risks, however, are difficult to anticipate and extreme, such as the abrogation of all commercial contracts upon a declaration of war. Under this definition, the phrase "risk arbitrage" is a contradiction and an obfuscation.

Ask price: The announced price at which a dealer who "makes a market" (q.v.) is willing to sell to a customer. Contrast with *bid price*.

Backwardation: A backwardation describes the pattern when the price of a commodity for later delivery stands below the simultaneously quoted price

216

of that commodity for earlier delivery. Of British origin, the term arose from the practice in the bond and share markets of continuing obligations from one delivery period to another. If a seller wanted to postpone delivery until the next balancing of accounts, he induced the buyer to take later delivery by paying him an explicit fee called a backwardation. (When the buyer had to pay the seller, the fee was called a contango.) In futures markets, this fee is implicit in the price differential someone committed to make delivery must pay to rollover (q.v.) the position to a later delivery month (q.v.). Thus, backwardation has come to describe a price relationship, just as does the American phrase *inverse carrying charge.*

Basis: Basis describes the difference from some other price, one commodity's price being "based" on the price of another commodity. Usually this second price is that of a nearby futures contract (q.v.). Thus, the basis is like a premium (or discount) for location, grade, or time to delivery, which traders will bargain over directly. The premium (or discount) can change over time; hence there can be "basis risk." Basis is distinct from "basis point," a common phrase in money markets, which means one one-hundredth of one percent.

Bear: A bear is a trader who believes that prices will decline. Thus, a bear typically takes a short (q.v.) position. A "bear market" is one in which prices are declining. News, such as crop forecasts or industrial usage, is thus often classified as "bearish" or "bullish." Contrast with *bull.*

Bid price: The announced price at which a dealer who "makes a market" (q.v.) is willing to sell to a customer. Contrast with *ask price.*

Broker: When arranging a transaction, a broker acts as an agent for a client rather than as a principal (q.v.) trading in his own name for his own account. "Brokerage" is the fee charged for this service. A "brokerage house" is a partnership or corporation that specializes in handling various buy or sell orders for many clients.

Brokerage house: See *broker.*

Bull: The opposite of a bear (q.v.), a bull is a trader who believes that prices will increase. Such an advancing market is called a "bull market." A bull typically takes a long (q.v.) position.

Butterfly straddle: A butterfly straddle (or spread) combines two straddles (q.v.), with one of the straddles short (q.v.) the nearby delivery month (q.v.) and the other straddle long (q.v.) the nearby delivery month. Also, one of the futures contracts (q.v.) overlaps, so that a butterfly straddle has, for example, one long contract for May delivery, two short contracts for July delivery, and one long contract for September delivery. If plotted, these positions would look like the shape of a butterfly from the front.

Carrying charge: See *spread*.

Cash: Cash refers to prompt payment with currency or its equivalent. Because most transactions in commodity markets call for payment on delivery, a purchase with immediate delivery is often said to be at the "cash price" and to have been conducted in the "cash market." Sometimes, cash refers to deals with neither immediate delivery nor immediate payment, although one party at least will be a commercial dealing in the physical commodity. In this sense, cash is meant solely to contrast with organized markets for futures contracts (q.v.).

CBOT: On the Chicago Board of Trade, founded in 1848, incipient trading of standardized futures contracts (q.v.) began in grains in the late 1850s, although the full components of margin (q.v.) and a clearinghouse (q.v.) took some more decades to reach their modern form. In recent years, some of the CBOT's most active markets have been in financial futures, notably the U.S. Treasury bond contract.

Certificated stocks: The amount of the commodity currently in the exchange-specified warehouses (or vaults) of the grade and variety eligible for delivery on futures contracts (q.v.). Thus, a synonym is "deliverable stocks." The exchange does not itself certify the commodity as eligible for delivery; rather that is the task of government inspectors or the warehouse (or sometimes the task of the producer or refiner).

CFTC: The Commodities Futures Trading Commission since 1974 has been the U.S. regulator of organized futures exchanges, determining along with the exchanges which commodities (including financial instruments) can be traded and which rules for trading apply. Headed by five commissioners appointed for fixed terms, the CFTC is an independent agency, much like the SEC (q.v.).

Clearinghouse: Begun as central locations where the clerks of members of informal clearing associations met to balance accounts, clearinghouses have evolved into official adjuncts of exchanges dealing in futures contracts (q.v.). The clearinghouse records transactions executed on the floor of the exchange and daily nets out any one trader's positions in the same contract and delivery month. In effect, the clearinghouse becomes the counterparty in any futures contract. Should a futures contract be settled with delivery, the clearinghouse oversees the recording of delivery notices (q.v.) and the passing of warehouse receipts (q.v.).

Clearing member: Those members of a futures exchange (q.v.) who deal in several commodities or specialize in brokerage for the general public are often also members of the clearinghouse (q.v.), a legal entity separate from the exchange. Typically, only some 10 percent of exchange members are clearing members. For a negotiated fee, clearing members register and eventually settle the futures contracts (q.v.) entered into by other members of the exchange and by outsiders. Responsible to the clearinghouse for the performance of the contracts, clearing members monitor the trading volume, size of outstanding positions, and creditworthiness of those for whom they clear accounts.

Comex: The Commodity Exchange in New York was formed in 1933 in a merger of four exchanges. In 1994, Comex in turned merged into NYMEX (q.v.). On Comex in recent years, the active trading of futures contracts (q.v.) has been concentrated in gold, silver, and copper.

Commercial: Commercial refers to a firm whose primary business is marketing, transporting, processing, or the physical commodity.

Contract grade: For each futures contract (q.v.), an exchange specifies a particular grade (or purity) of the commodity eligible for delivery, which must be made at one of the exchange-designated warehouses (or vaults) at one of the exchange-designated delivery points (q.v.). Sometimes the exchange also specifies the sources of the commodity, such as particular mines and refineries. For some commodities, exchanges set premiums and discounts for delivery of grades (or at locations) other than the contract grade, which in consequence is often known as the "par grade." Depending on the premiums and discounts prevailing at the time the futures contract matures relative to these official rates, the shorts (q.v.), who generally have the choice in the matter, usually find it advisable to use the "cheapest-to-deliver" grade.

Day trader: A day trader holds a position in futures contracts (q.v.) only during the trading day, offsetting (q.v.) it by the close of trading to have no exposure overnight. Thus, a day trader hopes to profit from moves in price over the course of several hours. A scalper (q.v.), in contrast, holds positions for a matter of minutes. Hedgers (q.v.) and speculators (q.v.) usually hold positions for a matter of weeks or months.

Delivery month: The delivery month on a futures contract (q.v.) is the span of time during which the short (q.v.) must make delivery, the particular day being at the short's option (for a few commodities, the particular day is the long's (q.v.) choice). As futures markets have evolved, the first and last days on which the short can initiate delivery do not necessarily span an exact calendar month, although the span is called "May," "June," etc., for convenience. Sometimes the usage is to refer to the May "expiry," the May "future," or the May "contract," this last usage despite the fact that many contracts for May delivery could be outstanding. See *delivery notice*.

Delivery notice: A short (q.v.) in a futures contract (q.v.) makes written notice to the clearinghouse (q.v.) of his intention to deliver the physical commodity in order to settle his contractual commitment. By the nature of futures contracts, once they have been cleared through the clearinghouse, there is no identifiable counterparty to the short's contract; the clearinghouse selects a long (q.v.) to receive the delivery, usually the long whose position is the oldest outstanding. A day or two following this delivery notice, the short passes the commodity (usually a warehouse receipt (q.v.)) and receives back payment, after any adjustments such as accrued storage fees. In some markets, a delivery notice is called a "tender." If the long who received the warehouse receipt decides later that same delivery month (q.v.) to sell it through the futures market (having first to establish a short position), she is said to "redeliver" or "retender" the warehouse receipt. See *certificated stocks*.

Delivery points: Futures exchanges designate the locations where delivery can be made to settle a futures contract (q.v.). For example, the corn contract of the CBOT (q.v.) can be settled with delivery at exchange-approved warehouses in Chicago, Toledo, or St. Louis, although Chicago is the contract grade (q.v.).

Exchange for physicals: An exchange for physicals, often abbreviated EFP, is a double transaction, one part in futures contracts (q.v.) conducted away from the trading floor of the futures market, the other part involving the physical commodity, typically not in the contract grade (q.v.) or at the delivery points (q.v.). For example, a dealer in copper may have a quantity of scrap and a short (q.v.) position in a futures contract. Another dealer, wanting to buy copper scrap, might hold a long (q.v.) position in the same delivery month (q.v.) as an anticipatory hedge (q.v.). As the first dealer delivers the scrap to the second, they cancel their futures contracts themselves, notifying the clearinghouse (q.v.). The price for the scrap itself most likely is negotiated in reference to the futures price, that is, as a basis (q.v.). In grain markets, this type of double transaction is called "ex pit," while in some other markets it is an "exchange for product."

Exchange member: Someone who has qualified for and paid for a "seat" on an organized market such as the CBOT (q.v.), Comex (q.v.), LME (q.v.), or NYMEX (q.v.). Exchanges typically limit the number of seats but the number is typically in the hundreds or thousands. An exchange member need not be present on the floor to trade, arranging with another member to act as a floor broker (q.v.), but, of course, many members are present in the trading pits (q.v.). Exchange members can trade on their own account or be employees of brokerage houses (q.v.) or dealers in the commodity.

Execution: The actual filling of a customer's order by a floor broker (q.v.) at the exchange.

Floor broker: A member of a futures exchange who stands on the floor in the pit (q.v.) for a particular commodity, acting as a broker (q.v.) for others rather than trading for his own account. Contrast with *floor trader.*

Floor trader: A member of a futures exchange, active on the floor of the exchange, who trades for her own account rather than as a floor broker (q.v.). Most floor traders are scalpers (q.v.) or day traders (q.v.). They are also referred to as "locals."

Forward contract: In its most general sense, a forward contract is any agreement calling for the execution of some act in the future, including, but not limited to, futures contracts (q.v.). Usually, the term is used not to refer to standardized futures contracts but to those contracts containing conditions tailored to the particular needs of the contracting parties and which, should either party's needs change, must be renegotiated privately rather than offset (q.v.).

Full carrying charges: When the difference between the price for a nearby delivery date and the simultaneously quoted price for a more distant delivery date exactly covers the warehouse fees, insurance premiums, and capital expenses of holding the commodity for that period of time, the price difference, which is a spread (q.v.), is said to be at full carrying charges.

Futures contract: Futures contract abbreviates the phrase "contract for future delivery." It usually refers to one of the standardized contracts traded in high volume on an organized exchange, with procedures for a clearinghouse (q.v.) and margin (q.v.) to ensure performance of the contracts. In effect, futures contracts become traded in their own right. In active futures markets, several delivery months (q.v.) trade simultaneously.

Handy & Harman: A dealer in precious metals, based in New York, whose cash prices (q.v.) for gold and silver are widely taken to represent the market for the physical commodity. The firm is also a major compiler of statistics on silver mining, stocks, and industrial consumption.

Hedge: A hedge is the position taken in futures contracts (q.v.) by a commercial firm dealing in the commodity or its products. When such a firm buys a futures contract, its position is called a long hedge. When it sells a futures contract, it has a short hedge. These positions could be part of relatively riskless arbitrage operations (q.v.), part of risk reduction strategies as hedge suggests, or part of speculations in the movement of some price relationship. Hedge refers less to the motive for the position than to who holds the position, namely a commercial (q.v.). See *anticipatory hedge*.

Hedger: Hedger is the term applied to commercials (q.v.) who take a position in futures contracts. Contrast with *speculator*.

Inverse carrying charges: Also known as backwardations (q.v.), inverse carrying charges are observed when the nearby delivery months (q.v.) have higher prices than those of simultaneously quoted futures contracts (q.v.) for later delivery.

Leg: A leg refers to one of the two positions constituting a straddle (q.v.) or a spread (q.v.).

Limit move: See *price-move limit*.

Liquidation only: See *trading for liquidation only*.

LME: The London Metal Exchange, founded in 1876, offers markets in the base metals, most active for immediate delivery and for delivery three months ahead. Not having a clearinghouse (q.v.), the LME has not been a true futures exchange, but the differences have been slight and decreasing.

Long: Long describes the market position of someone who has bought something, whether the physical commodity or a futures contract (q.v.). When making the trade, the person is said to "go long." Long has also come to indicate the person who holds the position. By the nature of futures contracts, for every long there must be a *short*.

Make a market: To make a market refers to the simultaneous offering to buy and to sell, albeit at a small difference in price. The "market maker" thus stands willing to trade without knowing the type of a prospective customer's transaction. Ideally, over the interval of a few hours or days, the amount he purchases nearly equals the amount he sells, his profits coming from the volume of transactions and the differential between his bid prices (q.v.) and his ask prices (q.v.).

Margin: Margin is a good-faith deposit, usually of money or exceptionally safe and liquid assets like Treasury bills, placed in the hands of a third party, that secures the execution of a contract. With a futures contract (q.v.), there is a chance that either the buyer or the seller might default if the market price moves against her, so it has been customary (and now obligatory) for both parties to the deal to deposit a set sum called "original margin." Depending on the status of the parties, the original margin is held by the brokerage house (q.v.), the clearing member (q.v.), or the clearinghouse. Whenever the price changes, a margin call (q.v.) is made. Additional funds called "variation margin" are required from the party against whom the price has moved so the contract remains secure; the other party receives those funds forthwith. Compare with *marking to market*.

Margin call: If prices move against its customer, a brokerage house (q.v.) demands additional funds, otherwise known as variation margin (q.v.), to ensure the performance of futures contracts (q.v.) that the broker has initiated on the customer's behalf. (The same happens between the clearinghouse and a clearing member.) If the customer fails to meet the margin call, the broker can close out the position.

Market maker: See *make a market*.

Marking to market: (1) Marking to market is a practice adopted to ensure that in the face of volatile prices the obligations of buyers and sellers are met. The effect of marking to market is to renegotiate a contract, by adjusting the good-faith deposit, the margin (q.v.), to include the difference between the original price within the contract and its current market price. The principle of marking to market would apply whether the adjustment were made hourly or monthly; on futures exchanges, the marking to market is made daily, using the settlement price (q.v.). (2) Marking to market is also used to refer to the accounting convention of relisting assets or liabilities at their current worth, typically using the current market price, rather than at the price at which they were acquired.

NYMEX: In the late 1970s, the New York Mercantile Exchange was a relatively small exchange for futures contracts (q.v.), with its main markets in the platinum group metals. By the early 1990s, NYMEX's new markets in energy products had become among the most active in the world.

Offset: To offset means to eliminate a position in futures contracts (q.v.) by an opposite transaction. (A synonym is "cover.") The sale of a contract for the same delivery month (q.v.) offsets a long (q.v.) position previously taken, just as a purchase offsets a short (q.v.) position. (Whether the position was profitable depends on the prices of the two trades.) The clearinghouse (q.v.) formally removes an offset position from the trader's account, rather than letting the two contracts run until they mature.

Open interest: Open interest refers to the number of futures contracts (q.v.) outstanding at a particular moment in time, that is, the number of contracts that have not been canceled by an offsetting trade (q.v.). The official publicized figures give the open interest by commodity and delivery month (q.v.) at the close of each day's trading.

Option: An option is a contract allowing one of the parties to choose whether he proceeds with the agreement. Thus, an option (which can be traded in its own right) is a conditional contract. Although futures contracts (q.v.) are unconditional contracts, they are sometimes, especially in the grain markets, referred to as options, because the short (q.v.) has the option of the exact day of delivery during a delivery month (q.v.).

Original margin: See *margin*.

Pit: A trading pit is a specially constructed set of steps, usually hexagonal, on the floor of a futures exchange. On some exchanges, this area is called a "ring" after a circular restraining bar.

Position limits: Futures exchanges and the CFTC (q.v.) typically set the maximum number of futures contracts any one trader can hold in any one delivery month (q.v.) and across all delivery months for a particular commodity. These limits apply more to speculators (q.v.) than to hedgers (q.v.).

Price-move limit: Futures exchanges limit the maximum advance or decline in price from the closing price the previous day. When prices are "limit up" or "limit down," either sellers or buyers find the price unrealistic, and trading ceases. Some exchanges do not impose price-move limits on a futures contract during the month it is expiring; others do not impose them at all.

Principal: A principal is the individual ultimately responsible for paying for a purchase or delivering on a sale. She will often appoint a broker (q.v.) to act as her agent.

Redelivery: See *delivery notice*.

Rollover: A rollover postpones an obligation either to take or make delivery on a futures contract (q.v.). The existing position is liquidated and simultaneously reinstated in another delivery month (q.v.). This is accomplished by (1) two distinct transactions, that is, taking a position in a contract that offsets (q.v.), and in effect cancels, an immediate obligation while opening the equivalent position in a more distant delivery month, or by (2) a single transaction, that is, arranging the appropriate straddle (q.v.). By either technique, a payment is made (or received, as the case may be) equal to the difference between the price for the two delivery dates. In this most common sense, rollover implies the special class of a "roll forward," namely rolling a nearby futures contract into a more distant contract. "Roll back," contrary to natural usage, means to roll a futures contract for distant delivery into a nearer month. A "transfer" is a rollover when the contract is just about to expire, that is, the delivery month has arrived.

Scalper: A scalper on a futures exchange tries to buy just a little below the market price and to sell just a little above it by anticipating the direction of price changes. At other times, scalpers act as wholesalers, accommodating a large order in the hands of a floor broker (q.v.) and then breaking it into smaller amounts. A scalper holds his positions for only a few minutes and hopes to make a small amount of money (just the top slice, as it were) on each of many trades. Although no one scalper will announce both a bid and an ask price (q.v.), collectively scalpers will make a market (q.v.).

SEC: The Securities and Exchange Commission since 1934 has been the U.S. regulator of the original issuing and subsequent trading of bonds and equities. The SEC's involvement with commodity markets has been primarily through its oversight of brokerage houses (q.v.), many of whose customers trade in futures as well as equity markets.

Settlement price: A settlement price is selected by a clearinghouse (q.v.) as representative of futures prices at a particular time of day, which provides a standard for the payment of differences on offsetting (q.v.) trades within the same day, the application of variation margin (q.v.), and the invoice price for delivery notices (q.v.). Usually the settlement price is the closing price. If price-move limits (q.v.) are in effect, the settlement price is not the price at which the futures contract would freely trade.

Settling: In its most general sense, settling refers to the actions taken to fulfill a contract. For example, the delivery of warehouse receipts (q.v.) settles a contract for the future delivery of corn.

Short: Short describes the market position of someone who has sold something, usually a futures contract (q.v.). If the sale called for immediate delivery, the position could not be kept open; hence, a short position usually has some degree of future commitment about it. Short has also come to indicate the person who holds the position. Contrast with *long*.

Short selling: Short selling is the selling of a good that has not yet been bought. A short seller hopes that the price of the good will fall, so that when he buys the good to deliver or offsets (q.v.) his short position, it will be at a lower price than that at which he has sold it.

Speculator: In futures markets, the term speculator is a catchall for anyone who hopes to profit from movements in price and who does not handle, market, or process the physical commodity. In practice, some commercials (q.v.) do, in fact, speculate.

Spot: The term "spot" refers to a good that is right at hand, and so is available for immediate delivery. The price paid for a good to be delivered immediately is said to be the "spot price." Compare with *cash*.

Spot month: Spot month refers to the futures contract (q.v.) whose delivery month (q.v.) is current. Because for some commodities, the delivery months do not include all the calendar months, spot month may refer to the nearest contract even though it may not yet be expiring.

Spread: A spread is the difference between the prices of a commodity for two different dates of delivery or at two different locations (the prices measured simultaneously). The term is also used to describe the trades necessary to achieve such an implicit position in the market, for example, by the purchase of a nearby futures contract (q.v.) along with the sale of a futures contract with a more distant delivery date. The difference in price between later delivery and earlier delivery is the "carrying charge" for that time period. Market-determined, the spread can range between full carrying charges (q.v.) and inverse carrying charges (q.v.). See *straddle.*

Straddle: Straddle is a synonym for spread, especially as it refers to the simultaneous taking of both a long (q.v.) and a short (q.v.) position in futures contracts (q.v.). On some futures exchanges, floor traders (q.v.) offer straddles directly and quote the price difference explicitly, not the prices of the two legs (q.v.) of the straddle. Someone forming and holding a straddle hopes to profit from the relative movement in the two prices, not their absolute movement. If she anticipates that the nearby delivery date will appreciate relative to the more distant delivery date (even if both prices decline), she goes long the nearby and short the more distant. If she anticipates that the more distant delivery date will appreciate relative to the nearby delivery date, she goes short the nearby and long the more distant.

Switch: Switch is a synonym for rollover (q.v.) through which a futures contract (q.v.) for one delivery month (q.v.) is transferred to another delivery month.

Tender: See *delivery notice*.

Trading for liquidation only: During an emergency, most often involving some extreme price moves in the nearby delivery month (q.v.), futures exchanges restrict trading to liquidation only. No new traders may enter the market and those who have existing positions may trade only if they reduce their position.

Variation margin: See *margin*.

Warehouse receipt: A warehouse receipt is the acknowledgment a warehouseman (or vaultkeeper) gives when he accepts goods into his warehouse. The receipt lists the good's condition and quantity, as well as the time it was placed into storage. Often these warehouse receipts become fungible and negotiable, allowing the owner to sell her good simply by passing the warehouse receipt to someone else. Indeed, possession of the warehouse receipt becomes proof of title.

References

Books and articles

Ackerman, Kenneth D. 1988. *The Gold Ring: Jim Fisk, Jay Gould, and Black Friday, 1869*. New York: Dodd, Mead.

Adler, Stephen J. 1994. *The Jury*. New York: Random House.

Amsterdam, Anthony G. 1960. "The Void-for-Vagueness Doctrine in the Supreme Court." *University of Pennsylvania Law Review* 109: 67–116.

Anderson, Ronald W., and Gilbert, Christopher L. 1988. "Commodity Agreements and Commodity Markets: Lessons from Tin." *Economic Journal* 98: 1–15.

Angrist, Stanley W. 1980. "On Facing Reality." *Forbes* 12 May.

Architzel, Paul M., and Connally, John P. 1981. "Delivery on Futures Contracts as a Legal Requirement." *Business Lawyer* 36: 935–52.

Baer, Julius B., and Saxon, Olin Glenn. 1949. *Commodity Exchanges and Futures Trading*. New York: Harper & Brothers.

Bailey, Warren, and Chan, K. C. 1993. "Macroeconomic Influences and the Variability of the Commodity Futures Basis." *Journal of Finance* 48: 555–73.

Bailey, Warren, and Ng, Edward. 1991. "Default Premiums in Commodity Markets: Theory and Evidence." *Journal of Finance* 46: 1071–93.

Baker, H. Kent., and Meyer, James M. 1980. "Impact of Discount Rate Changes on Treasury Bills." *Journal of Economics and Business* 33: 43–8.

Berger, Margaret A. 1989. "*United States v. Scop*: The Common-Law Approach to an Expert's Opinion About a Witness's Credibility Still Does Not Work." *Brooklyn Law Review* 55: 559–623.

Berle, A. A., Jr. 1938. "Stock Market Manipulation." *Columbia Law Review* 38: 393–407.

Bernstein, Peter W. 1980. "Engelhard's Not–So-Sterling Deal with the Hunts." *Fortune* 19 May.

Black, Barbara. 1984. "Fraud on the Market: A Criticism of Dispensing

227

with Reliance Requirements in Certain Open Market Transactions." *North Carolina Law Review* 62: 435-73.

Borgo, John. 1979. "Causal Paradigms in Tort Law." *Journal of Legal Studies* 8: 419–55.

Brennan, Troyen A. 1988. "Causal Chains and Statistical Links: The Role of Scientific Uncertainty in Hazardous-Substance Litigation." *Cornell Law Review* 73: 469–533.

Brennan, Troyen A. 1989. "Helping Courts with Toxic Torts: Some Proposals Regarding Alternative Methods for Presenting and Assessing Scientific Evidence in Common Law Torts." *University of Pittsburgh Law Review* 51: 1–72.

Broehl, Wayne G., Jr. 1992. *Cargill: Trading the World's Grain.* Hanover, NH: University Press of New England.

Bromberg, Alan R., and Lowenfels, Lewis D. 1980–93. *Securities Fraud & Commodities Fraud.* Colorado Springs: Shepard's/McGraw-Hill.

Browne, Harry. 1974. *You Can Profit from a Monetary Crisis.* New York: Macmillan.

Burt, Robert A.; Koskinen, John A.; Weiss, Elliot J.; and Whitford, William C. (Comment eds.). 1963. "The Delivery Requirement: An Illusory Bar to the Regulation of Manipulation in Commodity Exchanges." *Yale Law Journal* 73: 171–86.

Carney, William J. 1989. "The Limits of the Fraud on the Market Doctrine." *Business Lawyer* 44: 1259–92.

CFTC (Commodity Futures Trading Commission). 1981. *A Study of the Silver Market.* Washington: CFTC.

Cook, Timothy, and Hahn, Thomas. 1988. "The Information Content of Discount Rate Announcements and Their Effect on Market Interest Rates." *Journal of Money, Credit, and Banking* 20: 167–80.

Crane, Roger R. 1981. "An Analysis of Causation under Rule 10b–5." *Securities Regulation Law Journal* 9: 99–139.

Danovitch, David E. 1986. "Case Comments: *Strobl v. New York Mercantile Exchange.*" *Suffolk University Law Review* 20: 673–80.

Davidson, George A. 1985. "Squeezes and Corners: A Structural Approach." *Business Lawyer* 40: 1283–98.

Davis, L. J. 1981. "Silver Thursday." *Harper's*, May, 39–55.

Department of the Treasury, Securities and Exchange Commission, and Board of Governors of the Federal Reserve System. 1992. *Joint Report on the Government Securities Market.* Washington: U.S. Government Printing Office.

De Toro, Anthony. 1989. "Market Manipulation of Penny Stocks." *Securities Regulation Law Journal* 17: 241–56.

Easterbrook, Frank H. 1986. "Monopoly, Manipulation, and the Regulation of Futures Markets." *Journal of Business* 59: S103–27.

Edwards, Franklin R., and Ma, Cindy W. 1992. *Futures and Options.* New York: McGraw-Hill.

Edwards, Linda N., and Edwards, Franklin R. 1984. "A Legal and Economic Analysis of Manipulation in Futures Markets." *Journal of Futures Markets* 4: 333–66.

Ell, Douglas W. 1978. "The Right to an Incompetent Jury: Protracted Commerical Litigation and the Seventh Amendment." *Connecticut*

Law Review 10: 775–800.

Fackler, Paul L. 1993. "Delivery and Manipulation in Futures Markets." *Journal of Futures Markets* 13: 693–702.

Fama, Eugene F., and French, Kenneth R. 1988. "Business Cycles and the Behavior of Metals Prices." *Journal of Finance* 43: 1075–93.

Farber, Daniel A. 1987. "Toxic Causation." *Minnesota Law Review* 71: 1219–59.

Fay, Stephen. 1982. *Beyond Greed.* New York: Viking Press.

Federal Trade Commission. 1920–26. *Report on the Grain Trade.* 7 vols. Washington: U.S. Government Printing Office.

Finkelstein, Michael O., and Levenbach, Hans. 1983. "Regression Estimates of Damages in Price-Fixing Cases." *Law and Contemporary Problems* 46: 145–69.

Fischel, Daniel R., and Ross, David J. 1991. "Should the Law Prohibit 'Manipulation' in Financial Markets?" *Harvard Law Review* 105: 503–53.

Fisher, Franklin M.; McGowan, John J.; and Greenwood, Joen E. 1983. *Folded, Spindled, and Mutilated: Economic Analysis and U.S. v. IBM.* Cambridge: MIT Press.

Flynn, John J. 1988. "Legal Reasoning, Antitrust Policy and the Social 'Science' of Economics." *Antitrust Bulletin* 33: 713–43.

Frankel, Mark A. 1990. "A Trial Judge's Perspective on Providing Tools for Rational Jury Decision Making."*Northwestern University Law Review* 85: 221–5.

Freeman, George Clemon, Jr., and McSlarrow, Kyle E. 1990. "RICO and the Due Process 'Void for Vagueness' Test." *Business Lawyer* 45: 1003–11.

Freund, Susan K.; McDonnell, William E., Jr.; and Cadden, Hugh J. 1985. "Prejudgment Interest in Commodity Futures Litigation." *Business Lawyer* 40: 1267–82.

Friedland, Steven I. 1990. "The Competency and Responsibility of Jurors in Deciding Cases." *Northwestern University Law Review* 85: 190–220.

Friedman, Richard D. 1990. "Stalking the Squeeze: Understanding Commodities Market Manipulation." *Michigan Law Review* 89: 30–68.

Gibson-Jarvie, Robert. 1983. *The London Metal Exchange.* Cambridge: Woodhead-Faulkner.

Granger, C. W. J., and Newbold, Paul. 1974. "Spurious Regressions in Econometrics." *Journal of Econometrics* 2: 111–20.

Granger, C. W. J., and Newbold, Paul. 1986. *Forecasting Economic Time Series.* 2nd ed. San Diego: Academic Press.

Gray, Roger W. 1980. "When Does Aggressive Trading Become Market Tampering?" *Business Lawyer* 35: 745–50.

Gray, Roger W. 1981. "Economic Evidence in Manipulation Cases." *Research on Speculation: Seminar Report*, 108–20. Chicago Board of Trade.

Green, Michael D. 1992. "Expert Witnesses and Sufficiency of Evidence in Toxic Substances Litagation: The Legacy of 'Agent Orange' and Bendectin Litigation." *Northwestern University Law Review* 86: 643–99.

Greene, Berard H., and Rogers, William Dill (Comment eds.). 1951.

"Federal Regulation of Commodity Futures Trading." *Yale Law Journal* 60: 822–50.

Gross, Samuel R. 1991. "Expert Evidence." *Wisconsin Law Review* 1991: 1113–232.

Guinther, John. 1988. *The Jury in America.* New York: Facts on File Publications.

Harrington, William D. 1981. "The Manipulation of Commodity Futures Prices." *St. John's Law Review* 55: 240–75.

Harrington, William D. 1984. "Culpability and its Content under the Commodity Exchange Act." *Connecticut Law Journal* 17: 1–37.

Harriss, Barbara. 1979. "There Is Method in My Madness: Or Is It Vice Versa? Measuring Agricultural Market Performance." *Food Research Institute Studies* 17: 197–218.

Hart, H. L. A., and Honoré, Tony. 1985. *Causation in the Law.* 2nd ed. Oxford: Clarendon.

Heuer, Larry and Penrod, Steven D. 1990. "Some Suggestions for the Critical Appraisal of a More Active Jury." *Northwestern University Law Review* 85: 226-39.

Hieronymus, Thomas A. 1977a. *The Economics of Futures Trading for Commercial and Personal Profit.* 2nd ed. New Jersey: Commodity Research Bureau.

Hieronymus, Thomas A. 1977b. "Manipulation in Commodity Futures Trading: Toward a Definition." *Hofstra Law Review* 6: 41–56.

Hieronymus, Thomas A. 1981. "How the Practical Aspects of Testimony Directed Some Research." *Research on Speculation: Seminar Report*, 52–67. Chicago Board of Trade.

House Committee on Agriculture. 1980. *CFTC Regulatory Authority Review.* Washington: U.S. Government Printing Office.

House Committee on Agriculture. 1981. *Joint Agency Reports on Silver Markets.* Washington: U.S. Government Printing Office.

House Committee on Banking, Finance, and Urban Affairs. 1980. *To Modernize the Federal Reserve System.* Washington: U.S. Government Printing Office.

House Committee on Government Operations. 1980. *Silver Prices and the Adequacy of Federal Actions in the Marketplace, 1979–80.* Washington: U.S. Government Printing Office.

Hurt, Harry, III. 1981. *Texas Rich.* New York: Norton.

Imwrinkelried, Edward J. 1984. *Uncharged Misconduct Evidence.* Rochester, NY: Callaghan.

Imwrinkelried, Edward J. 1988. "The 'Bases' of Expert Testimony: The Syllogistic Structure of Scientific Testimony." *North Carolina Law Review* 67: 1–27.

Irwin, H. S. 1937. "Legal Status of Trading in Futures." *Illinois Law Review* 32: 155–70.

Jacob, Edwin J. 1985. "Of Causation in Science and Law: Consequences of the Erosion of Standards." *Business Lawyer* 40: 1229–41.

Jastram, Roy W. 1981. *Silver: The Restless Metal.* New York: Wiley.

Jeffries, John Calvin, Jr. 1985. "Legality, Vagueness, and the Construction of Penal Statutes." *Virginia Law Review* 71: 189–245.

Jegadeesh, Narasimhan. 1993. "Treasury Auction Bids and the Salomon

Squeeze." *Journal of Finance* 48: 1403–19.

Johnson, Philip McBride. 1981. "Commodity Market Manipulation." *Washington and Lee Law Review* 38: 725–79.

Johnson, Philip McBride, and Hazen, Thomas Lee. 1989–94. *Commodities Regulation*. 2nd ed. Boston: Little, Brown.

Jones, Carol A. G. 1994. *Expert Witnesses: Science, Medicine, and the Practice of Law*. Oxford: Clarendon.

Jones, Frank J. 1981. "Spreads: Tails, Turtles, and All That." *Journal of Futures Markets* 1: 565–96.

Kellman, Barry. 1985. *Private Antitrust Litigation*. Chicago: Commerce Clearing House.

Kern, John. 1987. "Price Manipulation in the Commodity Futures Markets: A Reexamination of the Justifications for Simultaneous Causes of Action under the CEA and the Sherman Act." *UCLA Law Review* 34: 1305–29.

Klejna, Dennis, and Meyer, Stephen H. 1990. "The Prohibition Against Commodity Manipulation: Review of Enforcement and Civil Actions." Paper presented at the conference "Market Manipulation: Law, Economics and Public Policy" sponsored by the Center for the Study of Futures and Options, Virginia Polytechnic Institute and State University, Washington, D.C., 8–9 November.

Kolb, Robert W. 1991. *Understanding Futures Markets*. 3rd ed. Miami: Kolb Publishing Co.

Kumar, Praveen, and Seppi, Duane J. 1992. "Futures Manipulation with 'Cash Settlement'." *Journal of Finance* 47: 1485–501.

Kyle, Albert S. 1984. "A Theory of Futures Market Manipulations." In Ronald W. Anderson (ed.), *The Industrial Organization of Futures Markets*, 141–73. Lexington, MA: Lexington Books.

Lempert, Richard O. 1981. "Civil Juries and Complex Cases: Let's Not Rush to Judgement." *Michigan Law Review* 80: 68–132.

Levi, Edward H. 1948. *An Introduction to Legal Reasoning*. Chicago: University of Chicago Press.

Levy, Bruce M. 1981. "An Analysis of the Commodity Straddle as a Tax Planning Device." *Taxes* 59: 467–81.

Lower, Robert C. 1991. "Disruptions of the Futures Market: A Comment on Dealing with Market Manipulation." *Yale Journal on Regulation* 8: 391–402.

Loss, Louis, and Ruebhausen, Oscar M. (Note eds.). 1937. "Market Manipulation and the Securities Exchange Act." *Yale Law Journal* 46: 624–47.

Lubet, Steven 1993. "Expert Testimony." *American Journal of Trial Advocacy* 17: 399–442.

Lunebury, William V., and Nordenberg, Mark A. 1981. "Special Qualified Juries and Expert Non Tribunals: Alternatives for Coping with the Complexities of Modern Civil Litigation." *Virginia Law Review* 67: 887–1007.

McCloskey, Donald N. 1985. *The Rhetoric of Economics*. Madison: University of Wisconsin Press.

McDermott, Edward T. 1979. "Defining Manipulation in Commodity Futures Trading: The Futures 'Squeeze'." *Northwestern University*

Law Review 74: 202–25.

McDonnell, William E., Jr., and Freund, Susan K. 1983. "The CFTC's Large Trader Reporting System: History and Development." *Business Lawyer* 38: 917–51.

McLaughlin, Michael A. 1983. "Questions to Witnesses and Notetaking by the Jury as Aids in Understanding Complex Litigation." *New England Law Review* 18: 687–713.

Markham, Jerry W. 1987. *The History of Commodity Futures Trading and Its Regulation*. New York: Praeger.

Markham, Jerry W. 1991. "Manipulation of Commodity Futures Prices – The Unprosecutable Crime." *Yale Journal on Regulation* 8: 281–389.

Mayer, Thomas. 1993. *Truth versus Precision in Economics*. Cambridge (UK): Edward Elgar.

Mermin, Arthur, and Pickard, Robert F. (Note eds.). 1947. "Regulation of Stock Market Manipulation." *Yale Law Journal* 56: 509–33.

Meulbroek, Lisa K. 1992. "An Empirical Analysis of Illegal Insider Trading." *Journal of Finance* 47: 1661–99.

Mitchell, Mark L., and Netter, Jeffry M. 1994. "The Role of Financial Economics in Securities Fraud Cases: Applications at the Securities and Exchange Commission." *Business Lawyer* 49: 547–90.

Morris, John R., and Mosteller, Gale R. 1991. "Defining Markets for Merger Analysis." *Antitrust Bulletin* 36: 599–640.

Peck, Anne E., and Williams, Jeffrey C. 1991. "Deliveries on Chicago Board of Trade Wheat, Corn, and Soybean Futures Contracts, 1964/65–1988/89." *Food Research Institute Studies* 22: 129–225.

Perdue, Wendy Collins. 1987. "Manipulation of Futures Markets: Redefining the Offense." *Fordham Law Review* 56: 345–402.

Petzel, Todd E. 1981. "A New Look at Some Old Evidence: The Wheat Market Scandal of 1925." *Food Research Institute Studies* 18: 117–28.

Pirrong, S. Craig. 1993. "Manipulation of the Commodity Futures Market Delivery Process." *Journal of Business* 66: 335–69.

Pirrong, S. Craig. 1994. "Commodity Market Manipulation Law: A (Very) Critical Analysis and a Proposed Alternative." *Washington and Lee Law Review* 51: 945–1014.

Pitofsky, Robert. 1990. "New Definitions of Relevant Market and the Assault on Antitrust." *Columbia Law Review* 90: 1805–64.

Poser, Norman S. 1986. "Stock Market Manipulation and Corporate Control Transactions." *University of Miami Law Review* 40: 671–735.

Reasoner, Harry M. (ed.). 1992. "Experts – Use and Abuse." Symposium *Antitrust Law Journal* 60: 335–413.

Roley, V. Vance, and Troll, Rick. 1984. "The Impact of Discount Rate Changes on Market Interest Rates." *Federal Reserve Bank of Kansas City Economic Review*, 27–39.

Roll, Richard. 1984. "Orange Juice and Weather." *American Economic Review* 74: 861–80.

Rosenak, T. W.; Blake, Harlan M.; and Rosenblat, Alan (Comment eds.). 1953. "Manipulation of Commodity Futures Prices: The *Great Western* Case." *University of Chicago Law Review* 21: 95–113.

Rowan, Roy. 1980a. "A Talkfest with the Hunts." *Fortune* 11 August.

Rowan, Roy. 1980b. "Who Guards Whom at the Commodity Exchange?"

Fortune 28 July.

Rudnick, Robert A., and Carlisle, Linda E. 1983. "Commodities and Financial Futures." *Journal of Taxation and Investments* 1: 45–55.

Rudnick, Robert A.; Carlisle, Linda E.; and Dailey, Thomas F. 1983. "Federal Income Tax Treatment of Commodity Transactions." *Boston College Law Review* 24: 301–40.

Rudzitis, Gundars. 1987. "Silver Prices and Market Speculation." In Harley E. Johansen, Olen Paul Matthews, and Gundars Rudzitis (eds.), *Mineral Resource Development: Geoplitics, Economics, and Policy.* Boulder, CO: Westview.

Russo, Thomas A. 1983–93. *Regulation of the Commodities Futures and Options Markets.* Colorado Springs: Shepard's/McGraw-Hill.

Schacter, Alan. 1986. "The Availability of Antitrust Treble Damages for Commodities Market Manipulation." *Fordham Law Review* 54: 853–68.

Schapiro, Donald. 1981. "Commodities, Forwards, Puts and Calls – Things Equal to the Same Things are Sometimes not Equal to Each Other." *Tax Lawyer* 34: 581–604.

Scheffman, David T. 1992. "Statistical Measures of Market Power: Uses and Abuses." *Antitrust Law Journal* 60: 901–19.

Scheffman, David T., and Spiller, Pablo T. 1987. "Geographic Market Definition under the *U.S. Department of Justice Merger Guidelines.*" *Journal of Law and Economics* 30: 123–47.

Schwager, Jack D. 1992. *The New Market Wizards: Conversations with America's Top Traders.* New York: HarperBusiness.

SEC (Securities and Exchange Commission). 1982. *The Silver Crisis of 1980.* Washington: SEC.

Selig, Stephen F., and Schmittberger, R. Wayne. 1977. "Tax Aspects of Commodity Futures Trading." *Hofstra Law Review* 6: 93–114.

Senate Committee on Agriculture, Nutrition, and Forestry. 1980. *Price Volatility in the Silver Futures Market.* Washington: U.S. Government Printing Office.

Silber, William L. 1981. "Innovation, Competition, and New Contract Design in Futures Markets." *Journal of Futures Markets* 1: 123–55.

Silberberg, Henry J., and Pollack, David C. 1983. "Are the Courts Expanding the Meaning of 'Manipulation' under the Federal Securities Laws?" *Securities Regulation Law Journal* 11: 265–81.

Silberberg, Henry J., and Pollack, David C. 1984. "Market Manipulation." *Securities Regulation Law Journal* 12: 69–75.

Simons, Joseph J., and Williams, Michael A. 1993. "The Renaissance of Market Definition." *Antitrust Bulletin* 38: 799–857.

Smirlock, Michael, and Yawitz, Jess. 1985. "Asset Returns, Discount Rate Changes, and Market Efficiency." *Journal of Finance* 40: 1141–58.

Smith, Jeffrey M., et al. (Comment eds.). 1973. "Commodities: Futures Control: Manipulation under the Commodity Exchange Act." *Minnesota Law Review* 57: 1243–56.

Smith, Jerome F. 1972. *Silver Profits in the Seventies.* Vancouver: ERC Publishing.

Stassen, John H. 1982. "Propaganda as Positive Law: Section 3 of the Commodity Exchange Act." *Chicago Kent Law Review* 58: 635–56.

Steele, Walter W. Jr., and Thornburg, Elizabeth G. 1988. "Jury Instructions: A Persistent Failure to Communicate." *North Carolina Law Review* 67: 77–119.

Stigler, George J., and Sherwin, Robert A. 1985. "The Extent of the Market." *Journal of Law and Economics* 28: 555–85.

Strawn, David U., and Munsterman, G. Thomas. 1982. "Helping Juries Handle Complex Cases. *Judicature* 65: 444–7.

Thornton, Daniel L. 1994. "Why Do T-Bill Rates React to Discount Rate Changes?" *Journal of Money, Credit, and Banking* 26: 839–50.

Thorup, A. Robert. 1990. "Theories of Damages: Allowability and Calculation in Securities Fraud Litigation." *Securities Regulation Law Journal* 18: 23–52.

Trustman, Alan. 1980. "The Silver Scam: How the Hunts Were Outfoxed." *Atlantic Monthly*, September, 70–81.

Van Smith, M. 1981. "Preventing the Manipulation of Commodity Futures Markets: To Deliver or Not to Deliver?" *Hastings Law Journal* 32: 1569–607.

Vinson, Donald E. 1986. *Jury Trials: The Psychology of Winning Strategy.* Charlottesville: Michie.

Wagster, John. 1993. "The Information Content of Discount Rate Announcements Revisited." *Journal of Money, Credit, and Banking* 25: 132–7.

Waud, Roger N. 1970. "Public Interpretation of Federal Reserve Discount Rate Changes: Evidence on the 'Announcement Effect'." *Econometrica* 38: 231–50.

Wemple, Peter H. 1985. "Rule 10b–5 Securities Fraud: Regulating the Application of the Fraud-on-the-Market Theory of Liability." *John Marshall Law Review* 18: 733–50.

Williams, Jeffrey C. 1986. *The Economic Function of Futures Markets.* New York: Cambridge University Press.

Williams, Jeffrey C., and Wright, Brian D. 1991. *Storage and Commodity Markets.* New York: Cambridge University Press.

Wolff, Elliot R. 1969. "Comparative Federal Regulation of the Commodities Exchanges and the National Securities Exchanges." *George Washington Law Review* 38: 223–64.

Working, Holbrook. 1948. "Theory of the Inverse Carrying Charge in Futures Markets." *Journal of Farm Economics* 39: 1–28.

Working, Holbrook. 1962. "New Concepts Concerning Futures Markets and Prices." *American Economic Review* 52: 431–59.

World Bank. 1992. *Market Outlook for Major Primary Commodities.* 2 vols. Washington: World Bank Report No. 814/92.

Wright, Richard W. 1985. "Causation in Tort Law." *California Law Review* .73: 1737–828.

Wright, Richard W. 1988. "Causation, Responsiblity, Risk, Probability, Naked Statistics, and Proof: Pruning the Bramble Bush by Clarifying Concepts." *Iowa Law Review* 73: 1001–77.

Yorio, Edward. 1989. *Contract Enforcement: Specific Performance and Injunctions.* Boston: Little, Brown.

Cases cited

Bartlett Frazier Co. v. Hyde, 65 F.2d 350 (7th Cir., 1933), cert. denied, 290 U.S. 654 (1933).

Cargill, Inc. v. Hardin, 452 F.2d 1154 (8th Cir., 1971).

Chicago Board of Trade v. Olsen, 262 U.S. 1 (1923).

Corbett v. Underwood, 83 Ill. 344 (1876).

Daubert v. Merrill Dow, 125 L.Ed.2d 469 (1993).

General Foods Corp. v. Brannan, 170 F.2d 220 (7th Cir., 1948).

Great Western Food Distrib., Inc. v. Brannan, 201 F.2d 476 (7th Cir., 1953).

Higgins & Gilbert v. McCrea, 116 U.S. 671 (1886).

In re. Indiana Farm Bureau Coop Assn. CCH Commodity Futures Law Reporter ¶20,964 [1977–80 Transfer Binder] (CFTC, 1979), affd., ¶21,796 [1982–84 Transfer Binder] (CFTC, 1982).

Irwin v. Williar, 110 U.S. 499.

Merrill Lynch v. Curran, 456 U.S. 353 (1982).

G. H. Miller & Co. v. United States, 260 F.2d 286 (7th Cir., 1958).

Peto v. Howell, 101 F.2d 353 (7th. Cir., 1938).

Strobl v. New York Mercantile Exchange, 768 F.2d 22 (2d Cir., 1985), cert. denied, 106 S. Ct. 527 (1985).

Trane Co. v. O'Connor Securities, 561 F.Supp. 301 (S.D.N.Y., 1983).

United States v. Scop, 846 F.2d 135 (2nd Cir., 1988).

Index

237

Printed in the United Kingdom
by Lightning Source UK Ltd.
128289UK00001B/325-330/P